Contents

Illustration Credits

Acknowledgments

Writing a book combines both extreme solitude and extreme communion with those that have anything to do with you. This book was also the case. For those of you around me during this time I appreciate your patience. The research for this book started at the beginning of the 1990s when I first left Australia and moved to Singapore. It was here that I became intrigued with the interrelatedness and differences of cultures and the role that architecture plays in the making of contemporary urban experience. During my time living in Singapore I was blessed to work with some amazing individuals and had the opportunity to travel and do projects throughout the Asia Pacific Rim. This experience set the foundation for many of the interests that I now take for granted. From Singapore I moved to Bangkok and then Kuala Lumpur. These cities and the people I met there are dear to me.

In the preparation of the manuscript I must thank my colleagues at the Harvard Graduate School of Design for their encouragement and constant advice, especially Dean Peter Rowe for his candid reflections and Professor Edward Robbins for his commitment to our ongoing dialogue and for his editorial insights. I would also like to acknowledge the work of my students Wenhui Shan, Hiroshi Koike, Hiroto Kobayashi, Yasmeen Sollas, Anand Krishnan, Joaquim Mitchell, Frank Ruchella, Kjersti Monson, and Maurice Roers for their assistance in translation, the preparation of research material and the presentation of the graphics found in this publication.

In addition I would like to express my appreciation to several people who contributed significantly to the production of the book – Daniel Francey of Phu My Hung Corporation, Vietnam, Ge Zhong of Tsinghua University, Beijing, Yang Guiqing of Tongji University, Shanghai, Toshio Tsushima of Tsushima Marshall Design, Tokyo and Sitthiporn Piromruen, Dean, Faculty of Architecture, Silpakorn University, Bangkok.

This research would not have been possible without the financial support of the Harvard University Milton Fund. This allowed me to travel once again to these remarkable locations and to hire research assistants without whose help this publication would not have been possible.

Lastly I would like to acknowledge the role that my students played in helping me to frame my ideas. The students of *GSD3470: Emerging Urbanity Case Studies of Pacific Rim Megaprojects* I humbly thank you. I am sure that I learned more from you than you did from me.

Richard Marshall
Cambridge MA, December 2001

1.1 Clusters of high-rise commercial office buildings now define the dominant form of urbanity in cities throughout the world. The dominant form then qualifies all other forms. The Bank of China, Hong Kong.

1 Emerging Urbanity

We live in a world that is both global and urban. We live in a time where our lives are increasingly based within similar lived experiences and we inhabit urban environments that in some respects are remarkably the same. More people are living in urban environments than ever before and in a few short decades urban life will be the primary experience for most of the world's population. At this time the experience of urbanity will become common to us all, a shared perspective. However, while we are all aware that our cities have undergone tremendous changes in the last century we are currently struggling to comprehend the enormity of the current condition of the urban, to the point where even the idea of urbanity, city culture, is highly contestable.

A confluence of complicated social and economic forces are impacting the way cities work, are thought about and operated upon. These are the focus of growing fields of study to understand their nature, production and influence, all of which deal with aspects of an amorphous discourse on globalization. While the discourse on the role of the urban in an age of globalization is energetic, there are as yet no conclusions that can be drawn. Rather there is general disagreement as to whether we are witnessing a convergence of sameness or a reinforcement of difference in cities, as to whether we are witnessing the emergence of a liberating "one world" phenomena or the maturation of an exploitive capitalist system. There is argument as to whether globalization is the key to wealth or the cause of greater spatial and social stratification. Nevertheless, there is ample evidence to suggest that there are powerful forces, which deliberately aim at the propagation of sameness in cities. This can be seen, for example, in efforts to market "world standard" real estate projects. These typically involve a group of international real estate investors and agents who market their products to a group of elite international investors. Further, there exists a powerful motivation on the part of some governments to create "world standard" projects to promote their national and city economic interests (see Marcuse 1997b).

Some see this as an inevitable sign of world progress, others as a sign of global corporate domination and of diminished cultural difference. As architects, however, we are increasingly being asked to provide "world standard" designs. Governments and clients from developing countries look to the glass and steel towers of New York, Chicago, Tokyo, London and Paris as symbols of success and representations of "progressive" and "modern" societies. In a glib way these governments attempt to accessorize their urban environments with the trappings of success by actively seeking to acquire a trophy case of buildings from the same select group of international architects (see Olds 2000). The results can be seen in any international architectural journal today.

Contemporary architectural practice operates over tremendous geographies. At the height of the building boom in Asia in the early 1990s, European and American firms were doing anything from one third to half of their work there. The 1997

1.2 The skyline of Lower Manhattan, prior to September 11, 2001, expressed the global financial power of New York in the global economy. This iconography is actively emulated by other cities in the quest for recognition in the global economy.

World Architecture Survey (taken in 1996 immediately before the Asian Economic Crisis) notes that Western European firms looked to Asia for nearly half of their work (World Architecture 1997: 17). Indeed that same survey notes that thirteen of the largest thirty firms operating in Asia were based in the United States, Australia or the United Kingdom. Whether this is a case of foreign firms exploiting the Asian situation or Asian clients demanding an international aesthetic, the result is a multitude of "international" projects that could be situated in any number of contexts. This leads inevitably to a collection of architectural projects that are remarkably the same in cities such as Tokyo, Shanghai, Singapore and Jakarta.

The sameness of the urban condition is an issue for all of us involved in thinking about, the design and construction of cities. Rem Koolhaas, one of the most influential thinkers on the contemporary urban condition, asks is the contemporary city, like the contemporary airport "all the same." If this is true, he wonders, to what ultimate configuration is it aspiring? In his essay entitled *Globalization*, he makes the point that increasingly in the "globalized domain of international architectural practice" large scale projects are being designed by architects not remotely connected to the context for which their works are intended – an ignorance that leads to what he describes as a "new purism" (Koolhaas 1998: 1248). This new purism is analogous to the writing of text on a clean slate, unencumbered by the existence of any previous text – a newfound freedom. Such uninhibited "freedom" has been lacking from architectural practice in the United States and Europe for almost half a century. The period of postwar rebuilding in Europe demanded immediate solutions and architects were empowered to make decisions with little mediation. In the United States too, Urban Renewal provided opportunities for architects to operate at unprecedented scale and scope. The rise of community participation and the increased restrictions placed upon architectural liberty are the direct result of this period of "freedom." The uninhibited freedom to which Koolhaas refers connects deeply with an architect's ego and sense of design authority. While there has been a diminution of architecture's authority in the United States over the past forty years, the emerging urban conditions of the Asia Pacific Rim provide architects with opportunities to exert their unbridled will. While this certainly raises issues of diminished cultural difference and the flattening of social and cultural spheres, it does raise a series of very interesting issues for contemporary architectural practice.

In a return to high modernism, "new purism" once again raises the idea and possibility of design purity. It questions whether there can be an unobstructed relationship between designed intention and constructed reality. Is a project that has not been mediated through a complicated public process, as often happens in the United States, better than one that has? While community activists may see inclusionary decision making as an unequivocal benefit, many architects continue to see this as interfering with creative vision. If architects were free to create visions that are not "interfered" with, would the finished project be a better piece of architecture and how or who should ultimately judge this? Can the same questions be asked about cities? Are designed visions of cities better or worse than cities produced through complicated, contested, long, difficult and costly public participation? For the most part the large urban projects examined in this book have been constructed in environments free from, or with limited, public process. As such they represent clear evidence of design intention manifest in physical form. In looking at them we can identify the designer's vision for how cities should be constituted and look like. In their form we see glimpses of the characteristics and possibilities of an emerging urban future – in future "ideas of the city."

1.3 View of Lujiazui, Shanghai, China. The construction of global imagery signifies Shanghai's global ambitions.

This book examines the idea of a convergence of sameness in the contemporary city in an age of globalization. Specifically it addresses one aspect of this convergence, in the development of global urban projects. Global urban projects are typically very large and expensive urban projects at the forefront of a nation's development agenda. These projects are produced with the purpose of enabling a stronger interrelationship with the global economy. As such, they have a very specific role to play. Because of this these projects do not represent broad visions of what a contemporary urbanity might be. On the contrary, because of the motivation behind their creation, these projects represent relatively narrow visions. The reason for this is simple. There is a rather particular environ-

ment that is deemed appropriate to attract and keep the global elite and it should come as no surprise that these spaces are indeed remarkably alike.

This vision, despite its narrowness, is an incredibly important one in the minds of many government officials for the real and perceived success of cities in the competitive global economy. Because of the power that this vision represents it has become the dominant vision of urbanity that in turn defines all other visions. While it is debatable as to whether this is good or bad, this dominant vision is inevitable given the logics of neoliberal global capitalism currently sweeping across the urban landscape of the planet. As architects we must

1.4 The primary experience of the city is the air-conditioned spaces of retail precincts. Raffles City, Singapore.

understand that we play an important role in giving form to this global urban landscape and must understand our position in relation to global capitalism. To be naive about the role of our work in this regard is a denial of our professional and ethical responsibilities. This book is about that role.

Emerging Urbanity is an examination of an urban phenomenon, which is the result of attempts by local and national governments, as well as the private sector, to secure economic advantage for their respective urban situations in the new global economy. These projects are initiated in a climate of intense competition between cities, where "competitive advantage" has become the new mantra of city governance. Among other things these projects provide two very important global advantages to their host locations. First they provide a particular type of urban environment where the work of globalization gets done and second, they provide a specific kind of global image that can be marketed in the global market place. These projects represent a new way of thinking about the role of planning in the city, which more than ever is concerned with marketing and the provision of competitive infrastructure.

In this way a city can announce to the world that it too is a global player and in doing so attract a greater share of the international pool of financial and human capital. And while we are all aware of projects established by this motivation in London with Canary Wharf, or New York with Battery Park City, for example, this book deals with this manifestation within the emerging urban conditions of the Asia Pacific Rim. *Emerging Urbanity* is an examination of the global forces that lead to the creation of these projects and a reflection on their implications for thinking about issues of contemporary urbanism and the role of urban design. It explores these issues by examining the contexts of a number of the largest and most

ambitious of these projects, which are critically examined to explore the consequences of global homogeneity and the implications of the resulting real and imagined lack of spatial distinction in our urban environments. Nine global urban projects are examined in the following chapters of this book.

Structure of the book

The book is divided into eleven chapters. This first chapter introduces a series of questions that relate to the making of these global urban projects. The second chapter outlines the general context of the tiger economies of the Pacific Rim and briefly explains why these economies developed as they did. It then describes the enormity of the globalization discourse and sets out a primary motivation for the development of this kind of urban project. This motivation deals with both the reality and perception of globalization, which creates an intense paranoia in the minds of decision makers in national governments; a fear of failing to capture a fair share of the wealth generated by the global economy. The chapter then sets out a series of issues that lie at the heart of the motivation for the book. This motivation can best be understood as a search for an answer to the following question. How might an evaluation of these very large urban projects in the Asia Pacific Rim redefine urban design operations in light of the contemporary global context? This chapter sets the framework for the examination of the individual projects.

The third and fourth chapters of the book deal with Tokyo Rainbow Town and Minato Mirai 21 respectively. These projects are two responses to the climate of booming development in Japan in the 1980s. They also respond to a desire to secure a profitable future in the new economy by promoting the possibilities of a new technological lifestyle, free from the inefficiencies of the Tokyo or Yoko-

1.5 The emerging urban contexts of cities such as Shanghai will fundamentally alter the way that we think about and design cities.

1.6 View of Minato Mirai 21. The modern Japanese city (copyright Christine Williams 2002).

hama urban situations. Both projects, additionally, show the relative inflexibility of urban development to respond effectively and quickly to changes in the global economy. They present different visions of how Japanese planners view city making and urban production and in their own ways are critical of their host locations. In their making they provide radically new visions of a possible "modern" Japanese city.

Chapter 5 deals with Muang Thong Thani in Bangkok, which is a privately owned and developed project. The story of Muang Thong Thani explains the emergence of the Asia Economic Crisis and the blind faith that developers placed in the Asian miracle. Its motivation comes from an attempt to capitalize on an expected population exodus from Hong Kong with the handing back of the British colony to Chinese control. Muang Thong Thani is the best example of a city created almost instantly in the midst of an inflated and unrealistic real estate market heavily influenced by global financial flows. The project represents the utopian vision of one man and its demise epitomizes the results of global capital flight and the fragility of place in the global economy.

Chapters 6 and 7 move the focus of the book to the emerging urban conditions of China. Lujiazui in Shanghai and Zhongguancun in Beijing represent the results of a tremendous experiment in the development of a socialist market economy. Lujiazui is only a decade old. Zhonguancun is currently under construction. Their stories provide insights into the growing urban situations in China and represent both a faith in China's abilities and a desire to engage more with the world. Created exclusively as portals into the global economy, each provides an infrastructure for China to claim a larger role in the global sphere. Their development histories provide insights into planning and design in these rapidly changing contexts.

Chapter 8 presents the situation of Vietnam's socialist market development and deals with two different projects – Hanoi North and Saigon South. For the past four decades Vietnam has struggled with conflicts and self imposed isolation. Today it is emerging as a competitive and stable country looking for quality investment. Vietnam's open door policies or *Doi Moi* represent a new initiative to engage with the world through global capital and political networks. Years of conflict and the retardation of their economy, however, have left the Vietnamese with little capacity to pursue development alone. Their strategy rather, is to create joint venture developments with internationals. Hanoi North and Saigon South represent two attempts to develop very large urban projects through partnerships with internationals. They also represent two very different realities in Vietnam. They were both created to secure competitive advantage for their host cities. The Vietnamese forged partnerships with foreign developers, who brought with them international designers and planners. Nevertheless, Saigon South is a success whilst Hanoi North has yet to eventuate. The story behind their making explains the differences between the North and South of Vietnam. It also displays the role that international investors play in helping governments to achieve their development ambitions.

Singapore's New Downtown in Marina Bay is the focus of Chapter 9. Singapore owes its existence to a long and profitable courtship with the global economy. It has developed from a colonial outpost into a major global financial hub and in doing so has created a specific kind of urban situation. In the matter of forty years Singapore has grown in size and wealth and boasts one of the highest home ownership rates and one of the largest capital reserves in the world. It is now in the process of embarking on one of its largest and most significant urban developments – its New Downtown, on reclaimed land in Marina Bay. The

New Downtown encapsulates a precise urban vision for how Singapore sees itself and what its ambitions are.

Chapter 10 deals with a global urban project of tremendous importance for the future of Malaysia. Situated within the Multimedia Super Corridor in Kuala Lumpur, lies the new Federal Administrative Center of Putrajaya. This project is Malaysia's version of Washington, Canberra or Brasilia. In making this project its creators aim to express a Malaysian identity capable of being marketed in a global marketplace. This is a project that will be the interface between Malaysia and the rest of the world. Within Putrajaya lays the global ambitions of the Malaysian people in their quest to claim a role in the future.

The final chapter deals with the implications of these urban projects for thinking about urban design and its role in the global world. It develops the notion that all urban projects contain specific urbanistic agendas or "ideas of the city" that are imbued in them by designers. It then attempts to understand the nature of the urbanity presented most clearly in these kinds of projects. By understanding the historical context from which urbanism is derived the chapter moves on to speculate on the future of urban design practice in a global world. It concludes with a series of principles that potentially might inform critical urban design thinking and practice and might help to resolve some of the issues that these projects raise.

2.1 As part of Hong Kong's development as a global financial center, the city constructed images that both expressed its success and its potential. This view is of the Bank of China and the Citibank Building, Hong Kong.

2 Urban Projects in a Global World

There is a future of architecture for the simple reason that no one has yet invented the building or architectural object that would put an end to all others, that would put an end to space itself. Nor has anyone yet invented the city which would end all cities or the body of thought which would end all thought. Now, at bottom, this is everyone's dream. So long as it does not become a reality, there is still hope.

Jean Baudrillard from BLUEPRINT
January 1999

Utopia is to be considered experimentally by studying its implications and consequences on the ground. These can surprise. What are and what would be the most successful places? How can they be discovered? According to which criteria? What are the times and rhythms of daily life which are inscribed and prescribed in these "successful" spaces favourable to happiness? That is interesting.

Henri Lefebvre *The Right to the City*

On the ebbs and flows of the global world

The first week of July 1997 was significant in the history of the Asia Pacific Rim. In this week two events occurred of world significance. The first of July was the day that Hong Kong was "handed back" to Chinese control, an event that had the world wondering about the future of the British colony. The first signs of a regional economic crisis overshadowed this however. On the next day, July 2, the Government of Thailand devalued the baht, a move that sent regional economies into turmoil after more than a decade of "miracle" growth. This led to regional financial instability of unprecedented scope and speed – the Asian Economic Crisis. What had been the fastest growing economy in the world was suddenly seen as a liability. The evaporation of the Asian economic "miracle" probably ranks second only to the unraveling of Soviet socialism as the greatest surprise of the last half-century (Bello 1997). It virtually destroyed the economies of Thailand, Indonesia, South Korea and the Philippines and as a result, the International Monetary Fund (IMF) stepped in to bail out South Korea to the sum of US$58 billion, Indonesia with US$43 billion, Thailand with US$17.2 billion and the Philippines with about US$1 billion in financial assistance. In addition, it raised many issues about the efficacy, stability and sustainability of the capitalist global economy. The resulting contagion also had a number of other consequences as well. It led, for example, to unprecedented unemployment in Thailand, to financial insulationism in Malaysia, and to political upheaval in Indonesia. Fundamentally it raised the question of how seemingly booming economies could turn so bad, so quickly.

Prior to 1997 the economies of the Asia Pacific Rim were remarkable for their growth and energy. Thailand, for example, enjoyed nearly a decade of acclaim as the world's fastest growing economy – the International Monetary Fund (IMF) and the United Nations Development Program (UNDP) cited it as a model for other nations to emulate.

Other Asian nations were similarly extraordinary. Between 1990 and 1996, the annual average GDP growth for Singapore was 8.3 percent, for Malaysia it was 8.8 percent, for Thailand it was 8.6 percent, and for China it was a staggering 10.1 percent (see World Bank 1993). In 1993, the World Bank published *The East Asian Miracle*, a document that heralded Asia as an economic success story (see World Bank 1993). The World Bank argued that the sustained economic performance of the economies of Hong Kong, Indonesia, Japan, South Korea, Malaysia, Singapore, Thailand and Taiwan was due to superior accumulation of physical and human capital in highly productive investments through the acquisition of technology. Further, the World Bank held these economies up as examples for emulation. It was a document that would prove to be overly enthusiastic.

The rise of the Asian countries can be described in three distinct phases. The first phase from about 1950 to 1990 can be described as the industrial, where nations rapidly developed extensive industrial operations in a game of technological catch up. This phase instigated rapid urbanization in cities throughout the Pacific Rim. The second phase is that of global positioning, where nations deliberately aimed at developing initiatives to claim a role for themselves in the highly competitive global economy. This phase included specific government led initiatives to develop advanced technologies, to streamline business and banking environments and to attract global investors. It also led to the establishment of many of the global urban projects examined in the following chapters. The third phase, which is yet to be developed, is the post crisis phase of development in the Asia Pacific Rim.

Four factors can explain the first phase of development activity. These are: the availability of new technology, access to large amounts of invest-

ment capital, large demographic shifts and the role that central governments play in development. For most nations in colonial Asia development was controlled by foreign powers intent on exploiting the strategic location of their assets in Asia. The priorities set by these colonial powers was often at odds with the priorities of local populations. Evidence of this can be seen in the different development agendas that existed during and after colonial rule ended. During the turbulent years of the 1950s and 1960s these nations shrugged off their colonial ties and, once independent, started their economic development in situations that lacked critical resources. Countries such as Singapore, Malaysia and Indonesia grew their economies from very primitive infrastructures. After World War II the gap between the industrialized world and the non-industrialized world was larger than even today. To reduce this gap required a "formidable effort" for non-industrialized countries to become competitive, leading to government led industrialization programs (Vogel 1991: 8).

Immediately after independence, Asian nations faced tremendous obstacles. Principal among these was the ability to access capital. The answer, for most, was to accept foreign aid and loans. Their respective governments initially controlled these foreign loans tightly. As many East Asian nations started to record impressive macroeconomic performance, their local populations, now freed from colonial rule and actively encouraged by Western capitalists, aggressively developed private enterprises in ways that were previously unavailable. Asia received massive aid from international lending organizations. The United States, in particular, was keen to provide economic and technical assistance as a way to stave off the threat of communism in Asia. As a result, Asian nations and private enterprises found easy sources of capital to fund their industrial expansions.

With the growth of the private sector, private companies began securing foreign loans to finance business expansions. This, naturally, resulted in a massive amount of debt in the Asian markets. The tremendous growth of these economies encouraged lending institutions to lend more money and a large amount of these funds were given without adequate securities. Organizations and individuals, which in other contexts would fail to secure financing, did so based to a large part on a blind faith in the Asian miracle.

This is true also in the world of property development. Families that owned agricultural land stopped producing palm oil or rice and became overnight property developers with dreams of building resorts, hotels, offices and golf courses. The landscape of Asia changed as kampongs gave way to high-rise luxury housing. And for a while it was too easy. Experience in development or adherence to acceptable real estate principals were not requirements in obtaining development capital. However, as Kotler and Kartajaya note, this, coupled with the high level of investor confidence in the future of the region, meant that Asia began to lose its grip on reality (Kotler and Kartajaya 2000: 16).

Through this massive economic expansion sites throughout the region grew in population terms as well. Rising productivity in agriculture reduced the demand for rural labor and this, combined with the emphasis on industrial production, created better income prospects in cities. Rural-to-urban migration expanded the population of cities, adding pressure to city infrastructures and services. According to United Nations estimates, 24 percent of Asia's population lived in urban areas in 1970, population figures for 2001 show that approximately 39 percent of the population in the Pacific Rim is urban, which is projected to increase to 52 percent by 2025 (United Nations 2001). These figures do not reflect the fact that although Asia is less urbanized than other regions, four of the world's ten largest cities are in Asia.

Migration into cities and limited resources only fueled governments' drive to create export-manufacturing markets in order to finance imports of food and raw materials that were necessary to provide for these new urban populations. Governments played a central role in coordinating the provision of infrastructure, managing new social conditions, maintaining political and social stability and managing emerging markets.

At the same time that Asian markets were expanding at tremendous rates, we became aware of new ways to understand economic, social and cultural activity. Globalization became the new mantra of the media, international business and national governments. It became a label that could be applied to just about anything. While the success of Asia over the previous twenty years certainly provided plenty of evidence that this new global economy was a powerful engine for growth, the collapse of the Asian markets exposed the dark side of the force as well. Globalization, it seems, is just the same as every other human construction in the sense that it has both positive and negative aspects to it.

In his essay entitled *Glossy Globalization* Peter Marcuse describes the duality of globalization. He writes:

> It creates an investment boom here, unemployment there; moves pollution from developed to developing countries; creates millionaires amidst abject poverty; stimulates migration but the burning of immigration reception centers too; builds shining skyscrapers but leaves the hovels in their shadows untouched where it does not render their former residents homeless; accelerates worldwide travel but produces

2.2 The empty shell of Muang Thong Thani stands testament to the false climate of property speculation in Bangkok prior to July of 1997.

massive congestion. All of these results are not neutral distributionally; most simply put, they help the rich worldwide and hurt the poor, and increase the polarization and divisions within societies.

(Marcuse 1997b: 29)

Marcuse goes on to describe that *Glossy Globalization* is the picture of globalization as a benign and inevitable process sweeping unstoppably over the world. His point is that it is neither benign, in that it is the result of human actions consciously undertaken by specific persons and groups, and that it is also not inevitable, in the current terms that it exists. It is important to understand this point. While the following discussion on globalization tends to explore the breathless aspects of the discourse this is done quite intentionally. Certainly the *glossy* nature of the discourse on globalization is responsible for a certain worldview, which leads to individual locations vying to attract business investment to that particular place and doing so often at the expense of other local priorities. It also leads to the conclusion that to not engage in these global games is an even worse future.

Most discussions on the global economy focus on the hyper-mobility of capital, the possibility of instantaneous transmission of information and money around the globe, the centrality of information outputs to our economic systems and emphasize the neutralization of geography and of places. What is ignored, however, is that even the most advanced information industries need a material infrastructure of buildings and work processes, and considerable agglomeration, in order to operate in global markets. Further, the globalization of economic activity has brought with it not only a vast dispersal of offices and factories, but also a growing importance of central functions to manage and coordinate such worldwide networks of activities. The work of Saskia Sassen is the clearest example of this kind of investigation (Sassen 1991).

The rapid growth of Asian cities has been taking place at a time when the impacts of free trade associations, the globalization of decision-making on investment location, and the impacts of new information-based industries are having a profound effect on manufacturing and service industry location, and hence on city development prospects. As the work of Dean Forbes notes among the most striking consequences of the impact of the global economy on the production of urban situations within the Asia Pacific Rim has been the accelerated creation of new urban forms (see Forbes 1999: 241; Forbes and Thrift 1987; Lin 1994). This includes the development of city-regions, which span across borders and generate their own financial resources (Rohwer 1995) and extended metropolitan regions, which comprise large cities and hinterlands of mixed rural and non-rural activities (Ginsburg *et al.* 1991; McGee and Robinson 1995). In addition the impact of the global economy on cities in the Asia Pacific Rim has led to the creation of "world city" services (Freidmann 1986: 72; 1995; Lo and Yeung 1996). These services define a city's importance in the global economy and lead to a hierarchically arranged ranking of cities based on the level of their urban services, not population (Yeung 1995). As we shall see in the coming chapters these urban services are clustered together to create new kinds of city infrastructure – the emergence of the global urban project.

On encompassing paradigms

To appreciate how the concept of globalization led to the creation of global urban projects it is necessary to explore some of the principal aspects of the globalization discourse. Of particular relevance is the proposition that the discourse itself establishes a powerful agent of fear in the minds of policy makers in national and city governments. The fear element of globalization is the fear of failing to capture the glorious wave of

2.3 The manufacturing of a global image to market the city as a node in the global economy is a major motivation for the constructed form of global urban projects such as Lujiazui, Shanghai.

node

globalization and being left stranded in the backwaters of economic despair. This fear leads to the development of policies and the provision of infrastructure, including urban projects, to secure competitive advantage and by doing so harness the opportunities offered by the global economy.

As a discourse globalization has created a plethora of terms and concepts, all of which aim at defining the forces that impact society, culture, economy and urban form. There is an incessant search to make sense out of what is happening in the world today. This is also true in urban dis-

courses, with the result that we are inundated with labels for these new descriptions of the urban condition – global city, 100-mile city, megacity, postmetropolis, cosmopolis, galactic metropolis, exopolis, edge city, simcity, fractal city, world city, and post-fordist industrial metropolis to name a few. Each of these terms is an attempt to adequately describe the complexity of forces shaping the modern city, and none being able to fully encompass the breadth of the issues.

The discourse on globalization is, as with the term itself, broad to the extreme. Dealing with it is a difficult task. As Edward Soja describes, it has become:

> the *fin de siècle*, a millenarian metaphor for practically everything that has been happening everywhere through the late twentieth century . . . [that] as an encompassing paradigm for all studies of the contemporary, globalization has become a particularly voracious trope, devouring and digesting a widening gyre of alternative discursive representations of what is new in our present world, while at the same time asserting itself as the necessary foundational concept for deciding what is to be done in response to this pervasively global newness.
>
> (Soja 2000: 190)

Soja describes well the pervasiveness of the concept. The assertion of globalization as the foundational concept for decision-making suggests that this self-perpetuation is inescapable. If globalization is both the problem and also the answer this creates a tremendous crisis for city decision makers. It sets up a condition where the negative aspects of globalization become freely apparent but unavoidable. To not engage with globalization creates even greater risk. It creates a mindset where the idea of not engaging in the global economy is not an option. Not to engage with globalization is to be left out of an encompassing paradigm that creates a certain worldview, is used to explain itself and becomes the ticket to global wealth.

While globalization, within the terms of this argument, can be seen to determine just about everything, the relationship between it and architectural production is an as yet underdeveloped discourse. Further, the relationship between globalization and designing the physical city is likewise underdeveloped. There is, however, a growing literature that deals with the Asian Pacific Rim city from a geographical perspective (see for example the work of Forbes and Thrift 1987; Forbes 2001; Ginsburg 1991; McGee and Robinson 1995; Friedmann 1986; Lo and Yeung 1996; Yeung 1995; and Olds 2001) however, this is less instructive of architecture's and urbanism's potential role in the formation of these new urban situations. Design discourse has been conspicuously silent on the issue.

To appreciate the complexity of the globalization discourse and the lack of physical design discussion within it requires a general overview of the constituent aspects of this multidimensional concept. There are principally three terrains, which define the concept of globalization; these are economic globalization, political globalization and cultural globalization.

Economic globalization

Most literature relates to the idea that globalization is the result of a tremendous expansion in the scale and scope of capitalist industrial production to the point where we have entered an era of global capitalism. It is characterized by a rapid growth in transactions and institutions that are outside the older framework of international relations. Global markets in finance and the multinational corporation are the major instances of the new transnational regime (Mittleman 1996; Sassen 1996). This is also marked by a new international division of labor, in which industrial urbanism is more widely distributed over the inhabited world than ever before. In this worldview commercial and financial circuits play a vital role in this restructuring process. The emphasis on an unprecedented expanding industrial urbanism and its accompanying economic globalization has developed principally in two disciplines of thinking. The first is based largely in economics and the second comes from geography. The geography perspective deals with impacts of globalization on cities and regions in ways that allude to the physical.

Evidence of economic globalization can be seen in physical development throughout Asia. An example of this is the Indonesia-Malaysia-Thailand Growth Triangle (IMT-GT) where economic cooperation pacts cut across borders and regions. The IMT-GT includes the development of common border towns, a road link between the Malaysian state of Perlis to Satun in southern Thailand, the construction of industrial estates in Northern Sumatra, and the development of the IMT-GT corridor between Songkhla/Haadyai in Thailand through Pulau Pinang in Malaysia to the Indonesian provinces of Belawan and Medan. The basis of this economic pact includes simplified border crossings using advanced information technology and industrial support infrastructures. The project aims at encouraging trans-border production networks. Another perhaps better-known example is the Singapore-Johore-Riau growth triangle, which in many respects can be seen as an extended metropolitan region crossing national boundaries (see Macleod and McGee 1996; Perry 1998).

Political globalization

The political discourse to globalization deals most directly with the manner in which globalization has eroded the sovereign power of nation-states. These political discourses are relevant to my discussions in as much as they describe the disempowering of nations to control their own destiny and feed into the fear element of globalization. It is this fear element that drives the sometimes frantic competitive positioning between nations and cities and ultimately leads, as we will see later, to the creation of competitive infrastructures, of which the global urban projects examined in this book are one type.

The political discourse on globalization focuses on the idea that nation states are, under the rubric of globalization, at the mercy of global markets and external political control. The Asia Economic Crisis fueled the idea that national governments were no longer in charge of their own destinies. This manifests both an intensification of the competitive agenda for most nations and the development of what Manuel Castells calls the establishment of the "super nation-state" (see Castells 1997: 267). The European Union is the best example of the type of political confederation to which Castells refers, however this has also manifest in economic regionalism with organizations such as the North American Free Trade Agreement (NAFTA) or the Association of South East Asian Nations (ASEAN).

The Association of South East Asian Nations (ASEAN) cooperation has resulted in greater regional integration. In addition to trade and investment liberalization, regional integration is being pursued through the development of the Trans-ASEAN transportation network consisting of major inter-state highway and railway networks, principal ports and sea lanes for maritime traffic, inland waterway transport and major civil aviation links. ASEAN is promoting the interoperability and interconnectivity of the national telecommunications equipment and services in order to defend regional economies from the influence of external players.

Cultural globalization

One of the most important texts in the realm of cultural globalization is Manuel Castells' *The Information City* which deals with a new informational mode of development arising from the restructuring of capitalism. At the heart of this new mode of development is information-based production. He writes that "we can see a major social trend standing out from all our observations: the historical emergence of the space of flows, superseding the meaning of the space of place" (Castells 1989: 348). This account privileges the capacity of electronic transmission over material infrastructure and electronic information output over everything else. In addition, it privileges the global elite of the new transnational corporate culture over other city groups.

Castells is not suggesting that place is not important. He is suggesting that relationships of place have changed. Importantly for concerns related to global urban projects he writes that the "new professional managerial class colonizes exclusive spatial segments that connect with one another across the city, the country and the world; they isolate themselves from the fragments of local societies . . ." (Castells 1989: 348). As we will see in the following chapters the global urban projects examined are to varying degrees removed from the context of the host city and operate separately from it, but are indeed connected to each other in various forms.

Global and local dimensions of globalization

The processes of globalization, and the informationalization of the processes of production, distribution and management, are profoundly altering the spatial structure of cities and the social structure of societies all over the planet. Among other things, globalization has increased competition among cities and towns for foreign investment. This occurs at all levels among different districts of a city, among different cities and towns, among different regions and provinces and between nations (see Borja and Castells 1997). To attract domestic and foreign investment, preferential policies are developed which in application are often not applied uniformly. The randomness of these policies creates tremendous problems for planning cities and towns, ultimately leading to a lack of cooperation in regional development. The implementation of planning policy and projects

without consideration for the regional implications of such acts is especially visible in regions that are developing very rapidly such as the Pearl River Delta in China where four international airports are to be built less than 50 kilometers from each other in Zhuhai, Macau, Hong Kong, and Shenzhen (see Fu-chen Lo and Yue-man Yeung 1996). The drive toward competitive advantage between nations, regions and cities results in a lack of coordination and a waste of resources. The socio-spatial effects of this articulation between the global and the local vary according to the levels of development of the countries, their urban history, their culture and their institutions. Yet it is in this articulation that the sources of new urban transformation processes lie (Borja and Castells 1997: 16).

Urban areas are not becoming redundant in the new information economy. Indeed, the global informational economy is organized on the basis of managerial centers capable of coordinating, managing and innovating the activities of companies structured in the networks for interurban, and often transnational, exchange. These nodes of economic activity are located within a matrix of strategic sites in cities all over the planet. At the heart of the new economic processes are activities concerned with finance, insurance, property, consultancy, legal services, advertising, design, marketing, public relations, security, information provision and computer system management (see Daniels 1993). These centers extend their influence into a surrounding area whose economic relations they then articulate (Friedman 1995: 22).

While advanced services are present in all large cities and nearly all countries, the higher levels of the advanced services networks are concentrated in certain nodes in some countries (see Harasim 1993; Daniels 1993). This concentration follows a hierarchical model among urban centers, with the most important functions, in terms of skills, power and capital, being concentrated in the chief metropolitan areas of the world (see Thrift 1996; Thrift and Leyshon 1997).

Amin and Thrift provide a hierarchical structure for this network. In their terms there exist: Global Financial Articulations (including London, New York and Tokyo), Multi National Articulations (including Miami, Los Angeles, Frankfurt, Amsterdam and Singapore), Important National Articulations (including Paris, Zurich, Madrid, Mexico City, São Paulo, Seoul and Sydney), then Subnational or Regional Articulations (which include, Osaka-Kobe, San Francisco, Seattle, Houston, Chicago, Boston, Vancouver, Toronto, Montreal, Hong Kong, Milano, Lyon, Barcelona, Munich and the Rhine-Ruhr region of Dusseldorf-Cologne-Essen-Dortmund) (see Amin and Thrift 1992). Yeung (1995) argues that a new hierarchic system of cities is emerging in the Asia Pacific Rim as well. In his formulation Yueng includes Tokyo, Osaka, Nagoya, Seoul, Taipei, Hong Kong, Manila, Bangkok, Kuala Lumpur, Singapore and Jakarta in this network. While this list may still be relevant today the ranking of the cities within it would have surely changed in response to the Asia Economic Crisis. While the order of this ranking is not critical for my purpose here, it is important to appreciate that there obviously exists tremendous competition between cities in the network to capture greater shares of global capital.

The issue at the heart of many national policy agendas is that if cities are not able to capture a significant share of the global capital market they risk the possibility of being fundamentally obsolete. The result is aggressive policies by national governments to ensure that they remain competitive. As soon as a region in the world becomes articulated into the global economy there is a concurrent demand for the establishment of an urban node to accommodate the required advanced services. The development of these high value complexes focuses on the production and processing of information. These are the urban nodes that locate the headquarters of companies, where financial firms can find both the suppliers they need and the highly skilled employees they require. They invariably include the extension or redevelopment of an international airport, a satellite telecommunications system, luxury hotels, English-language secretarial support, financial and consultancy firms familiar with the region, local and regional government offices capable of providing information, infrastructure to back up international investors and a local labor market with personnel skilled in advanced services. It is for these reasons that we find conditions of centrality in these urban development nodes and it should come as no surprise that all of the global urban projects examined in this book include these services and infrastructures. These are, in effect, the characteristics of the new global infrastructure.

Promoters and detractors of globalization

There are those in the international economic and political arenas who celebrate globalization. Soja describes this as the "most influential" ideoscape of the contemporary world. These are the power elites whose aim is to foster conditions.

> that facilitate the freedoms of global capitalism: increasing privatization of the public sphere, deregulation in every economic sector, the breakdown of barriers to trade and the free flow of capital, attacks on the welfare state and labor unions, and other efforts to reshape the power of established political and territorial authorities to control both the globality of production and the production of globality.
>
> (Soja 2000: 216)

There are two aspects of the most influential ideoscape that are important to highlight. The first is that the power of the global elite is both real and imaginary. It is real in the sense that today there exists the ability to move money quickly from one location to another. The crisis in Thailand displayed this and will be explained in more detail in Chapter 5. It is also imaginary in that the fear of this capacity establishes the fear element of globalization. In other words, national governments must not only compete to attract capital, but also to keep it.

The authors of the *Global Competitiveness Report 2000* produced by Harvard University's Center for International Development and the World Economic Forum, write that the

> evidence today still suggests that increased global integration of the 1990s will be seen eventually as one of the brightest events for millions of the world's poor . . . [and] many of the countries that have achieved rapid growth via global integration were relatively poorer countries in East Asia such as China, Malaysia, Thailand, Indonesia, Korea, and Taiwan . . .
>
> (Porter *et al.* 2000: 27)

They argue, naturally, that globalization brings with it the entrance of international companies who provide jobs and this in turn raises salaries. Further that even though globalization, in and of itself, will not solve the problems of the world's poor, that to resist it is even less of an answer. For the Center for International Development and for the World Economic Forum, the answer to many of the problems of the world is to promote globalization. Not to accept globalization is to be left out, which means having little or no access to the promise of the twenty-first century.

The *Global Competitiveness Report* (GCR) ranks some 58 countries from around the world according to two indicators. The first is the Growth Com-

petitiveness Index, which measures the factors that contribute to future growth of an economy, measured as a rate of change of GDP per person. The other is the Current Competitiveness Index, which aims to identify the factors that underpin high current productivity and hence current economic performance, measured by the level of GDP per person. For the GCR, "competitiveness" is defined as "the set of institutions and economic policies supportive of high rates of economic growth in the medium term" (Porter *et al.* 2000: 14). In order to grow, an economy must be competitive and to be competitive it must be integrated globally. Technology then plays an important role in allowing this integration. The GCR notes that sustained economic growth depends to a large part on a national economy's ability to upgrade technology, "either through innovation at home or through the rapid and extensive adoption of technologies developed abroad" (Porter *et al.* 2000: 19). We only need to think about Singapore, Malaysia, Thailand or China to see examples of extensive adoption of technologies developed abroad. In the case of Malaysia, in particular, this led to the establishment of the Multimedia Super Corridor to be discussed at some length in Chapter 10.

Globalization also has its detractors (see Starr 2000; Chin and Mittelman 1997; Mittelman 2000). Of concern to many is the question of who benefits from globalization's economic success? The recent World Economic Forum Summit in Seattle provided plenty of evidence that there are some that do not rejoice in globalization. World Economic Forum protesters, ranging from trade unions to anti-globalization campaigners and anarchists, disrupted the November 1999 conference and among other things attacked a McDonald's restaurant, a Starbucks café, several banks and a Gap clothing store – all viewed as proponents of the so-called "global corporate agenda." The World Trade Organization has become a

2.4 One city that has capitalized on its ability to present an image attractive to global investors is Singapore. View of the Padang, Singapore.

2.5 The global city of capital – Lujiazui, Shanghai.

target for angst about globalization free trade and corporate mega-mergers that have made average people worry about both the pace and the nature of change in the world economy. The detractors fear that the poor are being exploited and worry that under the terms of globalization that the common person is reduced to a unit of production and that value in the global economy is evaluated in extremely narrow economic criteria.

In terms of urban environments too there is a worry that cities are evaluated based upon extremely narrow economic criteria and that other criteria that have to do with quality of life, environmental concerns, social justice, or equity, for example, are not considered important. This kind of narrow evaluation leads to cities competing with each other and focusing increasingly on a narrow set of goals and objectives. Social services and other things that mark and describe our compassion and human culture do not fit into this narrow agenda. The globalization protesters voice loud concern over what they see as attacks on the welfare state, which for them erode the quality of life in cities. These protests equate the idea of the "world city" with the corporate city of capital and political control.

Ranking world cities

The modern usage of the term "world city" derives from Peter Hall's book entitled *The World Cities* (1966). Hall defines world cities as places "where a quite disproportionate part of the world's most important business is conducted" (Hall 1966: 7). For Hall, world cities were centers of great population, political power, trade, finance and communication. They were also centers of education, culture and the arts. As the world city discourse developed however, power and control became the important criteria for evaluating world city ranking. For later scholars, cultural aspects are ignored and instead primacy is placed on a city's

economic and political functions in the global economy.

John Friedmann took up the call of world cities in the 1980s and his work can be credited for setting the agenda for many others. Friedmann's "world city hypothesis" represents a conceptual framework for understanding the role of the global economy in the determination of urban outcomes. For Friedmann, a world city is a major site of concentration and accumulation of international capital and this concentration leads inevitably to growth distortions and social costs. For Friedmann key cities throughout the world are used by global capital as "basing points" in the spatial organization and articulation of production and markets. The resulting linkages make it possible to arrange world cities into a complex spatial hierarchy.

For Friedmann world cities are the sites where decisions are made that determine global financial operations. Importantly they are also, referring back to Marcuse, sites of spatial and class polarization which lead to social costs at rates that tend to exceed the fiscal capacity of the state (see Knox and Taylor 1995). This makes clear that there is both a belief that world cities are somehow accumulators of wealth and at the same time suffer as a result of these polarization tendencies. In their national economic agendas governments certainly play to the primacy of the positive side of this equation and although may indeed be aware of the negative, this awareness is not strong enough to deny their world city ambition.

The leading figure who took up Friedman's initial work was Saskia Sassen. Sassen's book *The Global City: New York, London, Tokyo* (1991), describes the new service economy concentrating on the finance, insurance, and real estate sectors (FIRE), which combine to produce what she calls "post industrial production sites." Her argument is that there has been a simultaneous dispersal of factories, offices, and service outlets and the reorganization of the financial industry have led to new clusters of control and management. There has also been the creation of a new type of market place "with a multiplicity of advanced corporate service firms and non-bank financial institutions [management consultancies, legal firms, personnel and marketing firms, etc.]." And most importantly that this new market place has been created through tremendous innovations in services and finance and that cities have emerged as key locations for the production of such innovation (Sassen 1991: 126). Further her work points to the fact that parts of cities and parts of that city's population are key to this production and that indeed to talk of a universal creation of wealth through globalization would be wrong.

The work of Friedman and Sassen poses an interesting possibility, could it be possible that the work of these scholars (and others), whose motivation was simply to understand the complexity of global interactions, might actually reinforce and indeed exacerbate the fear element of globalization in the minds of national and city decision makers? Could it be that as one begins to evaluate and rank cities in an order of global importance and power, one contributes to an environment of tremendous competition between them to achieve a higher ranking? One could imagine a government leader, a middle level policy advisor or a city planner in a lowly ranked city, deliberately plotting to improve their city's ranking in this global pecking order. This may indeed succeed in attracting new global capital and increasing a city's integration into the global economy, elevating its "world city" ranking. But it

2.6 New York is a global city that others attempt to emulate. Rockefeller Center Plaza, New York.

would inevitably also heighten social costs in that same location. Indeed the riots in Seattle suggest that many people believe that this is indeed what is happening in urban environments today. As the descriptions of the urban projects show such actions are indeed in evidence.

Competition and the quest for world city status and image

In the cities of developing nations competitive advantage is an essential element to many national policy agendas. Competition between cities is not new. Throughout time, cities have competed with each other for larger shares of capital and trade. Often competitive advantages have been due to location or natural features or secured through war and conquest. However, in a world of unprecedented technological advancement and the development of a truly integrated global economy the competition to attract wealth, in both physical and human terms, has become even more crucial and depends less on location and more on the availability of appropriate infrastructure.

The stakes are high as governments face increases in urban populations and strains on urban services. The World Development Report produced by the World Bank states that:

> At the beginning of the 21st Century, half the world's population will be living in areas classified as urban. As recently as 1975, this share was just over one-third, but by 2025 it will rise to almost two-thirds. The most rapid changes in the urban demographics will occur in developing countries. While the rate of urbanization has passed its peak in relatively high-income countries in Latin America, Eastern Europe and the Middle East, the transition is just beginning in Asia and Africa. Urban populations are expected to increase by almost 1.5 billion people in the next twenty-five years. The speed of urbanization and the enormous numbers make it one of the major development challenges of the 21st century.
>
> (World Bank 2000a: 46)

The changes in urban situations will be unprecedented and will have tremendous consequences for national and city governments. As urban populations increase governments will be forced to provide more urban employment opportunities, more urban infrastructure and more urban services. To do this governments will have to attract more capital to pay for these additional expenditures. To attract capital governments must compete with other nations, regions, or cities, creating a self-perpetuating development cycle of which governments have little control.

Since national governments are enmeshed within the "system of multilayered economic governance, their role and power continues to be qualified decisively by economic globalization" (Held and McGrew 2000: 27). The Asian Economic Crisis gave credence to the idea that governments are no longer able to regulate their own financial positions. With the increasing volatility of global capital, governments have been forced to adopt "increasingly similar (neoliberal) economic strategies ..." (Held and McGrew 2000: 27). This creates pressure for national governments to follow the line or be left behind. Ankie Hoogvelt describes that indeed, the governments of East Asia have been successful in developing stronger bonds with the global economy. He writes that "the state-led developmentalist project has succeeded in catapulting the economies of a small number of NICs [Newly Industrialized Countries] into the heartland of the reconstructed global capitalist system" (Hoogvelt 2000: 357). While this success has debatable merit it obviously raises many social and cultural issues.

The negative side of globalization is that as global competition intensifies, governments are forced to take increasingly aggressive positions which in the end lead to two concurrent ends. The first, as Held and McGrew note, is that to maintain competitive position, governments reduce levels of social protection. The second is that governments shift priorities to policies and infrastructures that both attempt to capture larger shares of this volatile capital and importantly, have the appearance of doing so. Thus projecting the "image of being global" is just as important as "being global" in the competitive global economy.

The idea that this global infrastructure has both a particular form and a projected image leads us to the relationship between urban projects and the notion of a global urbanism. Sharon Zukin makes the point that for global cities the presentation of a particular image is critical to their real and projected success and that the symbolic economy of a global city [here she refers to the image needed to attract investment capital] shapes the lingua franca of global elites and aids the circulation of images that influence "climates" of opinion and investment "mentalities". Zukin refers to the deliberate manufacturing of a particular image of the city by internationalizing it and "abstracting a legible image from the service economy" which results from the desire to gain competitive advantage (see Zukin 1992).

Concrete forms of globalization

Given that we understand that cities are competitive and that we have a general understanding of

2.7 Concrete forms of globalization appear in many guises. In Hong Kong, for example, it manifests itself in a clustering of a particular kind of real estate development, which results in a certain kind of urban situation. View of the urban space at the foot of the Marriott Hotel, Hong Kong.

the work of globalization, then one might assume that we would be able to develop a list of ingredients that cities should include in their strategic visions. As the following project descriptions make clear this is not an easy thing to do. The need for a clear understanding of the "ingredients" of these environments is an issue for governments, developers and also for designers, who are often asked to make them. This is quite a different question in the emerging urban conditions in the Asia Pacific Rim to the established environments of New York or London.

Unprecedented urbanization in Asia is creating urban conditions that we are just beginning to experience, analyze and understand. Rapid urbanization in China, for example is less than a decade old and the scale of future urban expansion will be unprecedented. This is also true for the rest of Asia as six of the ten most populous countries in the world are there (see Vernoorn 1998). Further, Asia has thirteen of the world's twenty-three megacities of at least 8 million inhabitants (Fu-chen Lo and Yue-man Yeung 1998). It is in this context, therefore, that the future of what we understand as "city" will be defined.

Global competition, modernization and unprecedented population growth has initiated a new phase of urbanization in Asia. New urban structures are challenging traditional ways of thinking about cities. The cities represented in this book – Tokyo, Yokohama, Bangkok, Shanghai, Beijing, Ho Chi Minh, Hanoi, Singapore and Kuala Lumpur represent nine locations where these new urban conditions are developing. These cities provide us with insights into how the future of urban form might look, how it might function and also what kind of culture it might be able to support. Despite the Asia Economic Crisis the future of the planet will be inexplicably determined by how cities in Asia develop.

The projects examined in this book are all responsive to the forces shaping the global sphere. In their own ways they manifest different visions for how the future of cities might be. Undoubtedly they all represent some of the most important real estate investments in their host cities. They all share the same general characteristics:

- They were all instigated in response to perceptions of global competition.
- They all attempt, in different ways, to secure competitive advantage for their host city.
- They provide a new kind of space occupancy not available prior to their construction.
- They aim to attract a very specific kind of occupant, the global elite.
- They are radically different in scale and articulation to the environment around them.
- They all attempt to secure celebrity status by projecting an image that can be marketed in the global market place.
- They encapsulate a specific and narrow definition of urban life and culture, and
- This urban vision becomes the dominant urban vision by which all other urban visions must relate.

The global urban projects represent a series of critical moments in the history of cities. In their development we are able to examine the emerging urban territories of the world. The Asia Development Bank (ADB) in its "Asia Development Outlook" (ADO) shows that the economic recovery of South East Asia has proved more rapid than anyone would have anticipated. All the countries in the region registered positive growth in 1999. The GDP growth rate for the region was 3.2 percent in 1999, in sharp contrast to a negative rate 7.5 percent in 1998. (At time of writing the world is once again dealing with economic uncertainty after the tragic events of September 11, 2001.) Fueled by strong domestic demand and favorable economic conditions, market analysts are assuming that Asia's economy will continue to be the fastest growing in the world, with economic growth rates eventually higher than those of industrialized countries such as the United States and Japan. In terms of industrial production, it took Asia less than two years to return to the pre-crisis level of output (Asia Development Bank 2000). If the future of the world economy will be found in Asia, then the future of the global city will likewise be determined there. This is of critical importance to urban design.

Toward an emerging urbanity

One of the interesting things about the globalization discourse is that despite its enormity and breadth, most of it ignores the physical design of the city and none of it provides an armature for thinking about the future of urban design. One of the few that deals with city making and urbanism is Deyan Sudjik's *The 100 Mile City* (1992). Trained as an architect, Sudjik provides a unique contribution for his attempt to understand the city making processes of the global city by looking at five cities: Paris, London, New York, Los Angeles, and Tokyo. Sudjik locates his work in the understanding that world cities operate in a singular economic system, one that leads to increased pressure to be competitive. He writes that the "metamorphosis [of these cities] into a system of interlinked, but also antagonistic cities has been the real legacy of the 1980s" (Sudjik 1992: 1). Sudjik's focus is on the boom building periods of the 1980s where the industrial city "mutated" into a different kind of urban condition, one that we have yet to fully comes to terms with. While Sudjik provides an explanation of and a critique of this new kind of urban condition he does not provide a direction for what urban design should be about or its direction in relation to this new condition of the city.

To arrive at an understanding of urban design's role in the context of globalized urban environments we must examine a series of urban projects created in response to forces induced by global competition. The following chapters will outline the contexts of some of the largest and most ambitious of these kinds of projects in the world today. While the urban projects examined are but one aspect of a much larger urbanization drama unfolding in cities throughout the Pacific Rim, what is remarkable about them is that unlike the multitude of separate policy, land use, development, design, infrastructure, transportation and economic decisions that combine to create the urban form of a metropolis, these projects offer a defined presentation of an urban vision. In their singularity they provide a clear articulation of an "idea of the city."

If one accepts that these are indeed the most important urban projects in an economic and political sense that it stands to reason that they should also be the most important in an urbanistic sense. In other words, they should somehow represent something more than expressions of power and capital and should, in addition, present a vision for what a particular city aspires to be, what type of urban form it deems appropriate and what type of urban culture it aims to cultivate. Urban projects in this sense are clearly physical representations or constructed evidence of the value that a culture places on built form. This kind of articulation necessarily requires the agency of design therefore to coordinate and establish the basis for city making.

The agency of design is indeed a fundamental aspect of making large projects. Dana Cuff describes that the scale alone of civic constructions requires them to be deterministic and that the effort required to bring a large project together is not only a long and arduous process it is also a matter of ideology, for there must be a "motivational narrative" to direct development when the

2.8 The provision of modern infrastructure in cities often results in the articulation of spaces that are not conducive to the establishment of a public realm. Tokyo Rainbow Town, Japan.

2.9 Minato Mirai 21 is a global urban project that presents an order untypical for Japanese urban situations.

initial enthusiasm wanes (see Cuff 2000). Large-scale urban projects must be directed toward some set of ambitions or toward some set of goals. In this way the direction of a project can be maintained during the long period of their implementation. Fundamentally all urban projects must include this element of directedness. It is this after all that defines the form of a project and separates each project from one another. The following chapters will show that there are common and foundational economic and political motivations in each of the global projects; the reason for their differences then stems from this issue of urbanistic directedness.

Given the *tabula rasa* conditions in which these projects locate themselves a designer must decide to create some kind of physical form, which is not an extension of any existing fabric. These are for the most part isolated projects, which requires that they be made and constructed within an absence of physical context, without traces of residual elements. Simply these sites do not provide any structures from which a scheme might extend and they must be started from scratch. The chosen form might emulate Paris or Detroit or Rome or New York or combinations of all of these. The point is that this is a conscious decision on the part of the designer. The basis of this decision is vested in a set of beliefs about what the "good city" should be, what it should look like and how it should function. Designers base such decisions within their own understanding of the idea of the city.

Regardless of one's own critique of the projects presented here, it is clear that they all grapple with this issue in various ways. In a time of tremendous uncertainty in planning and design in the United States what is perhaps most interesting is that these projects confidently present us with their specific visions. This contrasts with the situation in the United States, which today seems to be suffering from a crisis of confidence. In the Asia Pacific Rim the future is being boldly embraced while in the United States urban design seems incapable of describing the future at all and what future is presented is in reality the representation and repackaging of mythic notions of the past.

Although in some of these Pacific Rim projects there is clear evidence of certain nostalgia, this does not lead in the same way to a presentation of a mythic past. Putrajaya, as we shall see, certainly employs nostalgic references to reinforce its civic importance, but it does not attempt to reproduce an environment from the past. In the Pacific Rim urban design is engaged with issues of grandeur and visions of exuberance reminiscent of the great city making periods of Paris under Hausmann, Washington under L'Enfant and Canberra under Burley Griffen. This contrasts to the situation today in the United States where urban design is concerned with expressions of the ordinary and visions of conservatism. In the context of the Pacific Rim change is seen as good and the expression of it progressive. In the United States change is almost universally met with accolades of derision, and the expression of stasis is sought above all else. Over a period of some forty years urban design in America has gone through a process where the scale and scope of the field has diminished, resulting is an endemic reduction of vision.

This reduction has created a crisis of confidence in urban design, which is a significant issue for urbanism. The problem is that urban design lacks a definitive model to follow and a conviction for a particular path. This is complicated by the fact that the world is changing faster than us, as designers seem able to keep pace. Our understanding of what a city is and how to make it seem at odds with the way the world works today in an age of globalization. The models and precedents of what we hold to be the "good city" are no longer relevant for what the city has become or what it needs to be. Too often contemporary urban design is about the application of ideas that have their genesis in historically informed constructions. This is dangerous because it ties urban design to the notion that it is inherently a regressive act. What is needed, more than anything else in contemporary urbanism, is a recalibration of our ideas and an embrace of the current reality in which we find ourselves within an understanding of urbanism as a progressive activity.

As designers we must hold on to the idea that through the agency of design we can affect positive change, although perhaps in redefined terms. Too often the time lag required to design and then to construct an urban project means that our projects become a kind of historic catalogue of the past in our attempt to satisfy the needs of the present. The world changes so rapidly that by the time a city recognizes trends, studies impacts, plans for new accommodations, designs a response and builds a project, the trends that instigated the process in the first place have changed. One only need look to the story of the Amsterdam Waterfront Finance Company and its demise to understand how cities struggle to accommodate changing trends in real estate markets (see Marshall 2001). All too often planning cities today is about the provision of obsolescence.

In response to this there is a general move away from big ideas to strategic and engaged responses to urban design in the United States. There has developed a general distrust in the idea of the comprehensive master plan, where a singular intellect controls urban outcomes and the "big idea" often takes decades to construct. In the American context the results of comprehensive planning are evident in places with a deficit of infrastructure, office parks with a deficit

2.10 The future of the city is being made in places such as Lujiazui, Shanghai.

2.11 The iconography of a global urban project – Petronas Towers, Kuala Lumpur.

of urbanity and consumer and commercial agglomerations with a deficit of design (see Kaltenbruner 1999: 6).

The global urban projects presented in this book raise questions that lie at the heart of contemporary discourses in urbanism. From an evaluation of these very large urban projects in the Pacific Rim how might we redefine urban design operations in light of the contemporary context? The issue for urban design is what kind of urbanisms, if any, do these projects represent and how might an understanding of them inform future thinking and critical practice?

Japan

Tokyo and Yokohama

3.1 View across Tokyo Rainbow Town toward Kenzo Tange's Fuji Television Building with its signature orb. In the distance are the Rainbow Bridge and the context of Tokyo.

3 Tokyo Rainbow Town, Japan

Tokyo is not a city for only Japan anymore. Tokyo should be a world city that is open to the international society.

Mayor Suzuki "Symposium on the Tokyo District in the twenty-first Century" May 22, 1988

The city I am talking about (Tokyo) offers this precious paradox: it does possess a center, but this center is empty. The entire city turns around a site both forbidden and indifferent, a residence concealed beneath foliage, protected by moats, inhabited by an emperor who is never seen, which is to say, literally, by no one knows who.

Roland Barthes, *Empire of Signs*

Japanese society has been forced to deal with globalization in a very rapid way. For more than two centuries, from 1638 through to 1853, the Japanese resolutely refused contact with the outside world. This changed in 1853 when Commodore Mathew Perry, with the aid of the United States Navy, convinced the Shogun to allow American ships access to Japanese ports. Today Japan is completely dependent on accessing the global flow of trade and finance. The transition from isolation to complete integration is still an issue of considerable unease for many Japanese (see Reischauer and Jansen 1995). Japan's relationship to globalization is not clearly understandable. There exists a strange tension between an acknowledgment of themselves as world leaders and the idea that they are distinct and separate from the rest of the world. These tensions exist at many levels of society and express themselves in both a drive for internationalization (kokusai-ka), and at the same time a reinforcement of Japanese identity, particularly in living habits and immigration policy. There is a concurrent encouragement for Japanese businesses to operate in global arenas but a hesitancy to allow foreigners access into local markets. The refusal of the Japanese to allow Japanese citizenship to those from other countries is one indication of the attempt to preserve "Japanese-ness."

Japan's remarkable development since World War II was achieved through a series of deliberate and active measures to position Japan as a world financial power. The Japanese government envisioned Tokyo, the capital of Japan, as a center of world finance. This vision has led to a tremendous concentration of corporate headquarters, rising land values, and diminished housing supply in the center of Tokyo. Along with London and New York it is one of the leading financial centers in the global economy; however this center of world finance suffers from a series of urban problems, including congestion and competition for urban resources. In response to this Japanese planners sought new locations in which to construct the Japanese global city. The waterfront within Tokyo Bay offered such opportunities and Tokyo Rainbow Town is one such project.

Tokyo Rainbow Town is a global urban project envisioned as a silicon city for the twenty-first century on reclaimed land in the Tokyo Port. It was designed to incorporate the latest urban

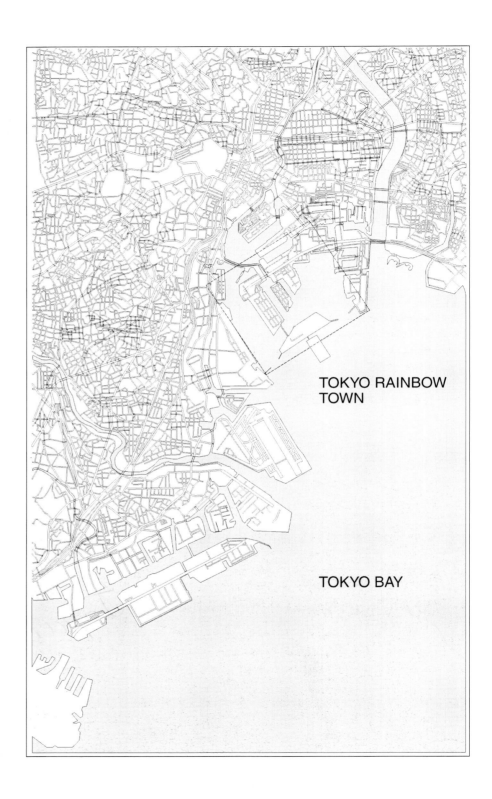

TOKYO RAINBOW
TOWN

TOKYO BAY

Map of Tokyo Bay showing the location of Tokyo Rainbow Town.

infrastructures and aimed at a balance of residential and business functions. Starting life as "Tokyo Teleport," it was conceived as a 24-hour business island. The Teleport would be an island that would never turn the lights off and look like a "wonder land" floating in the darkness of the bay. Inside this island an extremely competitive business environment would play an important role in the Japanese economy. The Tokyo Teleport [later Rainbow] Town project was an integral part of Tokyo's transformation from a single-centered structure to a multi-centered one, preparing Tokyo to be a twenty-first century international metropolis for the future's advanced information oriented society.

Tokyo is the center of all things in Japan. The Tokyo Metropolitan Area covers 4 percent of Japan's total land area yet accounts for 26 percent of the total population (see Tokyo Metropolitan Government 1999). Tokyo was the name given to the city of Edo in 1868 when the seat of the imperial family was moved there from Kyoto. At its center is the metropolitan prefecture (to), of Tokyo, Japan's capital and largest city. The three prefectures (ken) of Saitama (to the north), Chiba (to the east) and Kanagawa (to the south) border Tokyo. In 1996, Tokyo's population was approximately 33 million people in an area covering approximately 13,550 square kilometers (Tokyo Metropolitan Government 1999: 1). From the surrounding three prefectures almost 3.5 million people commute to Tokyo To everyday. Thirteen percent of these people are employed in Tokyo's three central wards, which accounts for only 0.3 percent of the Tokyo Metropolitan Area. The city of Tokyo refers to the 23 wards (ku) that constitute the city proper. There are three other major cities within the metropolitan area typically referred to as Tokyo – Yokohama, Kawasaki and Chiba. Yokohama, about 20 miles southwest of Tokyo, is the second largest city in Japan. The industrial city of Kawasaki lies between Tokyo and Yokohama. Both Yokohama and Kawasaki are in Kanagawa prefecture. Chiba, to the east of Tokyo, is also heavily industrialized.

3.2 View across the city of Tokyo. Despite its density surprisingly the majority of the city comprises small-scale buildings. However, as is obvious in this image Tokyo suffers from lack of open space.

Tokyo has a high population density with 24 people per hectare in comparison to the other global financial cities of New York with 6 people per hectare, and London with 10 people per hectare. Tokyo is the center for Japanese politics, economics and culture. Internationalization has created "time-zoneless" business within the city. More than 90 percent of all the databases in Japan, about 70 percent of strategic business think tanks, and 65 percent of the total sales of service industries are generated in the city. Information is distributed throughout Japan from Tokyo; with most Japanese television programs created by the key stations in the city. Publishing companies and bookstores are also concentrated there. This concentration of business causes a tremendously high demand for office space in the city.

The structure of the urban fabric and the problems of redeveloping areas in the city have created major obstacles to providing more office space in Tokyo. The city is structured historically around small housing lots, which are protected by law in Japan. This makes it difficult to redevelop urban environments. Japanese planners faced two issues in their desire to "internationalize" Tokyo – to find space to accommodate global business and in an environment of increasing globalization of business activities to produce urban space that could be evaluated by other countries (see Ito 2000). This became a major preoccupation for Japanese planners in the 1980s. Among other things, initiatives were developed to consolidate small properties to make larger development parcels, areas such as the high-rise district in Shinjiku are examples of this. However this strategy proved difficult. Frustrated with the difficulties of land adjustment Tokyo planners sought new spaces unencumbered by historical fabric. This search led them to Tokyo Bay and to a series of reclamation projects. Tokyo Rainbow Town is one of these projects.

Rainbow Town – Tokyo's global project

The economic centrality in Tokyo and the booming economy of the 1980s contributed to a situation where land prices began to double annually. Office vacancy rates fell to almost zero and the price of housing in the city moved beyond the reach of the vast majority of Tokyoites. The usual rate of land price inflation in the early 1980s was around 3 percent; however, it became 10 percent in 1987 and rocketed up to 77 percent in 1989 (Yamada 1989: 69). The demand for space for headquarter operations and service industries continued to concentrate on a relatively small area in central Tokyo. In 1986 the Nomura Research Institute estimated that twenty to fifty more sky-scrapers were required to secure the physical transformation of Tokyo into a world financial center. As Mike Douglass writes:

> . . . the stage was thus set for the tremendous price boom of commercial property that was triggered by the revaluation of the Japanese currency at the end of 1985. Commercial property prices more than doubled in 1986, and by the end of 1987 in prime locations in Tokyo they exceeded [US]$20,000 per square foot, almost ten times the average price in New York and twenty times that in Los Angeles.
>
> (Douglass 1998: 97)

This unprecedented demand led to two distinctive urban operations. On the one hand it led many developers to consolidate smaller land holdings into parcels large enough to support modern commercial buildings. However, this involved many complicated negotiations with small landholders and often these negotiations were unsuccessful. Within the fabric of Tokyo one can often see cases of unsuccessful negotiations, evidenced by tiny timber shops and houses wrapped by enormous newer developments. It also led to the provision of new land through reclamation activities in Tokyo Bay.

Tokyo – a city on the bay

Tokyo sits on the north and western shores of Tokyo Bay. As the Roland Barthes' quote noted at the beginning of this chapter, at the center of Tokyo lies the Imperial Palace. From this center a cobweb pattern of streets emanates. The cobweb survives in main arteries that radiate out from the center, leaving the old city through post stations called the Five Mouths. The most important of these was Shinagawa. Despite several reconstructions of the city, the pattern, if not the fabric, of Edo remains.

Edo consisted of the high and the low city. The high city, Yamanote, was where the Samurai had their mansions. This was in contrast to the low city, Shitamachi, where the hustle and bustle of the merchants was expressed in the tightly woven fabric of streets and houses. Shitamachi was a city lying between the hills of Yamanote and Tokyo Bay and until the explosion of growth after World War II Shitamachi had a close connection with the water. Before the war there was a network of canals and rivers that defined the form of the low city. As space became a valuable commodity, however, the waterways were filled and the boundary between the city and the water's edge was pushed farther back.

The establishment of Tokyo Rainbow Town follows a long history of growth and expansion in Tokyo. Planning for this growth has never been an easy task, made all the more difficult by rapid development. Given the amorphous nature and tremendous size of the city one might conclude that Tokyo is a city without planning. This is wrong. Tokyo is a highly regulated urban situation with a tradition of modern planning that dates to the end of the nineteenth century.

Planning for growth and expansion

To appreciate the history of urban expansion into Tokyo Bay, one must understand a little of this planning history. City planning, as a modern concern, began in Tokyo in 1889 with the *City Ward Improvements Plan*. This plan focused on improving the condition of roads, bridges, railroads, parks and public markets in the original fifteen wards of the city. This was modified and then repealed in 1919 and in its place the *City Planning Law and Urban Buildings Law* were enacted. This marks the first attempt at land use control in Tokyo and divided the city into three broad categories of residential, commercial and industrial uses.

Tokyo was significantly rebuilt twice in the twentieth century. The first rebuilding followed the Great Kanto Earthquake of September 1923. The fires that ensued after the earthquake destroyed about 40 percent of the urban area of Tokyo. This disaster allowed the city government to reorganize the city through the establishment of the *Disaster Recovery Plan* undertaken from 1924 to 1930, which included the reorganization of some 3600 hectares of the city. The city center and Shitamachi were completely renovated and many canals and waterways were filled. This effort included the provision of over a hundred kilometers of new trunk roads and the construction of new public parks, including Sumida, Hamacho and Kinshicho Parks. Despite the reorganization efforts the street pattern of central Tokyo resembles that of Edo. Old streets were widened and new streets cut through, but the city made itself in much the same shape that it was before.

The city expanded as an industrial metropolis through the early decades of the twentieth century to a point where new planning was needed to control the formation of urban areas. Green belts were introduced as a device to control the sprawling city. This was instigated with the *1939 Tokyo*

3.3 Japanese office workers in Idabashi, Tokyo. Evident is the visual complexity of the urban scene in Tokyo.

Green Areas Plan. In 1940, to commemorate the 2600th year of the accession of the Emperor Jinmu, tracts of land designated as Green Belts were acquired in Kinuta, Jindai, Koganei, Toneri, Mizumoto, and Shinozaki. Most of these areas remain as large-scale parks today.

Allied bombing decimated approximately 16,000 hectares of the city during World War II. Immediately after the war the Tokyo Metropolitan Government initiated the *Tokyo Postwar Recovery Plan* in 1946. The main elements of the plan were the establishment of satellite cities around the region with Tokyo as the hub and the idea that the population within the confines of the ward area was to be maintained at 3.5 million people. The plan also included a series of green rings covering some 19,000 hectares or about one-third of the ward area. The *Postwar Recovery Plan* however was invalid almost immediately because of the rapid population influx into the city. In 1947, for example, the population within the ward area was already at 3.82 million and rising. The *Postwar Recovery Plan* was reviewed in 1949 and severely curtailed. The period from 1950 onwards marks the beginnings of Tokyo's modern expansion and the development of the city as an important global financial center.

The Japanese compressed into twenty-five years an urban experience that spanned a century in the United States (Hill and Fujita 1993: 6). Between 1955 and 1965 the Tokyo metropolitan region increased from 15 to 21 million, adding an average of 600,000 people every year (Douglass 1993: 84). This brought with it severe social problems related to environmental degradation during a period of rapid economic growth. Government policies focused on industrial production alone and this exacerbated pollution, housing problems, and congestion within the city. Problems in accommodating population and economic growth led to the recognition of the need for planning and

this in turn led to the formation of the *First National Land Development Plan* in 1962. Aware of the fact that Tokyo was the center of population and industrial activity, this plan emphasized the creation of regional growth poles to diffuse economic benefits into the countryside. However, despite nearly forty years of government efforts to diffuse the dominance of Tokyo, the city remains as the central focus for nearly every economic activity in the country.

Several concurrent phenomena characterize the development of Japan during the 1960s and the 1970s. Japan's economy expanded at a tremendous rate. This led to rising incomes and the development of a consumer society. With this came a new confidence about Japan's role in the world culminating in the 1964 Olympic Summer Games and the Osaka World Exposition of 1970, which mark the emergence of Japan as a world power and a celebration of the remarkable development of the country since World War II. The 1964 Olympics led to a concerted effort to deal with traffic congestion in the city, starting with the *1959 Plan for the Metropolitan Expressway System.* At the same time, the growing service economy demanded a particular type of building in the city and during the 1960s the restriction on building heights was removed, allowing the construction of high-rise office towers.

With its growing wealth and the development of a national confidence about its future, Japan embarked on a significant restructuring of its economy, led in part by the establishment of the Ministry of Trade and Industry (MITI) in 1959. Under MITI's direction, Japan concentrated on the development of quality technology products designed for domestic and foreign consumption. Japan became a world leader in shipbuilding, electronics, automobiles and high technology. This coincided with infrastructure development in Japan's ports, needed to transport Japanese exports to their overseas markets. The 1960s saw Japanese exports expand at an annual rate of more than 15 percent, and by the mid-1960s Japan was producing a trade surplus.

During this period the population of the country stabilized as the birth rate slowed. With increasing industrialization more people moved off the land to industrial jobs in the cities. In the Meiji period (1868–1912) the urban population of Japan was about 15 percent; at the end of World War II it was about half. However at the end of the 1960s it had risen to about 80 percent. The dominance of Tokyo within Japan's urban hierarchy meant that by the beginning of the 1970s one in every nine Japanese lived in Tokyo. Space became a very limited resource in all of Japan's urban areas. It was particularly scarce in Tokyo. Urban dwellers in Tokyo lived with far less space than their global counterparts and the provision of affordable housing remained the chief flaw in Japan's postwar economic "miracle."

As Japan began to claim an increasingly important trade and financial role for itself, its position in the global economy changed. The rise of Japan in world trade and the development of Japan's financial strength created a new kind of Japanese business climate in the 1980s. Partly through historical circumstance, partly through design and partly due to synergy, Tokyo attracted and kept nearly all of the headquarters of Japan's emerging global financial empire. The result was that the city became the center of nearly all decision-making in the country. As a result, Tokyo dominated Japan as a center for technology, information, and financial services.

The environmental situation of the city was a major cause of concern for the city government. In 1968 a *New City Planning Law* was enacted and in 1970 the *Building Standard Law* was revised. These amendments allowed for far greater control over the form and structure of new development in the city. This was further refined in 1980 with the introduction of a *District Planning System*. Despite the chaotic impression, Tokyo is a highly regulated urban context. The Japanese planning system is two tiered and only applies to areas designated by prefectural governors as "city planning areas" (CPA). The first tier actively promotes development, in what are called Urbanization Promotion Areas (UPA), while the second actively restricts it, in Urbanization Control Areas (UCA). A UCA protects, for example, green belt areas or agricultural areas.

Within an Urban Promotion Area zoning is organized under three categories – housing (seven classes), commercial (three classes) and industrial (two classes). A major difference between the Japanese city and the American city is that in the Japanese city zoning lists the type of use prohibited whereas American zoning lists the use permitted. Officially land is segregated by use into residential areas, commercial areas and industrial areas. However, the law allows one to build houses in the commercial area and vice-versa. All land use zoning allows more than one use and as a result, the commercial uses that generate higher investment returns tend to encroach into residential areas worsening the supply of adequate housing within the city. This not only creates a looser zoning environment. It is one of the major factors in the formation of the complexity of the city (Reza, Parsa and Kawaguchi 1999: 112).

Planning Tokyo as a multi core city

The fourth *National Capital Region Development Plan* (1986–2000) divided the National Capital Region into the Tokyo Megalopolis (Tokyo, Saitama, Chiba, Kanagawa and the southern part of Ibaraki Prefecture) and the Neighboring Region. One of the central concerns for this plan was the singular dominance of Tokyo with the aim of

3.4 In the early 1990s cranes filled the skyline of Tokyo. This image, near Tokyo Dome, displays the juxtaposition of buildings, railway lines and elevated expressways in the city.

3.5 Sunday afternoon in Takeshita-dori, Harajuku, Tokyo. Japanese people seem to seek out the small and intimate spaces of older parts of the city and feel quite at home amongst masses of people.

reorganizing the region into multi-core urban zones. The idea was to strengthen the subcenters around the Central Ward Area of Tokyo. These subcenters are Kinshico-Kameido, Asakusa-Ueno, Ikebukuro, Shinjiku, Shibuya, Osaki and the Water-front-Subcenter. Yokohama is a separate city and not a subcenter. Within the concept of the *National Capital Region Development Plan* each subcenter has its own character and function.

It is difficult for the metropolitan government to solve the problem caused by the concentration of Tokyo. Subcenters were established in order to mitigate this concentration, however as Hiroshi Yamada notes the distance between these sub-centers was not large enough to accomplish this. Rather, they expanded the metropolis and created one huge core in the city (see Yamada 1989). The idea of a waterfront subcenter has its origins in the decline of industrial operations on the waterfront concurrent with the demand for more commercial space in the city.

The rise in urban incomes, the maximization of workers and the worldwide decline in heavy indus-try led to a change in the Japanese economy in the 1970s. The OPEC fuel crisis of 1973 ended the era of cheap energy in Japan. This led to a shift in economic priorities and the country began to diversify its markets, with tremendous success. The 1980s were a period when American cities were coming to grips with the emptying of central cities and a resultant lack of investment. Tokyo, on the other hand, saw a simultaneous emptying of residential population and the filling in of head-quarters, bringing with it rising land values. This led to the dual expansion of the periphery, as people sought affordable housing, combined with the domination of the center by high-end corpor-ate concerns.

By the 1980s, the Japanese economy had become one of the most important in the world.

Japan's economic position was buoyed by exports in automobiles, high-quality steel, precision optical equipment, and electronic products. Japan's trade surpluses increased tension with key trading part-ners in Europe and the United States who accused Japan of unfair trading practices and the pursuit of its own "narrow-minded interests" (a situation that has not changed very much, see Kahn 2001). Japan was put under tremendous international pressure to deregulate its financial markets. Accordingly Japan's financial markets were dereg-ulated and liberalized. The revision of the Foreign Exchange Control Law in 1980 allowed many foreign financial companies to establish their branch offices in Tokyo (Yamada 1989: 60).

Foreign investment remained very low throughout the 1960s. Between 1980 and 1985 however, there was a steady increase in foreign investment but after the incorporation of *endaka*, the revalu-ation of the yen against major currencies begin-ning in late 1985, it rose dramatically. The revaluing of the yen and the deregulation of trade barriers marked a tremendous change in Japan's global economic position. With *endaka*, "eco-nomic restructuring in Japan turned into a fixation on transforming Tokyo into a world financial and transnational corporate command center" (Doug-lass 1998: 90). The 1990s, marked a different kind of change in the Japanese economy. The "bubble economy" of the 1980s, which was typified by easy credit and unbridled speculation, popped. This ushered in Japan's worst postwar recession and a period of economic maturation in Japan. However, prior to the popping of the bubble there existed a tremendous demand for new space in the city and one of the areas to receive consider-able attention was Tokyo Bay.

Utopia in Tokyo Bay

The modern "boom" in waterfront development comes from the shift of the economy toward information and financial services and the concurrent decline in the role of heavy industry. It is a familiar story in cities around the world. This economic shift has had similar results in many other cities. At the same time that industry was being restructured and industrial space was being consolidated, there rose a tremendous demand for a new type of space in cities. In Tokyo, this created a particular type of high-end intelligent office environment in lands that were previously industrial ports.

Since World War II, Tokyo has paid a heavy price for the speed of its economic growth. The lack of space in the city has been a major concern for both planners and architects. Expansion into Tokyo Bay always provided the city with new space. The rise of Tokyo in the global economy inspired utopians to make proposals for its ultimate form. Perhaps the most famous example is Kenzo Tange's Metabolist project in Tokyo Bay of 1961.

Tange's scheme was the first of the modern designs for Tokyo Bay. It was presented as a critique of the *First National Capital Region Development Plan for Tokyo* of 1956. Tange's proposal invades the bay with a complicated structure of expressways and housing pods. Tafuri writes that the scheme was a polemic against "the two dimensional tradition of planning, with its theories of territorial equilibrium based on decentralization by means of satellite towns" (Tafuri 1986: 385).

Another similarly grand scheme is the New Tokyo Plan 2025 by Kisho Kurokawa, which dates from 1987. Kurokawa's proposal came later although it bears an uncanny resemblance to Tange's, if not in form then certainly in concept. His New Tokyo Plan 2025 was part of a larger proposal to reorganize the entire urban system of Japan through the construction of a series of networked urban projects. As part of this network Kurokawa pro-

posed the distribution of metropolitan functions that are concentrated in Tokyo to a new Tokaido Corridor to run from Osaka to Tokyo. The project takes a position that Tokyo will inevitably be internationalized and in order to facilitate this it should be drastically renovated. As part of this renovation, Kurokawa proposed the construction of a new metropolitan island within Tokyo Bay. The scheme called for the relocation of the Diet Building, other government agencies, embassies and international facilities. The middle of the island included golf courses and residential districts while around the periphery commercial high-rise buildings would define its edge. The island laid out a grid reminiscent of Heian-kyo, the ancient capital of Japan. On top of this grid a system of canals looped through the fabric of the island. The proposal called for the relocation of the Port of Tokyo to the Pacific coast (Chiba Prefecture) with a huge canal linking it to Tokyo Bay. The soil dug up from the canal providing the land necessary for the construction of the island.

Kurokawa's proposal extended to the city as well. His scheme called for the construction of Boso New City, a major metropolis in Chiba linked by expressway and subway through the island to Old Tokyo. His scheme really was the reconstruction of Tokyo as a global metropolis. While both schemes are polemic they speak to the idea that the Bay was a territory for occupation and that such development would be a panacea for Tokyo's ills. These projects represent real ambitions and provide us with a way to think about the development of Tokyo Rainbow Town.

Rinkai Funu-Toshin (Rainbow Town)

The Tokyo Waterfront Subcenter or *Rinkai Funu-Toshin* (Rainbow Town) is Tokyo's seventh subcenter and a modest project compared to those envisioned by either Tange or Kurokawa. The project was announced by the Governor of Tokyo,

Map of Tokyo Rainbow Town.

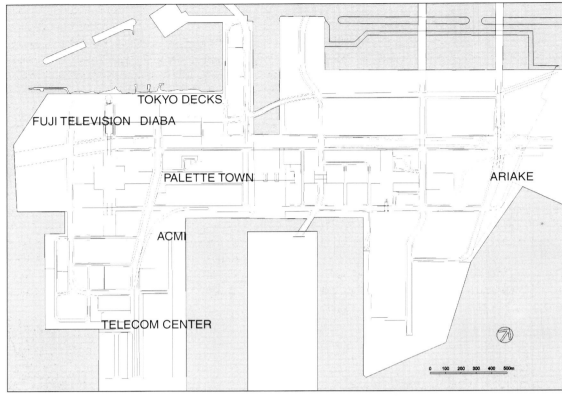

TOKYO DECKS

FUJI TELEVISION   DIABA

PALETTE TOWN

ARIAKE

ACMI

TELECOM CENTER

0 100 200 300 400 500m

Shunichi Suzuki in 1985 and after a period of consultation from advisory committees the *Waterfront Subcenter City Development Promotion Plan* was produced in 1987. This plan defined the form, character, function and phasing of the project. The project site covers the reclaimed islands No. 10 and No. 13 and part of the Ariake District in Tokyo Bay. With the coming of the information age, Japanese planners saw telecommunications as a critical infrastructure for an aspiring global city. The Tokyo Waterfront Subcenter was conceived of as a *teleport*, a center of information technology and telecommunications. However the 1987 proposal extended the concept to a major urban development which was to include housing, business and convention facilities.

Globalization was a major motivation behind the articulation of the Waterfront Subcenter Plan by

enhancing global communications and information networks in the city to secure Tokyo's future prosperity. Mention has already been made of the difficulty in redeveloping existing parts of the city because of the nature of land holdings and the rights of those owners under Japanese law. The land designated for the Waterfront Subcenter, by comparison, was owned by the Tokyo Metropolitan Government and free of any such restrictions. This issue alone made the prospect of developing the project exciting for the Japanese planners. In this context they were free to create their own utopia.

When one examines the location of the site in relation to the rest of Tokyo, several "advantages" are evident. The site is centrally located in the Tokyo conurbation, less than six kilometers from the city center with excellent access to Haneda Airport and the International Airport at Narita. The worldwide restructuring of port operations did not leave the Port of Tokyo untouched. The consolidation of industrial activities common in ports all around the world also occurred in Tokyo. This "emptying" of port activities from the waterfront allowed for remarkable redevelopment opportunities. While industry was receding from the waterfront, there developed a growing awareness of the potential of these sites to solve some of Tokyo's development problems. This ultimately led to government initiatives to take advantage of this situation and in 1986, the ruling Liberal Democratic Party of Japan announced what was referred to as the Amano Proposal (see Seguchi and Malone 1996).

The Amano Proposal, named after Masanori Amano from the ruling Liberal Democratic Party, was a national policy in response to globalization. The proposal highlights the globalization of business activities and the resultant demand for commercial office space in Tokyo, which it recognized as contributing to the unprecedented rise in property prices. The plan also acknowledged the need for the Japanese to shift from an export driven economy to one based on domestic consumption (a demand from the United States and Europe). The Amano Proposal was an initiative to satisfy both criteria at the same time. In essence the proposal aimed at boosting domestic consumption by invigorating the Japanese construction industry and by doing this create much needed commercial office space to address the escalating real estate prices. The Amano proposal made three recommendations for massive construction projects – Tokyo Central Station, Shiodome Station

3.6 Rinkai Funu-Toshin. The spaces of the project define a new scale in the city. Enormous buildings are located in enormous spaces.

3.7 In Tokyo Rainbow Town an idealized global image is presented and carefully controlled. View of the Telecom Center – a land station for satellite telecommunications.

3.8 The older fabric of the city operates at the scale of a medieval village. The perseverance of the block structure of Edo maintains this kind of urban intimacy. reinforcing culturally held spatial understandings.

and the waterfront in Tokyo Bay. However it was clear that the main focus was to be Tokyo Bay.

In traditional Japanese fashion the government decided to establish study groups for each construction effort. These groups were made up of government officials, representatives from public agencies and other necessary experts and, depending on the project, possibly private landowners. Interestingly, with the tremendous affluence of Japan during this time and despite the realization of huge developer profits, it was decided that the public sector would be responsible for all of the infrastructure of these projects.

The Amano proposal inspired a series of large-scale waterfront proposals in Tokyo Bay from a number of different groups (see Seguchi and Malone 1996). Projects ranged from Kisho Kurokawa's New Tokyo Plan 2025 (previously mentioned) as well as Garden City Islands by the Kaiyo Sangyo Kenkyu-kai Corporation. While these proposals were for the most part hypothetical, they did raise to new levels of interest the issue of waterfront development within Tokyo Bay.

In the case of the Tokyo waterfront development, owing to the fact that the government owned much of the land, the Tokyo Metropolitan Government was charged with producing the development framework for the waterfront. In 1988, the framework plan was produced which also included the adjoining areas of Harumi and Toyosu. The framework plan for the Waterfront Subcenter covered an area of 448 hectares. The scheme imagined a resident population of 60,000 and a worker population of 115,000. The Subcenter was divided into four areas – Aomi, Ariake-Minami, Ariake-Kita and Daiba. In the Aomi district business and commercial facilities were located. The Ariake-Minami district included convention and hotel facilities. The Ariake-Kita district

included housing. The Daiba district was designated for leisure and entertainment facilities.

The Tokyo Metropolitan Government imagined launching the scheme through a spectacular World City Exposition event, known as "Tokyo Frontier." However, due to the economic downturn in the early 1990s the exposition stalled, was delayed and finally abandoned. Hence, lacking any fanfare the Waterfront Center emerged surreptitiously. Perhaps due to its bad start the project has had its fair share of problems. Since its inception it has battled political criticism, community groups and environmentalists. Despite these concerns, which dealt mostly with the need for the development at all, the Tokyo Government planners held steadfastly to their original proposal.

Space of the Rinkai Funu-Toshin

To appreciate the design of Rinkai Funu-Toshin one must appreciate something of the relationship between formal codes, those written into law, and informal codes, customs and traditions, which combine in the Japanese situation to form the specificity of a city such as Tokyo. The Japanese sense of city space is informed by this and one gets a reading that in the older parts of the city there exists a certain layering of space, which for the most part is completely outside of the realm of perception and understanding of non-Japanese. This typically Japanese phenomenon has traditionally been expressed in terms of *omote* (front) and *ura* (back) leading to descriptions such as *omote-dôri* (main street) and *ura-dôri* (back street), *omote-mon* (front gate) and *ura-mon* (back gate), long considered characteristic of Japan, although of course it is not confined to there (Maki 1997).

While it is not the intention to explain the Japanese conception of city space it is important to highlight that there is a fundamental difference between

3.9 The scale of the infrastructure of Tokyo Rainbow Town can be appreciated in this image. Running along the middle of the project is the No. 357 expressway. Evident also in the center of the image is the pedestrian bridge that links the Tokyo Joypolis to Palette Town.

Japanese and Western concepts of space making. *Oku*, a spatial concept peculiar to Japan, is a good example. The existence of a centripetal *okusei*, or inwardness, has always been basic to urban space formation in Japan. The use of the term invariably involves the concept of *okuyuki*, or spatial depth, signifying relative distance or the sense of distance within a given space. *Oku* has a number of abstract connotations, including profundity and unfathomability, so that the word is used to describe not only physical but psychological depth. It is interesting to note how often the Japanese use the word in adjectival form. Such usages include *oku-dokoro* (inner place), *oku-guchi* (inner entrance), *oku-sha* (inner shrine), *oku-yama* (mountain recesses), and *oku-zashiki* (inner room), all relevant to the notion of physical space; *oku-gi* (secret or hidden principles) and *oku-den* (secret or hidden mysteries of an art), referring to things invisible but nevertheless present; and *ô-oku* (wife of a shôgun) and *oku-no-in* or *oku-gata* (wife of an aristocrat or nobleman), terms suggesting social position (see Maki 1997). Evident in the use of all these words is a social character that positively affirms the existence of what is hidden, invisible, or secret and incomprehensible to most foreigners.

While these visible and invisible characteristics of form are present today, globalization, modernization and ever-increasing urban population densities encourage the further loss of the sense of place in the Japanese urban context, resulting in the dispersion of inner space. Maki notes that this inner space becomes more and more compartmentalized, being relegated to one portion of an apartment, for instance, and thus ceases to participate in the kind of collective inner space formerly seen in both downtown and uptown sections of Tokyo. These powerful culturally derived, and relativistic, concepts have given way to "modern" rational planning in projects such as Tokyo Rainbow Town. This loss is exacerbated by the separation that exists between the disciplines of planning and architecture in Japan. The role of defining urban form is vested with planners who decide the principal aspects of every project.

Planning in Japan derives from a scientific rationality and leads to the notion that a plan is the result of a series of logical decisions that have to do with solving problems of providing urban infrastructure. This is evident, for example in the procedural aspects of plan making, which can be seen in the implementation of Japanese new towns such as Makuhari in Chiba. In Rainbow Town too infrastructure drives the conception of place making in these locations. While there is no denial of physical thinking in Japanese planning, there is an obsession with the physical only as it relates to these infrastructural considerations such that Japanese planners start their conception of a project by articulating circulation systems. Once the plan has been "solved" in these terms, the residual spaces are divided into parcels. In addition, the planners in the Japanese context define a maximum envelope for each parcel. At this point architects are included in the process. The dominance of these formal codes is puzzling given that Japanese have a highly developed sense of culture and history and yet traditional space making concepts seem to be ignored in these newer urban situations.

In the case of Tokyo Rainbow Town the result is a kind of disconnected assemblage of large forms rather than any sense of a connected tissue. Connection, as an idea that might consolidate the project, becomes ornamental such that these disconnected elements are linked via a beaux-arts inspired promenade, which cuts across the landscape. This element is 80 meters wide and cuts across the entire 4-kilometer length of the project. Rather than connecting these isolated objects however, the result appears diagrammatic and pastiche. The end result of this rational process is

3.10 View toward the Telecom Center.

that large-scale urban projects in Japan operate at a scale completely at odds with the way the rest of Tokyo works. The most densely populated areas of the city are often very finely scaled and small spaces seem to attract large numbers of people. Perhaps this is due to the fact that these kinds of urban situations offer possibilities where the hidden, invisible and secret characteristics of Japanese space are most readily accessible to people able to perceive and understand them.

In projects such as Rainbow Town this fine scale is missing. Given that the planners faced little restrictions on the site they could have chosen to replicate aspects of this fine grain development. The fact that they did not speaks of two possible conclusions. It suggests that this fine grain development is incompatible with the global ambitions

of the project and it suggests that its planners might be critical of such smallness and intimacy. It seems evident that the project is a critique of the chaotic nature of "old Tokyo" and the problems that this older fabric brings with it. In the articulation of Tokyo Rainbow Town there seems to be a latent desire to tidy everything up, to organize it, to make it more efficient. For a society based in a strong sense of order and control the happenstance nature of their own urban environment might be seen to be a thorn in the side of rationally trained Japanese planners who see it as their mission to "fix" and "correct" such chaos. Small-scale intimate spaces may, in addition, be seen as old, while large-scale efficient spaces might be equated with progress and modernity. While there is no evidence that would make a case either way, it remains curious why spaces such as Tokyo

3.11 View toward the northern edge of the Daiba Area.

45

3.12 Compared to older parts of the city one's experience of being a pedestrian in Tokyo Rainbow Town is very different. Public pedestrian space is the residual space between enormous buildings and infrastructure. This view was taken in front of the Fuji Television Building.

Rainbow Town exist, which seems at odds with a strong cultural tradition of urban space making.

Perhaps this is evidence of the power of the global sphere to flatten social and cultural difference. Perhaps this is an example of the dominance of the global over the local such that these hidden, invisible and secret characteristics become imperceptible to those that rely on them to understand their position in the city. The old part of the city, protected by well-established laws that protect the rights of landholders, is difficult to "fix." The waterfront subcenter, by comparison, offers a tabula rasa from which to project a scheme of the utmost efficiency. The result, however, is an urban environment, which prioritizes the space of the car over the space of the pedestrian and reduces open space to that space that is left over between

large commercial projects. In Rainbow Town there is a deliberate attempt to separate the pedestrian from the car and in doing so the space of the street becomes a purely functional space in the city.

Rinkai Funu-Toshin is in essence a collection of isolated projects on a large flat surface. These are linked by the Yurikamome transit system that loops around the island. The four areas of the Rinkai Funu-Toshin each have a character of their own. The Aomi district, designated as the business and commercial zone, includes the Telecom Center at the end of the West Promenade and adjacent to the Aomi transit stop is Palette Town, a 125,000 square meter shopping and entertainment project. Palette Town houses the Toyota City Showcase, a gigantic showroom of the entire range of Toyota automobiles, History Garage, marketed as "a trip down memory lane to see cars from around the world" from the 1950s and 1960s and Future World which highlights transportation systems of the future. Palette Town also includes Venus Fort, a "theme park for ladies" it is a two level shopping mall made to resemble a medieval Italian townscape.

The Daiba area, designated for leisure and entertainment, hosts the Decks Tokyo Beach (with its Tokyo Joypolis) and Aqua City Odaiba. Hotel Nikko Tokyo and Hotel Grand Pacific are located here. The FUJI Television headquarters building by Kenzo Tange, with its signature orb is adjacent to these projects. Other commercial projects located in Daiba are the Nissho Iwai headquarters, the Daiba Frontier Building, the SUNTORY office headquarters and the ITOKI headquarters.

Ariake-Minami, designated as the convention and hotel zone, includes the Washington and Marriott Hotels and the International Exhibition Center. Tokyo Fashion Town is also located there. Ariake-Kita includes a range of housing and the International University Village for Research and Exchange.

The current status of the Tokyo Waterfront Subcenter

The Tokyo Waterfront Subcenter (Tokyo Rainbow Town) is in a constant process of being rethought and reproposed in response to the changing nature of the global economy. For such large-scale urban development, the time lag between "global" trends and construction of the project is a major issue. Simply, urban projects cannot respond quickly to changes in the nature of the global economy. This is their major flaw and one of the basic problems that planners and designers face in dealing with the city. Rainbow Town is no different in this sense. With the popping of the "bubble" in the early 1990s, combined with the problems of the Asian Economic Crisis in the late 1990s, the

project is posing a major problem for Tokyo's planners. This is somewhat reminiscent of the problems faced by Canary Wharf in response to a downturn in financial services in London in the late 1980s.

The reduction of demand for office spaces due to the collapse of the Bubble Economy has meant that private companies have not moved to the "peripheral" areas of Tokyo Bay. On the contrary, any new office space that has eventuated has continued to concentrate in central Tokyo (Ito 2000: 12). In the current context the possibility of businesses moving from Tokyo center to Tokyo Bay seems small. And while the fact that the government owns the majority of land on the waterfront is an advantage for the planners, private companies, wishing to develop in these sites are made to comply with urban planning regulations, which are more stringent than in other areas of the city. This combined situation has forced the government to rethink its development of the project.

The current version is expressed in the *Waterfront Subcenter City Development Promotion Plan* formulated in March 1997. This plan actively seeks citizen participation and the government's ambition is to advance the project steadily with the understanding and cooperation of citizens. One of the most significant changes is the schedule. The provision of the basic infrastructure was completed in 1995. Stage II will run through to 2005 and Stage III through to 2015. The final stage begins in 2016. Other changes include a working population of 70,000 and a resident population of 42,000 (the number of housing units will be 14,000 of which 2015 are currently completed). As for land use, 234 hectares (53 percent of the total 442 hectares) are slated for public infrastructures such as roads and parks, 192 hectares (43 percent) for business, commercial and residential uses and 16 hectares (4 percent) for disaster prevention bases (Tokyo Metropolitan Government 2001).

Rinkai Funu-Toshin is a project that started as an ambitious attempt to position Tokyo as a global city. In addition it was created to reduce the dominance of Tokyo To. In these terms the project seems marginal to both Tokyo's success as a global financial center and the government's attempts to diffuse development in the city. Planning in Tokyo continues to struggle with one major issue – the difficulty in controlling where development will occur in the city. This creates tremendous stresses on urban infrastructure and a concentration of investment in the center of the city. The project does present us with an interesting insight into how planners in Tokyo see the ideal form of cities. The space of Rinkai Funu-Toshin is abstract, characterless and functional. Here we see one ultimate configuration of the modernist project. Is it little wonder that developers want to be in Old Tokyo?

4 The Project of the Century

Minato Mirai 21, Yokohama, Japan

At Minato Mirai 21 we saw the emergence of a particular type of building typology, one we will soon have to recognize as the dominant typology: a completely inarticulate container with no architectural pretensions, whose only purpose is to accommodate certain processes or offices, and which simply represents a massive quantity of square meters imposed on an urban site without any more positive contribution.

Rem Koolhaas, SMLXL

The skyscraper with 70 stories above ground and a height of 296 meters is a symbol of Yokohama. At the Land Mark Plaza you can enjoy shopping in the surrounding area. It also features hotels and halls. The view from "Sky Garden" on the observatory 69th floor is extremely wonderful.

Yokohama Convention and Visitors Bureau

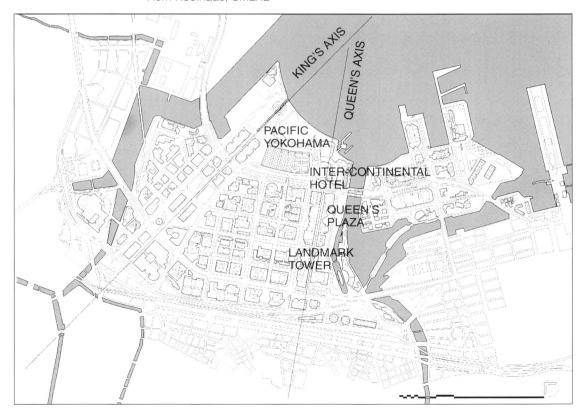

Map of Minato Mirai 21, Yokohama.

4.1 Minato Mirai 21 – view of the Landmark Tower
(copyright Christine Williams 2002).

Located in the city of Yokohama, some 30 kilometers south of Tokyo (30 minutes by both train and car), is Minato Mirai 21 (meaning "future seaport of the twenty-first century"). Minato Mirai 21 (MM21) is an information city designed to attract global financial and other business institutions and companies. Located on a former Mitsubishi shipbuilding site it is a self-proclaimed "project of the century." It is also the site of Japan's largest urban complex, Queen's Square (500,000 square meters) and Japan's tallest skyscraper, the Landmark Tower (296 meters). Designed to be a new urban core for the twenty-first century, Minato Mirai 21 is a large global project intended to promote the independence of the City of Yokohama. It plays an important role in the "*core city concept*" conceived by the Japanese Govern-ment in the *Third National Capital Region Plan* of 1986, which aimed at reducing the dominance of Tokyo To.

The project lies between two important nodes in Yokohama, the Kannai-Isezakicho District and the Yokohama Station District. It is the third element to a new conception of Yokohama and aims to not only fill the gap in a geographic sense but to provide everything that the city has not been able to provide anywhere else. MM21 is an ambitious undertaking aimed at the creation of a twenty-four hour cultural *cosmopolis*, an information city of the twenty-first century and a city with a "superior environment, surrounded by water, greenery and historic monuments" (Yokohama Minato Mirai 21 Corporation 1996: 7). MM21 aims to be nothing short of a viable international cultural city, a location where the world comes to Japan. MM21 exemplifies an attempt by a local government to aggressively pursue global interaction. However, the project did not begin life as a global project; rather it developed into one, starting as a vision to help make Yokohama a better place. Through time

4.2 Image taken from the observation deck of the Landmark Tower looking at the sail-shaped Inter-Continental Hotel and the adjacent Rinko Park.

this vision became increasingly global in scope. This is evident in the increasing fascination with the idea of a teleport and with intelligent infrastructure.

The designers of MM21 provide us with a clear expression of what they see as a global project. MM21 is a radically different place to the rest of Yokohama with the articulation of urban spaces and the scale of the elements (buildings, blocks, and green space) clearly setting it apart. In addition the project is physically separated by road and rail infrastructure, which further isolates the project from its immediate context. But while separate from the city, MM21 provides a picture postcard view – the enduring image that proclaims that Yokohama too has reinvented itself and is ready to play in the global game.

MM21 today sits uncompleted. After almost forty years of vision and development the project is only a quarter complete. MM21 is a project that has struggled to overcome both the vagaries of global project production and the complete dominance of Tokyo as the center of all things in Japan. MM21's creators have tried in vain to lure companies away from Tokyo. The supply of space in the project, and the continued belief in the provision of that supply, seems to be radically at odds with the demand. The reality and the myth of the global urban project appear as radically different visions in MM21.

Minato Mirai 21 has three primary objectives: the promotion of Yokohama's independence from Tokyo, the decentralization of the commercial and administrative dominance of Tokyo and the cre-

4.3 View of the Yokohama Bay Bridge.

ation of a waterfront environment for recreation, conference and central port administration services. In its evolution, the capacity of the idea for the project has grown in complexity and integration into the global sphere. It has developed from an idea to address local needs and demands for a better environment, through various iterations to its current projection as a global project. One can trace the history of the project and discover the emergence and development of the "global" idea in MM21.

Yokohama and the Waterfront City

Minato Mirai 21 has a history that dates to the early 1960s, a period of tremendous expansion in all Japanese urban environments. This expansion and urban transformation is likewise true for the city of Yokohama, the capital of Kanagawa ken (prefecture). The city is part of the Tokyo agglomeration and acts as one of the major dormitory areas for workers in Tokyo. Yokohama is a bustling city with a population of more than 3 million people, making it Japan's second largest city. Yokohama and Kawasaki (which lies between Yokohama and Tokyo) form the center of the Keihin Industrial Zone where much of the industrial and heavy manufacturing activities for the Tokyo area are concentrated. The port of Yokohama, one of the largest in Japan, handles imports of raw materials for the surrounding industry and a wide range of exports.

Until 1858 Yokohama was a small fishing village. In 1859 Townsend Harris, the first United States consul to Japan, negotiated the opening of five ports to foreign trade and the exemption of foreigners from Japanese jurisdiction. For Yokohama the agreement meant that the neighboring town of Kanagawa became a foreign trading port. Harris was able to persuade the Japanese Shogun that it would be to their advantage to negotiate a treaty with the United States rather than to fight the

British and French as the Chinese had attempted to do, with no success. A year previously, the Chinese refused to accept the Treaties of Tientsin, which resulted in continued hostilities and the eventual burning of the emperor's summer palace in Beijing in 1860. The Shogun relented but with the proviso that the American fleet anchor in Kanagawa and not in Edo (later Tokyo). This meant that American cannons would not be able to attack the capital.

Historically, Yokohama was always Japan's gateway to the world. It was always very receptive to Western industrial technology and adopted the idea of *wakon yosai* or "Japanese spirit to western knowledge." The port and its industrial facilities provided Yokohama with a tremendous engine for growth and the population of the area grew rapidly. Through the early part of the twentieth century planning in Yokohama closely resembled that of Tokyo. Similar to Tokyo's *City District Plan*, Yokohama introduced the *General Principles for the Construction of Greater Yokohama* in 1920. After the Great Kanto Earthquake of 1923 almost 90 percent of Yokohama was destroyed. This event established the *Rehabilitation Plan* and as a result was to take on an even more important role with the construction of larger port facilities. However, because of funding restrictions, this plan actually had little impact on the rebuilding efforts in Yokohama.

The city suffered severe bomb damage in 1945 with 42 percent of its population becoming victims of the bombing and almost 100,000 buildings destroyed by fire. Postwar reconstruction in Yokohama was a slow and difficult process. Much of the city center was requisitioned by the allied occupation, which slowed commercial development. Ninety percent of the port facilities were taken by the U.S. Military, which caused a retreat of trading and financial companies to Tokyo (Saito 1990: 40). Real growth only occurred well into the second half of the 1950s and through the 1960s. With Japan's increasing industrialization and urbanization after 1960, Yokohama became critical to the country's development efforts. The port of Yokohama, one of the largest in Japan, played a vital role in feeding raw materials to the adjacent industry and in shipping completed products out of Japan. The industrial emphasis of Yokohama's development meant that much of the waterfront was filled to accommodate heavy industrial occupations and the port, once commercial, became a heavy industrial port (Saito 1990: 40).

As a result of rapid industrialization, the waterfront was occupied by industrial complexes and huge factories, which brought with them many trucks. This ultimately led to an impoverishment in the environmental quality of the waterfront. In 1963, "Six Projects" were proposed by the local government of Yokohama that would lead to the remaking of the city (Tamura 1989: 189). These projects aimed at the reinforcement of the city center, the reclamation of Kanazawa shore for the provision of industrial space south of the city, the development of Kohoku New Town to the north of Yokohama, the construction of highways and subways and the construction of the Yokohama Bay Bridge. The "reinforcement of the city center" included the rehabilitation of port properties and development of a waterfront city project, which would eventually be called MM21.

The construction of a waterfront city was proposed in 1963 and announced by Mayor Asukada in 1965. With a growing sense that Yokohama needed to address its growth issues, the City of Yokohama announced a redevelopment plan of which a new "waterfront city" was part. Despite the reliance on the port for much of Yokohama's economic activity, the project called for the relocation of the Mitsubishi shipyard. In 1967 talks began between the city and Mitsubishi Industries and throughout the 1970s each negotiated their respective positions, ultimately leading to the announcement in 1981 that Mitsubishi Industries would relocate.

The population of Yokohama increased rapidly in the same period. Immediately after the war the population of Yokohama was 750,000 people. By 1951 the population had returned to prewar numbers of approximately 1 million. Between 1951 and 1968 another million people had moved to Yokohama. In 1973 the population was over 2.5 million. The combination of growth in heavy industry and the fact that Yokohama quickly assumed a "bedtown" role to Tokyo meant that by 1978 the city's population exceeded that of Osaka, making it Japan's second largest city with a population of 2.7 million people. The *Third National Capital Region Plan*, which promoted the idea of multiple cores within the metropolis of Tokyo, meant Yokohama was to be a major core within this conurbation. The idea was to expand the business functions in Yokohama to provide office space where residents of Yokohama would work, reducing the amount of people who commuted daily to Tokyo.

The rate of population growth brought with it a series of congestion problems. Throughout the 1960s the environmental quality of the city deteriorated leading to problems of pollution as agricultural lands were developed into housing. While some trunk roads were constructed, roadway infrastructure lagged behind the increase in population creating massive traffic congestion issues in the city. The population increase was so rapid that the city could not provide enough park space, to the point where in 1969 the area of park per person in Yokohama was less than one square meter (Editing Committee 1989: 378). In 1972, the City of Yokohama announced that they would tackle "five major urban problems." These were pollution, trash disposal, traffic, sewerage and the lack of public owned land for such things as schools.

4.4 View of Yokohama, clearly showing the density of the urban fabric and the lack of open space.

It is apparent therefore that the original aim of the waterfront project was to contribute to the solution of some of these problems. The project aimed to connect the Kinnai/Isezaki area, the oldest center, with Yokohama Station, a newer center, which had developed since World War II. This would lead to the establishment of three city centers in Yokohama – the Kinnai Area, the Yokohama Station Area and MM21. The new area was to be efficient, clean, and provide public open space for the city. MM21 would provide the functions required by the future metropolis in a setting of "abundant water and greenery" (MM21 Corporation 1996).

Future seaport of the twenty-first century – Minato Mirai 21

In 1981 an agreement was reached between the city and Mitsubishi Industries regarding the relocation of their industrial facilities to the Kanazawa area. The removal of the Mitsubishi shipbuilding activity opened up a tremendous development opportunity, which is reflected in the third master plan for Yokohama entitled Yumehama 2010 (meaning "dream for 2010"). The plan was initiated in 1981 and for the first time presented the framework for the waterfront city project. In the same year the Project Promotion Committee headquarters for MM21 was established and the interim report on the master plan for the Yokohama City center and waterfront area was announced. In this same year the project was officially named Minato Mirai 21.

After two years of effort, the plan for Minato Mirai 21 was released in 1983. At the same time the relocation of Mitsubishi Industries shipyard was completed. Toward the end of 1983, the Minister of Transport authorized the landfill project on public waters and the Minister for Construction authorized a Land Readjustment of over 35 hectares. Thus the Minato Mirai 21 project was officially launched. In 1984, the Yokohama Minato

Mirai 21 Corporation was established and the cornerstone ceremony was held. The Yokohama Minato Mirai 21 Corporation was established as a public-private partnership, which included the City of Yokohama, Kanagawa Prefectural Government, Japan Railways, local landowners and local business circles. Its role was to attract new business participants, coordinate and promote community development, promote a series of green initiatives, the management of public and other facilities and to deal with public relations for the project.

MM21 Corporation is what is known in Japan as a "Third Sector" corporation and is neither publicly nor privately owned. This kind of corporation operates between the public and the market. It has control of its own actions and thus avoids strict governmental surveillance. The roles of the public and the private participants in the corporation are different. The public sector, which includes the City of Yokohama, the Japanese government, and the Kanagawa Prefecture, is responsible for the overall planning and coordination of the project. Further, it is responsible for land reclamation, the construction of port facilities, the construction of all public facilities and the infrastructure for the project. The Housing and Urban Development Corporation (HUDC), an additional player in the public sector, is responsible for land readjustment in connection with developing roads and building sites.

The joint public-private sector players have specific responsibilities. MM21 Corporation is responsible for survey work and for the promotion of the project. Pacific Convention Plaza Yokohama Corporation is responsible for the development and management of Pacifico Yokohama facilities. The MM21 District Heating and Cooling Corporation is responsible for the development and management of the heating system. The Seaside Subway Yokohama Inc. is responsible for the development and operation of the MM21 Line (subway). Media City Yokohama Co., Ltd. is responsible for the provision of interactive information services. The private sector, which includes a variety of corporations, is responsible for the construction of all the office, commercial and private housing facilities for the project.

An early priority of the MM21 Corporation was the provision of parks, responding to the need for more public green space in the city. In 1985, a section of Nippon-Maru Memorial Park opened adjacent to Kitanaka Bridge at the mouth of the Ooka River. This small park, now the site of the Yokohama Maritime Museum, proved very successful, both in terms of providing much needed open space and also as a platform where people could watch the project unfold before them. In a city with such a low amount of public green space, the provision of this park was a major public relations success.

The same year the Minato Mirai Teleport Plan was announced. This concept shifted the idea of the development from one that responded principally to local desires and needs into an increasingly global territory. The concept developed a series of interrelated ideas. MM21 was to be a cultural cosmopolis operating around the clock and responding to the growing Japanese adoption of the new economy. It was also going to be an information city of the twenty-first century and bring with it international monetary rewards.

International Telecommunications Portal – Teleport

The promotion of advanced technologies as a necessary aspect of life for the Japanese was an idea promoted by the Japanese government (and in particular MITI) from the early 1980s. The teleport idea deals with the creation of "intermodal broadband hubs" or gateways that connect satellite circuits with terrestrial fiber optic and microwave circuits. The teleport concept includes the provision of intelligent office buildings that use broadband communications as a value-added lure to attract leading-edge companies as tenants. For city governments, teleports were seen as economic development projects that, in much the same way as seaports and airports, were to become magnets for urban development and create jobs for knowledge workers in fast-growth industries. The teleport was promoted as a necessary ingredient for many projects in order for Japan to continue to be competitive in the twenty-first century.

In MM21's case the idea was to create an urban environment that provided a comfortable and convenient lifestyle, by "emphasizing advanced technologies to facilitate urban activities" (Yokohama Minato Mirai 21 Corporation 1996: 10). For the MM21 Corporation this meant that, as far as possible, buildings developed within the project must have "advanced information functions" by making use of advanced communication systems. In this way the project could tap into the global information flows and secure immediate access for all those that lived and worked in the project. The aim was to provide both a working and living environment that would be "competitive" with other locations, in particular Tokyo. This was reinforced in 1988 when the Japanese government (MITI and the Construction Ministry) designated the Pacific Convention Plaza and Exhibition Site (Pacifico Yokohama) as a National Conference Facility and the Minister of Construction authorized the Intelligent City plan for MM21.

MM21 was imagined as a place for the interchange of international culture. The National Conference Facility was seen as an effective strategy for these types of interchanges. Indeed Yokohama is the only city designated as an "international convention city" in the metropolitan area of Tokyo

by the Ministry of Transportation. The notion of people gathering for the interchange of knowledge and information followed the global positioning strategy of the project. However, the reality of broadband and satellite communication today invalidates the need for such projects. The idea of a singular project as the only information portal in the city has given way to the idea that information technology is not spatially bound. Every house and every office now has access to advanced information technology through standard phone lines. Nevertheless, despite the changing nature of information technology and the invalidation of MM21's basic premise, the MM21 Corporation has not revised the basic planning parameters for the project. The project still presents itself in terms of a global project, although in redefined terms. Conspicuous by its absence

today, for example is much of the "information" marketing material for MM21. The project no longer proclaims itself as a teleport. Indeed the project struggles to justify itself on many levels and in this sense it is the same as Tokyo Rainbow Town.

Themes of MM21

In 1988, Minato Mirai 21 Corporation reached agreement with all of the landowners of the project and established the basic rules for urban development within the project. The agreement establishes rules for urban community development based on an understanding that participants share the same values in creating a "harmonious, enjoyable urban environment." It defines the role of fundamental elements of development, such as, water, greenery, skyline, and street scenery. It also delineates participants' thinking regarding development themes and land use. In addition, it establishes standards for construction, building heights, layout of pedestrian networks and concerns of approaches to advanced information needs, recycling, disaster prevention and surrounding area requirements. While these are by no means exhaustive they are significant in Japanese terms. Most development in Japan has little control placed upon it and despite these limited controls this, among other issues, may explain the reluctance of Japanese property developers to locate in MM21. Japanese city zoning lists the type of use prohibited and beyond very simple design controls architects are free to create whatever they wish. This not only creates a looser zoning environment. It is one of the major factors in the formation of the visual complexity of the Japanese city. In situations where planners have attempted to control the form of development, developers are hesitant to invest.

The basic foundation of MM21's vision can be seen in a series of themes that the Minato Mirai 21 Corporation has articulated for the project that reinforce the project's ambitions as a global conduit. They are:

- The creation of a viable town accommodating various urban activities, through efforts to highly integrate urban functions conducive to the creation of a new information base and culture.
- Creation of a unique coastal urban core as a gateway to the world, thus establishing a new image of the port city of Yokohama so that the sea or port atmosphere can be felt anywhere in the town.
- Creation of a lively town through development of superior urban infrastructure, with particular emphasis on the provision of continuous space

where people – the most important element of the town – can enjoy walking and relaxing.
- Creation of a town whose various facets, as the center of urban activities, are combined in a unique style and simple harmony.
- Creation of a town ensuring a comfortable and convenient lifestyle, by emphasizing advanced technologies to facilitate urban activities (MM21 Corporation 1996: 10).

These themes display a series of interesting aspects of the Japanese experience in making global projects. The first is that in the minds of the planners and developers is the idea that technology will provide a better life. There is a preoccupation with the idea that these advanced information environments will ultimately lead to a new information culture with "a unique style and simple harmony." There is a belief that this will somehow solve many of the lifestyle problems faced by many Japanese as they go about their work and life. It is evident, however, that these "development" themes are also incredibly abstract and do not in any way describe or delineate between a multitude of urban models. Nor are they suggestive of an appropriate urbanism. It is clear in the planning and making of MM21 that the planners had a very clear vision of what they thought the city should be like. This idea can be seen clearly if one compares the rational and ordered environment of MM21 to the chaotic and less structured environment of Yokohama itself. A new model is being proposed that replaces the old. The translation from development theme to constructed project highlights many things about the nature of functional thought for the Japanese urban context. As is the case in Rainbow Town we see in MM21 a deliberate attempt at creating something other than what exists in Yokohama. At MM21 we see a different version of a Japanese utopianism.

Components of Minato Mirai 21

MM21 involves everything from land readjustment and reclamation to port development and building construction. The port of Yokohama was reorganized with the improvement of container terminals and other advanced port facilities in order to strengthen and maintain the competitiveness of the port as an international port in the center of Japan. This involved the improvement of the port-side transport system in order to ensure a smooth flow of cargo and improving the navigating environment of the port itself. As the port was reorganized, there was an active effort to improve the port environment and to promote the public's use of waterfront areas.

The public use of the waterfront is facilitated by an elaborate engineering component to Minato Mirai 21. The project is just as extensive under the ground as on top of it. Underground service tunnels beneath all trunk roads are used for electrical wiring, gas and water pipes, telecommunications and fiber optic cables as well as waste disposal and area-wide air conditioning systems. The project has Japan's largest area-wide air conditioning system to produce, distribute and control heat. Waste from various facilities is routed systematically via the service tunnels to a central cleaning center and then transported to incinerators. A new subway system, the Minato Mirai 21 Line, is under construction. It runs from Sakuragi-cho Station to Motomachi via the center of the MM21 complex. Scheduled to open in the year 2003, this all-underground train system will be operated jointly with the Tokyu Toyoko Line allowing access to Tokyo. All of this is provided to attract people and development to MM21 and is paid for through public finances.

One of the major functions of MM21 is to attract people from Yokohama, from other parts of Japan and from around the world. To do this MM21 includes the Pacific Convention Plaza Yokohama (Pacifico Yokohama), the core facility of Yokohama Convention City and one of Japan's best-equipped convention centers. The National Convention Hall of Yokohama (the only national auditorium in eastern Japan and one of the world's largest) opened in April 1994. It comprises a conference center, exhibition hall and hotel. The National Convention Hall, the key element of Pacifico Yokohama, has over 5000 seats and is one of the world's largest convention halls. The conference center consists of about sixty conference rooms of various sizes. The exhibition hall includes over 10,000 square meters of column-free space. The Pacifico Yokohama and the Yokohama Grand Inter-Continental Hotel were completed in 1991. The hotel sits at the very northeast corner of MM21 and has become one of the key images for both the project and for Yokohama. It is a thirty-one story, 559-room and forty-one suite hotel with a striking silhouette, designed to resemble a sail. The project has appeared in international design and planning journals and appears on the cover of Ann Breen and Dick Rigby's book entitled *The New Waterfront*. It has become an international symbol for waterfront revitalization.

Global urban projects construct a particular kind of image around themselves, which is then presented into the global market place. In this way projects claim a certain celebrity. MM21 does this as well by claiming both the tallest building in Japan and the largest urban complex. The Landmark Tower is Japan's tallest skyscraper rising to a height of 296 meters, it incorporates some 392,000 square meters of office space as well as a hotel, shopping mall, a sports club, a multi-purpose hall, restaurants and observation floor on the sixty-ninth floor. The building also boasts one of the fastest elevator rides in the world. From the Sky Garden one can view the City of Yokohama and on certain days Mount Fuji can be seen to the west. The Landmark Complex

4.6 Landmark Tower – global icon and tallest building in Japan (copyright Christine Williams 2002).

4.7 MM21 boasts a continuous publicly accessible waterfront (copyright Christine Williams 2002).

4.8 Yokohama Grand Inter-Continental Hotel.

is the entry point into MM21. One enters the building from a moving walkway, starting in front of JR Sakuragicho Station. The walkway is directly linked to the five-story atrium of the shopping mall, Landmark Plaza, which occupies the base of the Landmark Tower. Most people moving into the territory of MM21 pass through the entrance to Landmark Tower on their way to other parts of the project.

Japan's largest urban complex is Queen's Square. Immediately adjacent to Landmark Tower, it is a composite business complex, which integrates business, commercial and hotel services, including a concert hall. The project consists of three office towers and a hotel sitting on top of the Queen's Mall. The towers provide an important façade for the east edge of MM21. This elevation is the most important for the project because it presents the most complete view of MM21. This view is most often portrayed in promotional material for MM21 and has become the global image for all of Yokohama. Situated between the enormous Landmark Tower and the Grand Inter-Continental Hotel at the northern edge, the towers of Queen's Square attempt to relate the scale of these two elements by stepping down in height (Tower A is 172 meters, Tower B is 138 meters, Tower C is 109 meters and the Hotel is 105 meters in height). The Queen's Mall, which sits under the four towers, is a gigantic passageway that links the Landmark Plaza to the Pacifico Yokohama. For most people accessing MM21 this space is the complete experience of the project. It acts as the major circulation path through MM21, thereby making redundant the need for pedestrian scaled streets in the project. MM21 is largely an internal environment. This reduces the open space of the master plan to the level of being merely gestural.

Minato Mirai 21 does incorporate a network of parks and greenery, known as the "Green Network." Open space is in abundance in MM21,

in direct contrast to the lack of such space in Yokohama itself. The pedestrian network provides a clear example. It consists of three wide malls extending across the entire Minato Mirai area. It links open spaces and blocks and provides pedestrians free access to every part of the project. The Green Network also provides attractions within MM21. The Sail Training Ship *Nippon Maru* is permanently moored and maintained in Nippon-Maru Memorial Park and with the adjacent Yokohama Maritime Museum, provides tourists with a narrative of the history of the port. This park was one of the first elements completed in MM21 and provided an excellent vantage point to view the progress of the project. One of the major open spaces in MM21 is Rinko Park, along the northern shore of MM21. It is an expanse of waterfront lawns, walkways and tidal pools with views across the harbor toward the Yokohama Bay Bridge. The park is some distance from the population of Yokohama and so includes 100 underground car-parking spaces in order to attract people to the very edge of MM21.

In an urban context with so little open space, Rinko Park is popular and people do drive and park to access the space. The Grand Mall Park, at the very center of MM21 is made up of a series of smaller plazas. The area in front of the Yokohama Museum of Art and the walkways to the Landmark Tower, Yokohama and Queen's Square, Yokohama are known as "Art Plaza," "Yoyo Plaza" and "Cross Patio," respectively. Cross Patio is aptly named as a zone of crossing between the Landmark Plaza Mall and Queen's Mall. It is the only external moment in an otherwise enclosed walk from the entrance of the project to the end of Pacifico Yokohama.

The historic Aka-Renga Park in the Shinko District is dedicated to the continued use of the site's old redbrick warehouses to preserve some aspects of the industrial heritage of the port. Aka-Renga Park will preserve parts of the former Yokohama Customhouse and Yokohama Minato Station. A promenade has been constructed along a narrow, abandoned railroad track bed. This track includes a truss bridge, the Kishamichi Promenade, which is the major pedestrian access to the Shinko District and spans across the mouth of the Ooka River, leading to Unga Park. Shinko Park sits opposite the Intercontinental Hotel of Pacifico Yokohama. This park offers a series of embankments and lawns for people to view MM21 and the port. Adjacent to this is one of the icons of MM21, the Yokohama Cosmo World Amusement Park. Cosmo World provides Yokohama with a year-round entertainment facility including the well-known Yokohama Ferris wheel. The Green Network culminates Pukarisanbashi Pier, at the tip of MM21 in front of the Hotel Continental. From the pier one can catch shuttle boats to Yamashita Park, the east exit of Yokohama Station and Hakkeijima Sea Paradise as well as sightseeing cruises around the port of Yokohama.

Despite the extensiveness of the "green network," open space within MM21 has a very precise use. Except for small moments one's entire journey from Landmark Tower to Pacifico Yokohama is internalized. Open space then is for purely recreational pursuits. It is not part of the constitutive fabric of the urban experience. Public space is not part of the primary experience of visiting and moving through MM21. The design of the streets and the arrangement of the open spaces clearly display this. The idea of the street as public condenser and container of urban culture, as in cities such as New York or Paris or Tokyo, finds no root in MM21. In their search for comfort the planners of MM21 have created a completely hermetic environment. One's everyday engagement with the project does not include any exposure to these open spaces nor to any aspect of an exterior pedestrian zone. In doing so MM21 expresses a clear "idea of the city."

The space and structure of Minato Mirai 21

Minato Mirai 21 is a wholly new entity on vacant land in Yokohama Bay. Its planners were unencumbered by the presence of existing infrastructure or buildings and free to articulate the plan in a manner that was fitting with their projection of what an ideal project should be. A number of key elements define the structure of the plan. MM21 is divided into five zones. These zones are the Business Zone, the Promenade Zone, the International Zone, the Commercial Zone and the Waterfront Zone.

The Business Zone sits in a band against the Yokohama-Hanada expressway and is intended to accommodate company headquarters and cultural and retail facilities designed to support the functions of the central business district. The Promenade Zone lies in front of the Business Zone and accommodates museums and other cultural facilities. The International Zone is a band of development in front of the Promenade Zone and includes hotels, shopping centers and housing. The International Zone faces Rinko Park and includes amusement facilities and "international exchange facilities" such as conference and exhibition facilities. Of all the zones, the International is the most complete. The Commercial Zone is located around the Yokohama Railroad Station and includes a variety of assorted commercial facilities. The Waterfront Zone encircles the project and includes the Rinko Park. It is designed as a passive recreation space. However it does include some functional piers and other port facilities.

Three principal axes define the structure of the plan. The first called the King's Axis, runs along the western side of the project and links Yokohama Station to the Rinko Park. The second is the Queen's Axis, which runs up the eastern edge of the project from Sakuragicho Station through the

4.9 View across Cross Patio, with people moving between Landmark Plaza and Queen's Mall.

4.10 This image shows the current status of the majority of MM21. The size of the development parcels can be compared to the existing fabric of the city beyond.

Landmark Plaza, the Queen's Plaza and culminates at Pacifico Yokohama. The third is the Grand Mall Axis, which is a major axis running east–west through the center of MM21. These axes define both the traffic and pedestrian circulation patterns for the project. Of these the most complete is the Queen's Axis, along which the majority of the completed buildings are located. Two arterial roads, Kokusai Boulevard and Minato Mirai Odori Boulevard, connect to Yokohama and cross the site from east to west. These form the two major circulation spines of the project. In addition, the Yokohama-Hanada expressway forms the southern edge of the project. Perpendicular to these three east–west elements are a series of arterial roads that provide access north and south and link under the expressway to Yokohama proper.

Overlaid on top of the traffic circulation is an extensive pedestrian circulation system. This system is laid out in accordance with the King's Axis and the Queen's Axis and is linked across the site by the Grand Mall. Harking back to one of the articulated themes for MM21 the pedestrian system is conceived of as a continuous space where people can move freely. What is interesting and curious in MM21 is the separation of the car from the pedestrian. In their efforts to create a "comfortable" environment within the project, these two realms have been completely segregated. The result, as one might expect, is that the car space is ultimately utilitarian. Devoid of any humanizing elements these arterial roads are designed as efficient vehicle movement infrastructures. This is symptomatic of the Japanese planners' "engineering" of the project. The inverse is

4.11 MM21 is isolated from the rest of Yokohama by infrastructure. In the bottom left of the image one can see the start of the moving walkway that connects Landmark Plaza with Sakuragicho Railroad Station.

also true for the pedestrian spaces of the project, where the "safe and comfortable" becomes homogenized and hermetic. In the case of the Queen's Axis, the space of the pedestrian is taken out of the space of the city and inserted, for the most part, into commercial space. Real street life is thus internalized. The pedestrian space for the most part does not occur in relation to how people would move through the site, even if the project were completed. In addition, the articulation of this pedestrian zone denies the possibility of an urban vitality that occurs in older areas of many Japanese cities. What is lost in MM21 is the grittiness and congestion that makes older city centers in Japan so interesting.

MM21 global project

Isolated from the fabric of Yokohama, MM21 is a significant change in the scale and density in comparison to the city. On one side of the expressway, streets in the Kannai and Noge districts of Yokohama are very small scale, between five and ten meters wide. MM21, in contrast, introduces 50-meter wide boulevards. The block structure proposed in MM21 is likewise of a very different scale from the rest of Yokohama. In Noge or Kannai the largest block would be in the order of 100 meters wide. In MM21, the smallest block is 150 meters wide. This has a significant impact on the generation of public life in the city. The larger block size internalizes activity and takes it off the street. This diminution of public life is extended with the introduction of elevated walkway systems

Minato Mirai 21

4.12 The experience of visiting MM21 is mostly an internalized one. This view is of the interior of Landmark Plaza.

4.13 Start of the Grand Mall Park, looking down upon Cross Patio.

that separate pedestrians from the car dominated ground plane.

In comparison to Yokohama there is nothing familiar about MM21. MM21 stands out as something completely different. This lack of the familiar does not equate to a heightening of urban experience in the city. On the contrary, the life of the street, focus of public life in the traditional city has been subdued. The project works best in terms of the creation of the image of the global city. The Landmark Tower and the Inter-Continental Hotel, along with the Yokohama Bay Bridge, create the necessary "postcard view for the new economy" which is important in marketing an international city image to the rest of the world. MM21 raises the question of whether it is possible to produce a global urban project that accomplishes both a vital urban situation and an image suitable for the global "marketing" of the project.

Thailand

Bangkok

5.1 The postcard view of Muang Thong Thani. Lakeview Apartments – 24 buildings each 30 stories tall.

5 The Golden City in the City of Angels

Muang Thong Thani, Bangkok, Thailand

It [Muang Thong Thani] is a dazzling complex of two dozen huge gray-white buildings soaring nearly 30 stories high, and surrounded by streets lined with shops, town houses and detached homes. Walk closer and it feels eerie, for it is a ghost city.

New York Times February 16, 1999

Most of the western world has forgotten what life in a city is like ... where a surveyor's grid, laid out with pegs and string in open fields, can mushroom into a skyline of skyscrapers with an urgency that suggests time lapse photography.

Deyan Sudjic writing about Muang Thong Thani, BLUEPRINT 1993

Bangkok of the Future, Now.
Muang Thong Thani advertising slogan.

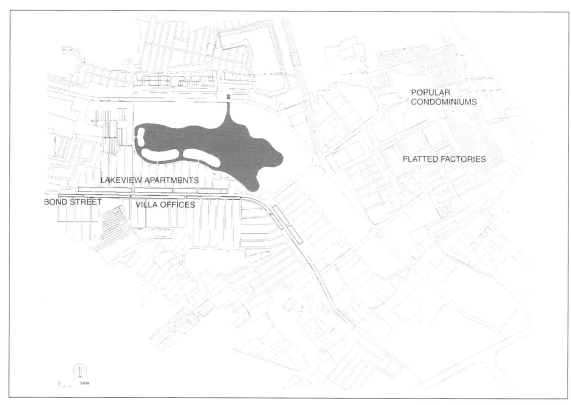

Map of Muang Thong Thani, Bangkok.

Located on the outskirts of Bangkok, in Chaeng Wattana close to Bangkok's Don Muang International Airport, lies one of the most remarkable examples of a city created almost instantly in the midst of unprecedented optimism for Bangkok's role in the future of Asia. This optimism was buoyed by Thailand's remarkable record of growth. Between the middle of the 1980s and the middle of the 1990s, Thailand experienced a period of economic development of which there exists little equivalent in the twentieth century. Thailand recorded the strongest growth of any country in the world during this period with an annual rate of increase in its gross domestic product in excess of 10 percent, reaching a maximum of 13 percent in 1988 (World Bank 1993). Integral to Thailand's remarkable growth was the construction sector. Muang Thong Thani (Golden City) is a global urban project that characterizes the rise of Thailand as a miracle economy in the 1990s and also its fall.

Over a period of forty years Muang Thong Thani's developer, Bangkok Land, quietly went about securing land to accumulate some 750 hectares on the outskirts of Bangkok. Initial development on the site resembled many other residential developments on the outskirts of the city. In 1989, however the trajectory of the project changed. The management of the family business shifted from the older and more conservative generation to a younger and aggressive one. This new generation, representing Asia's emerging entrepreneurial spirit, guided the project toward a dramatic new direction. No longer would the project be yet another residential development on the outskirts of Bangkok; instead a brand new city, designed to house a million people would be built.

Despite being a privately owned and developed development, Muang Thong Thani utilized the same characteristics as other global urban projects. The project was instigated in response to perceptions of global competition and was an attempt, in its own way to secure competitive advantage for its host city. In addition, it aimed to provide a new kind of space occupancy not available prior to its construction and aimed to attract a very specific kind of occupant, in the Thai middle class or the displaced Hong Kong elite. Further it is radically different in scale and articulation to the environment of the rest of the city and this was done, in part, to secure a kind of celebrity status by projecting an image that could be marketed in the global market place.

The Golden City's skyscraper apartment blocks, once a glowing symbol of Thailand's booming economy, stand as a beacon in the landscape of Bangkok, visible on approach by air to the airport and from the elevated expressway leading into the city. Today these towers sit mostly deserted. Most are in a state of disrepair and several are uncompleted. The story of Muang Thong Thani epitomizes both the blind faith invested in the Asian miracle and the volatility of development in the global market place.

Muang Thong Thani – The Golden City

Muang Thong Thani is the flagship development of Bangkok Land, owned by one of Bangkok's most influential families, the Kanjanapas. In the 1990s, the Kanjanapas family controlled an enormously profitable retail and property empire and Bangkok Land was the biggest capitalized stock on the Bangkok Stock Exchange. In 1992, *Fortune Magazine* estimated the Kanjanapas family's personal worth at US$2.1 billion, making them one of the world's richest families. The following year combined profits from their four listed companies reached an all-time high of US$266 million. However, by 1995 the Kanjanapas family empire was overextended with debt when the financial crisis struck leaving their companies vulnerable. Unable to service its debt Bangkok Land was forced to negotiate new payment terms with Bangkok Bank and Siam Commercial Bank, who together were owed a total of 4 billion baht (US$101 million). Muang Thong Thani remains an important project for Bangkok Land and its attempts to repay this money will be determined by how they reposition the project. The company is hoping that the Golden City will eventually become profitable. However, the level of global and domestic uncertainty facing Thailand today may make Bangkok Land's ambitions impossible to fulfill (see World Bank 2000d).

For several decades Bangkok Land had been accumulating properties in Chaeng Wattana close to Bangkok's Don Muang Airport and by the late 1980s they held 750 hectares. Initially the company was involved in fairly modest residential development, of a type common in the outskirts of Bangkok, under the guidance of empire founder Mongkol Kanjanapas. Mongkol was born in Bangkok in 1921. In the early 1960s, he moved to his ancestral village of Shantou near Hong Kong. In 1963, he established a watch-making company in Hong Kong that would become Stelux Holdings International. Mongkol moved back to Bangkok in the late 1960s where he began to move into the property market in the early 1970s. Anant Kanjanapas, the eldest son of the family, began his business career at Stelux in Hong Kong, where he developed an aggressive Hong Kong business acumen. In 1989, Anant returned to Bangkok to head Bangkok Land. The family's influence continued to expand and Anant was able to cultivate powerful political connections. Since 1991 he has been a government-appointed senator.

After listing Bangkok Land on the Stock Exchange in 1992, the family pursued a strategy of expansion in all of its business interests in both Hong Kong and Thailand. The aggressive Anant, buoyed by his political connections and family wealth, set about redefining the vision for their 750-hectare site at Chaeng Wattana. Four factors may have informed his vision for Muang Thong Thani. The first was his perception of an emerging Thai middle class in the market for luxury items in that there was definite potential in being able to satisfy a need for luxury housing. The second is that Bangkok is a difficult and inefficient place to live and there was potential to provide a new concept of living in an environment of order and efficiency. The third and fourth may be traced to Anant's knowledge of urban development in Hong Kong. With the transfer of Hong Kong to Chinese rule the potential existed to provide a "Hong Kong style" housing product in Bangkok that would be attractive to Hong Kong people looking to set up life in other situations, possibly Thailand. However, Canada proved a far more attractive destination for the majority of Hong Kong expatriates. The fourth can be traced to Anant's understanding of the tremendous profits that Hong Kong developers made constructing satellite towns in the New Territories. Given the perception of the Bangkok real estate market, there was an obvious hope to reproduce those profits in Muang Thong Thani. It is within these terms that the basic concept of Muang Thong Thani was formed.

Globalization and Thailand's tiger ambitions

In July of 1997, the devaluation of the baht (Thai currency) by the Thai government signaled the beginning of a regional economic crisis that shook the world. Between July and December of that year the baht went into a free fall and the Thai stock market crashed. Foreign capital fled and Thailand, once held up by the World Bank as a miracle of sound financial policy and sustained growth, was bankrupt (World Bank 1993). In August of 1997, faced with a debt of US$89 billion (of which over half was due within the following months), the Thai government asked for a "rescue" package from the International Monetary Fund (IMF). The IMF welcomed the request, confident that the financial support would contribute to stability in financial markets in Asia. This proved to be optimistic. As the crisis exerted its influence almost 3 million Thai workers lost their jobs, but the most visible signs could be seen in the construction projects that stopped all over Bangkok, leaving a host of unfinished high-rise towers scattered across the skyline. The crisis marked the end of a remarkable period of development in the city and nation.

Thailand began its road to modern development in the late 1950s. The World Bank played a crucial role in providing funds and Thailand began a period of rapid industrialization and infrastructure development. Initially the Thai economy was based upon import substitution but shifted to export-oriented industrial operations in the 1970s. This was spurred by foreign investment, particularly from Japan. Efforts to attract foreign direct investment (FDI) were supported by proponents of free markets in the United States and Europe and Thailand began introducing economic policies to integrate the Thai economy into the global economy through accelerated trade, investment and financial liberalization. Between 1985 and 1995 Thailand's economy grew by 10 percent per annum, the fastest rate of growth in the world and Thailand became the "economic miracle" poster child for the World Bank (World Bank 1990: 3). In the early 1990s, the Thai government managed to create an environment conducive to foreign capital and the country benefited from Japan's bubble economy during this period. The Japanese were the largest foreign investors in the Thai economy. The availability of FDI had important consequences for the economic climate in Thailand during this period.

5.2 Older developments in Bangkok Land resemble this villa, typical of many residential developments on the outskirts of the city. Behind, the Lakeview Apartments can be seen, creating an artificial ridge in the otherwise featureless plain of Bangkok.

One of the factors that would later destroy the Thai economy was that this capital was not invested in productive sectors of the economy but into short-term high profit ventures such as the stock market, real estate and credit creation. As a result, the city of Bangkok began to change rapidly as foreign capital was used to finance the construction of luxury housing, hotels and office developments. This could be seen with new developments sprouting all over the city. This rapid building boom gave the impression of prosperity and many investors, developers, financiers and analysts became seduced by the appearance of success. However, Thailand's booming real estate development was not based on the creation of wealth, rather on a climate of speculation made possible through borrowed funds. The ease at which developers secured financing led to a massive amount of construction. With a tremendous oversupply of commercial real estate and the burgeoning external debt, foreign investors started to look for other avenues to invest their money. As funds were pulled out of Thailand the banks faced a massive liquidity problem, triggering the financial crisis.

The appearance of prosperity had been achieved by rapid industrialization, the creation of an environment attractive to FDI, minimal regulation and an engagement with the global economy. One of the most alarming aspects of Thailand's predicament was how quickly the Asia crisis destroyed a seemingly "miracle" economy. The speed at which Thailand was devastated changed attitudes toward globalization. Once seen as the source of success it was now seen as the cause of major problems. Anti globalization was embraced by people in the street, by business and by government policy. The Thais actively sought to insulate themselves from the global economy through a series of legislative changes. However this only occurred after the Asia Crisis had taken hold. Globalization was targeted as the reason for the economic crisis; however Thailand's embrace of globalization did not cause its downfall. The ease at which capital left Thailand, however (the ease of movement of funds being

5.3 The influx of FDI into Thailand can be seen in the number of high-rise commercial developments in Bangkok. This view is taken from Silom Road looking toward Sathurn Road.

one characteristic of the global economy), contributed to the speed of an inevitable collapse.

It is a mistake to assume that problems faced by the Thai economy were unforeseen or unpredictable. It now appears that poorly managed fiscal policies may have had a greater influence than anyone had expected. The International Monetary Fund was aware of the problems in the Thai economy and repeatedly warned the Thai government that they should initiate changes to their economic policies. As far back as March 1993, the IMF issued a series of confidential letters to the Bank of Thailand and the Thai government cautioning that the rapid growth in capital stock had brought in an excess of supply in several sectors such as commercial and luxury residential construction. A total of five letters were delivered by the IMF, all of which stressed that a combination

of high current account deficit, rising short-term debts, along with rapid growth in credit and asset prices had increased the economy's vulnerability (The Nation Section 1999). But while the going was good Thailand and Bangkok thrived in a bubble of artificial confidence and the Thai government paid such warnings little credence.

Building the empty city

One of the most active sectors of the Thai economy during this period was the property sector. Immediately prior to the crisis, property development in all its aspects – construction, building materials, mortgages, loans, legal fees and all manner of other financial service activities – contributed 30 to 50 percent of annual GDP growth (Paisley 1996: 61). Bangkok began to grow both upwards and outwards and in doing so exuded architectural excess. This period produced lavish and outrageous architectural expressions such as the glass towers of the Siam Commercial Bank Complex with its golden pyramid roofs and the comical Bank of Asia Building designed to resemble a robot! Easy supply of money, combined with the emergence of a powerful social pressure to appear successful, created an environment that supported the construction of luxury projects. The annual production of office space reached its top in 1994, with the construction of more than one million square meters (Bangkok Post 1994). In the same year the annual production of residences exceeded 150,000 units. In addition, 1994 saw the launching of more than 250,000 units of residential construction (Wonghanchao 1996: 63).

The unprecedented construction of offices and residences was in part due to population increases in the metropolitan area of Bangkok of approximately 2.5 percent per year during this period. To satisfy this increase required slightly more than 50,000 additional units of housing each year. At the same time, the incomes of people in Bangkok increased in real terms by more than 10 percent per annum. This increased the purchasing power of the emerging middle class in Thai society. However other influences added to the increasing demand for housing as well. Young people, suddenly far more prosperous than their parents' generation, desired both luxury and independence and actively sought to leave the family home to either reduce their commute to work or simply to satisfy lifestyle ambitions (see Chalermpow Koanantakool 1993: 72). However, while this was true it cannot explain the total volume of housing constructed in the city.

One issue that was overlooked by Thai property developers and an issue of particular relevance for Muang Thong Thani, was that in 1995 less than 60 percent of households were able to acquire

residences on the open market. This was true for even the least expensive residences, which were apartments of thirty to forty square meters on the outskirts of the city (costing approximately US$12,000). With interest rates at 12 percent, only those whose monthly income exceeded US$450 could afford this type of housing. The minimum wage of a workman or a saleswoman, for example, was fixed in 1995 to US$6 per day (US$150 per month). Only double income families or lower-level civil servants were earning over US$450 per month in 1995.

The property market in Bangkok was in a desperate situation of rampant oversupply. In 1993, the vacancy rate of residential units approached 10 percent; it reached 11.5 percent in 1994, then 14.5 percent in 1995 (more than 300,000 vacant residences on the whole). In the office market the situation was hardly better, since the rate of vacancy approached 32 percent in 1994. On the outskirts of the city almost 40 percent of the offices were unoccupied, compared to 24 percent in the central business district (see Wonghanchao 1996; Charms 1999). Despite this, Bangkok Land continued to aggressively move forward with the planning and design of Muang Thong Thani. As with many other developers in Bangkok at the time they were either ignorant of the true reality or blind to its implications.

It now appears these vacancy figures were underestimated. Real estate companies artificially inflated the rates of reservation and sales figures in order to create the illusion that their projects were selling and therefore highly desirable. Developers were manufacturing a myth around their projects to lure investors by suggesting that others had seen value in their product. In some cases the payment of a ridiculously small amount was enough to validate a commitment to purchase. These tactics masked inherent problems in the real estate sector and ultimately delayed any

5.4 View of Silom Station. Bangkok's elevated rail system locates itself on top of the roadway, plunging the congested streets into darkness.

recognition of the economic crisis. This was certainly the case with Muang Thong Thani.

The emerging Thai middle class became a consumer generation who by necessity relied on credit to support its lifestyle habits. Developers tried to cash in on this lust for luxury by building projects that would satisfy this lifestyle ambition. In an incredibly competitive market however, developers were forced to go to great lengths to gain the attention of this consumer set. Combined with the absence of planning in the city and little zoning or building control this created a cacophony of built form in the city. High rise office and residential projects could be located essentially anywhere. This created situations where high-rise buildings could occur in alleys surrounded by one- and two-story houses, instead of along main roads. This further overloaded Bangkok's inadequate city infrastructure and contributed to the absurd traffic conditions for which the city is renowned. The motivation to develop Muang Thong Thani came from both the desire for luxury and an appreciation of urban problems in Bangkok.

Bangkok – Krung Thep – City of Angels

To appreciate the critique of Bangkok's urban problems it is necessary to briefly examine the planning and physical context of the city. Bangkok (Krung Thep) is the capital and largest city of Thailand. It is located in the central part of the country, on the Chao Phraya River delta near the Gulf of Thailand (Siam). The origins of the city relate to the relocation of the capital of Ayuthaya after the Burmese army sacked it in 1767. The original site of settlement was Thonburi on the east bank of the Chao Phraya River before it moved to Krung Thep (Thai for "city of angels") in 1782. Bangkok is the royal capital of the Chakri dynasty, starting with King Rama I and continuing today with King Bhumibol or Rama IX. The city has

always been the center of administration in the kingdom and a major commercial center attracting other Asian, principally Chinese, as well as European merchants. Characteristically Thailand always had an open door policy with the outside world. To maintain Thai sovereignty, Europeans were allowed to set up banks and commercial operations with little restrictions, thereby avoiding the "colonization" suffered by many other South East Asian countries.

This strategy of partnership before conquest led to Thailand allying itself with Japan during much of World War II (1939–45). The Japanese were allowed to use Thailand as a base of South East Asian operations in exchange for not laying claim on Thai sovereignty. As a result of this alliance Bangkok suffered serious allied bombing in the last year of the war. After 1945 the country was politically unstable and indeed much of the recent political history of Thailand has been characterized by a series of political upheavals. The country has experienced seventeen coups and several periods of military rule since World War II, the last being in 1991. Despite the political instability the city began expanding quickly in the 1960s. Bangkok played an important role in supplying produce and other materials in support of the American efforts in Vietnam and as a result its economy flourished.

Bangkok is quite unlike any other city in its form and organization. About 12 million people live in Bangkok and its extended metropolitan area (World Bank 2001). It is one of the largest primate cities in South East Asia with approximately 20 percent of all Thais living in the city. Bangkok is also a city with tremendous problems. The World Bank notes that Bangkok continues to suffer with the worst possible traffic congestion, urban poverty, poor air quality, limited sanitation facilities, inadequate garbage disposal, insufficient green space, and recurrent flooding (World Bank 2001).

Driving into the heart of the city from the Don Muang Airport on the elevated expressway one is struck both by its sheer enormity, sprawling away to the horizon, and also by the randomness of high rise development that pops up all over the city. It is apparent that the city does not obey the same kinds of rules that one has come to expect in other cities. This is because although in theory Bangkok has a documented planning system with both zoning and building controls, in practice these are mostly irrelevant to how the city has developed. Rather, development in the city is spontaneous and opportunistic. The cacophony of form that characterizes Bangkok displays a general disregard for location "rules" as one with even a cursory understanding of real estate development might expect.

Planning in Bangkok is "controlled" by the Town and Country Planning Act of 1975. However, under the Act a developer is not required to obtain planning approval. Instead there is a requirement to obtain building approval (Building Control Act 1975), where the use of the building is considered in relation to the approved plan for any given area of the city. This is a rather weak planning tool and does little to direct where development will occur. The Bangkok Metropolitan Authority understands that the Comprehensive Plan fails to provide a framework to control or direct development and to address this failure two international consultants were engaged to redefine the planning system in Bangkok in 1995. A team from the European Community focused on the system itself while Professor Gary Hack and a team from the Massachusetts Institute of Technology (MIT), produced a draft new plan.

This new plan sought to normalize development in the city. As such it aimed to guide growth in line with how one generally thinks cities should behave. The plan aimed to create higher densities around transportation nodes, to redistribute land use to create a more even pattern of employment in the city, thereby reducing the amount of commuting in the city and also to provide a series of open spaces and lakes in the fabric of Bangkok to help control the city's flooding problem (MIT *et al.* 1996). A change in the administration of the Bangkok Metropolitan Authority, combined with the economic crisis has meant that these recommendations have yet to influence the planning system or the physical fabric of the city.

The city of Bangkok generally refers to the Greater Bangkok Metropolitan Region (BMR). Called Krung Thep Mahanakhon in Thai, the BMR consists of the Bangkok Metropolitan Administration (BMA) covering an area of some 1500 square kilometers and the neighboring provinces of Nakhon Pathom, Nonthaburi, Pathum Thani, Samut Prakan, and Samut Songkhram. The total area of the BMR is in the order of 7800 square kilometers. Unlike Tokyo's growth, which occurred in expansive bands from the center, Bangkok's expansion was, and continues to be, uneven. While areas of housing and industry can be found as far as 40 kilometers from the center, there still exist vacant sites closer to the center. This is due to the patchwork nature of the road system, which means that some areas within the urban landscape are simply inaccessible. Indeed, the arterial road system to a great extent has defined the form of the city. This patchwork produces a "leap-frogging" of development activity as projects respond to the chaotic roadway organization. Better road access exists to the north and east of the city and subsequently the city has expanded in this direction. While land use planning does not influence the form of the city, transportation planning certainly does. The problem with this is that transportation planning in Bangkok is inefficient and open to political interference.

The first attempts to control the form of the city through the articulation of expressways came with the creation of the *Greater Bangkok Plan 2533*, produced by the American firm of Litchfield and Associates in 1960. This plan aimed to make Bangkok a modern city with the construction of a super highway system encircling the city. Although Bangkok was to follow the spirit of the Litchfield plan and embraced automobiles with the construction of the ring road, the construction of other highway infrastructure did not occur. The rising affluence of Thai society, combined with no restrictions on car ownership and inadequate road infrastructure inevitably led to a situation for which Bangkok has become renowned – almost paralyzing traffic congestion.

In response to the inadequacies of road construction in the city and the tremendous traffic congestion, the 1990s saw the planning and construction of major expressways and the planning of mass transit in the city. This included the construction of the First Stage Expressway, part of the Second Stage Expressway, the At Narong-Ramintra Expressway and the Don Muang Tollway leading from the center of Bangkok to the Don Muang Airport in the north. This construction totaled only 91 kilometers, far short of the 1042 kilometers planned. The lack of coordination in the provision of highway infrastructure means that the road system is ineffectual in dealing with the volume of traffic in the city. One of the strategic advantages that Muang Thong Thani has is that it is located adjacent to the Don Muang Tollway, which provides excellent access to both the airport and the center of the city. This was indeed no accident. Political connections certainly played a part in securing Muang Thong Thani access to the Don Muang Tollway.

Designing the Golden City

Muang Thong Thani is an urban development wholly designed by one firm of architects, Nation Fender. Robert Nation and Karl Fender, writing in 1992, describe how:

. . . the design process commenced in April of 1989 with an initial master plan concept and the design of the first proposals for high-rise buildings which combine residential (flats) and industrial (factories), as stage one of the development. Work proceeded slowly and intermittently during the remainder of the year, while the client investigated potential markets in Asia. One year later [1990] the process assumed an urgency that has yet to subside.

(Architecture Australia 1992: 34)

From June 1990 to July 1991, construction contracts to the value of US$1 billion were awarded to the French construction company, Bouygues-Thai. The speed at which Muang Thong Thani was constructed is remarkable and called for a radical modification of the relationship between client, architect and contractor. The client formulated briefs and delivered them in the form of a "biro doodle" to the architects. Within a day an indicative image and broad solution would be approved for sales content and viability and transferred to computer documentation. This documentation formed the basis for sales packaging, building permit applications and preliminary negotiations with the contractor. It was not uncommon for preliminary agreements between the client and the contractor to be in place within eight weeks of the initial "biro doodle" (Architecture Australia 1992: 35). The speed of the process was assisted by a minimum of regulatory procedures within the Bangkok planning system and more than any other global urban project Muang Thong Thani represents a "just add water" approach to urban development – an instant urbanism.

The most striking aspect of Muang Thong Thani, visible both on air approach to Bangkok and from the expressway linking the center of the city to the airport, is the line of twenty-four apartment towers standing thirty-storys tall marching down one side

5.5 View of the deserted streetscape in Muang Thong Thani.

5.6 Lakeview Apartment Towers, view from the lakeside.

of an artificial lake. Situated amongst a sea of red, green and brown tiled villa roofs the towers rise like some enormous mountain range on the otherwise flat alluvial plain of Bangkok. These concrete towers are arrayed at intervals along a 2-kilometer long road called Bond Street. The towers, called Lakeview Housing, sit on top of a continuous six-story plinth of shopping and parking that runs the entire length of the street. On the roof of this plinth the designers envisaged recreation spaces for the apartments. The towers have been designed to present their most elegant profile to the street with concrete fins protruding from the face of the structures creating both visual interest and a breakdown in scale to the elevations. Housed within this row of towers are 3500 residential apartments, the majority of which today stand empty. The entire ensemble is painted white, further highlighting the silhouette of the development on the Bangkok skyline.

On the southern edge of Bond Street, immediately opposite the Lakeview Housing with its 2-kilometer plinth, sit ninety office-retail-residential-mixed-use buildings. These are known as the Villa Offices, which consist of five levels of flexible commercial or light industrial space, upon which two-story penthouses sit. There is also basement car parking. The Villa Offices are also mostly deserted and many have fallen into a state of disrepair. The facades of the buildings incorporate curtain wall glazing and protruding aluminum canopies were intended to create a visual energy within the streetscape. This is futile however as Bond Street itself stands deserted. The sidewalks are now cracked and the palms lining the median are in desperate need of attention but the obvious care in which the designers articulated the landscape is evident.

Standing in the eerily empty street one can certainly imagine the vision of the designers. Indeed, if Muang Thong Thani were created under different circumstances Bond Street would have radically altered the way one thinks of streets in Bangkok and perhaps would have validated the idea that well designed streets have a place in the city. However, Bond Street encapsulates the tragedy of Muang Thong Thani. It represents wasted architectural effort and the failed potential of a new urbanism. At the end of Bond Street, Nation Fender's master plan included a project known as Park Lane Center, which was to be a mixed-use shopping and office development of two thirty-story office towers and 55,000 square meters of retail. This part of Muang Thong Thani was not built, although the project appears in many of the renderings carried in professional journals in the early 1990s.

On the other side of the development sit the Flatted Factories and Popular Condominiums. The design of the eight flatted factories, which consist of ten story 65,000 square meter buildings, is one of the signatures of Muang Thong Thani. In the 1993 July/August issue of *Blueprint*, Deyan Sudjik wrote an article entitled "Bangkok's instant city" and included several photographs of the factories, one of the images being a photograph showing several female construction workers, a vendor with his three-wheeled bicycle and a security guard standing in front of the "slick" factories. This image exemplifies one of the hidden issues in the wealth through globalization argument and captures the income gap between those that have and those that can only dream in Thailand. The people in the photograph, displayed like props, will never be able to partake in the kind of success that Muang Thong Thani aims for.

5.8 Entrance canopy to one of the vacant villa offices.

5.9 View along Bond Street. On the left of the image of the Lakeview Apartment Towers and on the right the Villa Offices.

5.10 View of the Villa Offices.

The factories themselves consist of a car park upon which eight levels of flexible factory space sit. The "big box" program is wrapped in a skin of aluminum panels and blue curtain wall glazing. The bulk of these buildings is moderated by a series of horizontal projections, in the form of fins and balconies and further accentuated by the exposure of the car parking ramps, which are fashioned into sculptural elements within the larger composition of the building form. Interest is further generated by the incorporation of large-scale graphics designed by 8vo in London. These large numerals create both a visual interest and an ordering system for the uniformly designed buildings. Although these factories are mostly empty, Bangkok Land has been successful in selling some of them to the Ministries of Defense and Trade, amongst others (Stelux 1997).

The Popular Condominiums, which consist of low-cost housing developments in twenty-seven blocks of fifteen stories (totaling 27,000 apartments) are the most successful part of the original scheme for Muang Thong Thani. The apartments, some as small as 40 square meters, were sold for approximately US$12,000. This type of housing proved very popular with civil servants and teachers. The design of the apartments however, expresses the economic rationalism of the project. Sudjik is pointed in his description of them, writing:

[that] negotiating the double-loaded corridors of the popular condominiums at night is going to feel like a journey through the lower decks of a crammed migrant ship crossing the Atlantic. The flimsy walls and cheap doors are going to provide little in the way of privacy.

(Sudjik 1993: 19)

5.11 View toward the Flatted Factories.

5.12 View toward the Flatted Factories. In the distance are the Popular Condominiums.

5.13 Each Flatted Factory is numbered. These numbers, along with various color schemes, differentiate one building from another.

5.14 The most active areas in Muang Thong Thani are the streets around the Popular Condominiums. Each street is fronted by ground floor retail, which brings activity to these spaces.

The environment created around the popular condominiums is intriguing. Nowhere else in Thailand do people live in such densities. Estimates of how many people live in Muang Thong Thani vary; however Anant Kanjanapas states that about 75,000 people live in the popular condominiums (Bangkok Post 2000). If this number is indeed correct then the resulting density within the popular condominium district is in the order of 700 people per hectare. Even by Asian standards this is high. The result of this density is a remarkable active street life facilitated by retail and services stores located on the ground floors of the condominiums. The street becomes a hive of activity and similar to conditions in Hong Kong where apartments are small, people actively seek street life as a way to escape the claustrophobic housing conditions. In this area of Muang Thong Thani Nation Fender's vision for a redefined urbanism finds form.

The Asia Crisis impacted Bangkok Land in the same way that it did other developers. Thailand's lax liquidation laws, however allowed the company to survive. The family's companies were overextended when the liquidity problems arose and the situation in Muang Thong Thani reflects the changing fortunes of Bangkok Land. The company was desperate for revenue and sales of its commercial, industrial and residential properties were not able to produce any cash flow. The company's only asset was land and Anant looked for new possibilities to make productive use of this asset. The 1998 ASEAN Games provided an excellent opportunity to change the direction of Muang Thong Thani. Despite the fact that the company could not repay its debts, Anant was able to secure financing to construct the Bangkok Land Sports Complex (later renamed the IMPACT Arena). During the ASEAN Games the Sports Complex hosted events such as boxing, gymnastics and weightlifting, while athletes from ASEAN nations stayed in the vacant Lakeview Housing apartments.

In addition, the Impact Exhibition Center (IMPACT), the largest in South East Asia, was constructed in 1999. Eighty-four fairs, mainly local shows, were booked for the Impact Center in 2000. The events provide an additional two billion baht revenue (approximately US$44 million) for Bangkok Land (Bangkok Post 2000). Other facilities are under construction including a two-story convention center, covering 25,000 square meters. The new center will cost 800 million baht to build (approximately US$17 million). Upon completion the Impact site will have 20,000 square meters of exhibition halls and 25,000 square meters of convention space. Bangkok Land is also planning a new project, the New Century Plaza, a retail-entertainment development, opposite the IMPACT Arena. The 1.5 billion-baht project will be a joint venture between Bangkok Land (60 percent) and the Asian Land Fund of the United Kingdom (40 percent) (Bangkok Post 2000). However, despite these development initiatives, investment analysts are uneasy about Bangkok Land's shares because of doubts about the company's financial stability. It has massive debts, big losses and a poor image because of empty units at Muang Thong Thani. According to the Stock Exchange of Thailand, Bangkok Land had outstanding debts totaling 10.4 billion baht (approximately US$220 million) at the end of 1999 (Bangkok Post 2000).

Modernist utopia in the rice fields

Muang Thong Thani owes its pedigree to the modernist utopias promulgated through Congrès Internationaux d'Architecture Moderne (CIAM) manifestos. Indeed in its own way, Muang Thong Thani reinforces CIAM's promotion of modernism and internationalism in architecture. Robert Nation and Karl Fender describe their desire for a modernist architecture, which would create:

clean, elegant and lasting building forms, comfortable in Bangkok today and appropriate for the future. It is not cluttered by token cultural references but is deeply committed to the living patterns of Thai society.

(Architecture Australia 1992: 35)

However, CIAM modernism combined two forms of utopian thinking, architectural and social, into a new conception of urban order. Muang Thong Thani, by comparison, is utopian only in that it captures a sense of a completely new vision of architectural construction yet lacks an accompanying new egalitarian social vision. In other words the project lacks the pretensions to change the social foundation of Thai society.

The project follows the CIAM model in other ways as well, particularly in terms of defamiliarization and dehistorization of the project vis-à-vis its context. It utilizes a modernist strategy of defamiliarization in that it proposes a new urban structure radically different from the existing city in its form and organization. However, this strategy does not imply the same critique of the capitalist city inherent in CIAM utopias. Rather, there is a bold embrace of the capitalist city in Muang Thong Thani, which can be seen in both the system of the project's production and the kind of accommodation provided within the project, where Muang Thong Thani is undoubtedly a project designed for profit. The strategy of dehistorization can be seen in the employment of the aesthetic of universal design principles. However, unlike other modernist projects this is not done, as James Holston notes in reference to Brasilia, to mask an agenda for social change (Holston 1989). This is done to secure a new and different place for the project by simply removing the history of the city and establishing Muang Thong Thani in a free position with relation to the history of the city. In utilizing these strategies it removes the project from the chaos and inefficiency of the city and sets it apart as

something else. In this way it resembles such Modernist utopias as the Cité la Muette, Drancy in Paris by Bodoin and Lods in the appearance of dwelling units of uniform height and appearance grouped into residential super blocks with high-rise residential towers rising from a row of lower rise development marching along in a line (see *Can Our Cities Survive?* by José Luis Sert: 1942). But where Cité la Muette does so for social and political reasons, Muang Thong Thani does so to enhance the imageability of itself in the global market place.

The instant urbanity of Muang Thong Thani is both enlightening and overwhelming. It is enlightening in the sense that if one thinks of Muang Thong Thani as an enormous experiment, forgetting for a moment the morality of such a proposition, then one finds a fantastic environment which reinforces the architectural ego in the sense that it validates the idea that such projects are possible, although in narrowly defined terms. One can certainly see why Nation Fender would have been seduced by the idea of designing Muang Thong Thani. At some level the ego in this project represents the desire of all designers to construct their own version of utopia, to create a holistic vision of the world imagined in the mind's eye. In this project Nation Fender were given a remarkable opportunity to articulate and build their idea of the city. One can appreciate how the designers must have felt tremendous excitement at the prospect of creating a project at the scale and scope of great projects imagined by Le Corbusier and others. In these terms the project is worthy of examination; however the potential of the design of Muang Thong Thani is unfortunately wasted.

The project is overwhelming in the sense that although the project is possible to construct physically, where it has failed, perhaps not surprisingly, is in the construction of a social sphere. In this sense Muang Thong Thani invalidates the architectural ego and validates the idea that projects must be born from a context broader than just the physical setting. They reside within a context constructed from cultural, social, ecological, economic and physical realities. Muang Thong Thani's failure is the failure to understand the plurality of the context in which it was created. This project is an example of the limitations of design in its ability to cope with designing the global sphere. Increasingly design must address its relevance to an understanding of the forces that shape international money circuits and global politics. In this case the developer and the designers were unaware that the context in which they were working was a false one, a bubble of inflated wealth that was more image than reality. Muang Thong Thani was born into a false context, the empty shell of a potentially great project stands testament to that falsity.

China

Shanghai and Beijing

6.1 Artist's impression of Century Boulevard, Lujiazui, Shanghai (copyright EDAW Ltd.).

6 The Focal Point of China

Lujiazui, Shanghai

It is a good time to be a designer in China. Unlike America there are no rules in China. We can do what we want. We can do good design!

Xie Xiaoying, Landscape Architect, China

The speed of change occurring in urban environments in China is unprecedented and astonishing. In world terms no other country has urbanized as rapidly as China since it started its engagement with the socialist market economy. This is certainly evident in the tremendous changes that have occurred in cities such as Shanghai, where ten years ago the Lujiazui Financial District did not exist. On one side of the Huangpu River sat the majestic Bund and on the other sat an array of industrial facilities, workers' housing and farmland. Today, this same territory hosts a dazzling display

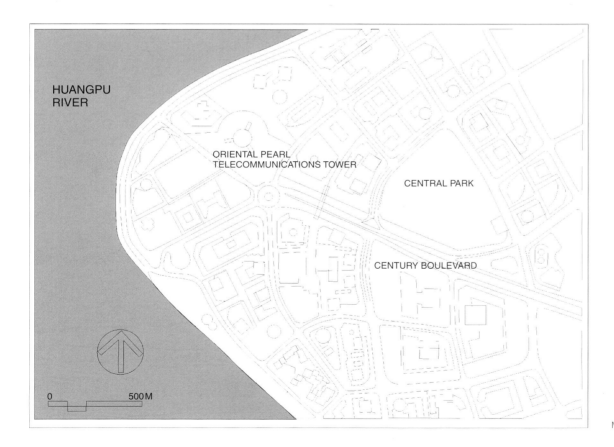

HUANGPU RIVER

ORIENTAL PEARL TELECOMMUNICATIONS TOWER

CENTRAL PARK

CENTURY BOULEVARD

0   500 M

Map of Lujiazui, Shanghai.

6.2 Lujiazui as seen from the famous Bund on the other side of the Huangpu River. A statue of Chairman Mao sits staring at the steel and glass high rise towers.

of steel and glass high-rise office towers, symbols of the New China. This is the Pudong New Area, the focal point of China's economic development strategy for the next fifty years. At its head is Lujiazui, the central business district or "international trade and finance zone" of the Pudong New Area, one of several critical projects propelling the emergence of China as a world financial leader. This is the Shanghai for the twenty-first century.

Standing on the banks of the Huangpu today one can see both the international city of the past reflected in the majestic facades of the famous Bund and on the other side of the river the glistening towers of a new Shanghai beginning to reclaim its title as a global financial center. Lujiazui presents an uncompromising vision of the future of the Chinese city. Its genesis comes from a new era in Chinese history. Emerging from nearly fifty years of imposed isolation China is now seeking to capture a larger role in world affairs. Lujiazui is one of the primary vehicles to propel this emergence. Its creators aim to develop it into the business center of Asia with a focus on finance, trade, commerce and other tertiary industries. It is a project rich in the aspirations of a nation just beginning to realize its position in the world. It is also a global urban project whose creation stems from an understanding of a potential relationship between the globalization dynamics of finance and business and urban space creation. Lujiazui recognizes the importance of place in the new global economy and seeks to capitalize upon it.

To measure the success of the Pudong New Area is difficult. The vagaries of global financial and business transactions create an environment of extreme instability. This means that success can only be phenomena measured in the present. However, in 1999, the Pudong New Area Administration approved 470 foreign-invested projects with contractual foreign capital of US$1.1 billion. In July 2000, it reported a 55.5 percent rise of foreign trade to reach US$12.4 billion. Imports rose 71.6 percent to US$7.74 billion and exports grew by 34.4 percent to US$4.6 billion. Japan was the largest trading partner with Pudong, followed by the United States and Germany during the period (see Shanghai Lujiazui (Shanghai Pudong New Area Administration) 2001a).

The Pudong New Area is an enormous project imagined as the new economic engine for Shanghai and Eastern China. It is divided into four zones, each with a different emphasis: free trade in Waigaoqiao, finance in Lujiazui, export processing in Jinqiao and high-tech in Zhangjiang. At present, the total construction area of commercial facilities has reached 600,000 square meters, which includes built and committed projects. This represents double the amount of commercial floor space that exists in Shanghai's historic commercial center of Nanjing Road on the other side of the Huangpu River.

The Shanghai Urban Planning and Design Research Institute is obviously proud of its handiwork. In fact, Shanghai is so proud of its city building efforts that it built a museum of planning to commemorate the city's change from industrial engine to financial capital. Since the beginning of China's industrialization, Shanghai has always been the largest and most productive of her industrial cities. It is a city with a remarkable history of foreign occupation and much of the older fabric of the city resonates with the glory of days past. It is also a city that shows marked evidence of the impact of globalization. This often shocks a foreign visitor, who struggles to overcome stereotypes of what a Communist city is presumed to be.

Walking down Nanjing Road one cannot help but see the commercialization of the streetscape proclaiming the lure of McDonald's, Kentucky Fried Chicken or Coca Cola. Crossing the Nanpu

6.3 On the Puxi side of the river sits the majestic Bund, international trade and finance center of the early part of the twentieth century.

6.4 The Nanjing Road pedestrian mall displays the vibrancy of "open door" Shanghai.

Bridge, as one enters the city from the new airport, one cannot fail to see the mushrooming landscape of office towers, hotels, department stores and high-rise residential towers. Shanghai is evidence of a new reality, a reality where centrally controlled planning embraces a Las Vegas free-for-all and Communists embrace capitalism more fervently than capitalists themselves. This landscape of commercial glam and exuberant energy is fast becoming the new China.

The open door policy

The pace of urban development in Shanghai accelerated tremendously after the central government announced the development of the Pudong New Area in 1990. Indeed, Shanghai has invested three times more in its urban infrastruc-

ture in the last five years than the total invested in the previous forty (Zhang Hui Min 1999). These infrastructure projects include the construction of the Nanpu, Yangpu and Xupu bridges across the Huanpu River, Metro Line One, the elevated Inner-Ring road and the North–South elevated road, as well as the Shanghai–Nanjing expressway. Projects already approved or in planning include four new bridges, four new tunnels and a new footbridge over the Huangpu River.

Since the announcement of the "open door policy" in 1978, foreign direct investment in Shanghai has increased substantially and its foreign trade grew rapidly as exports rose to promote economic growth and pay for the increased volume of imports. Among the results of the open door policy, therefore, was a rapid increase in trade volume, a gradual shift in trade composition due to greater Chinese flexibility in economic policy and a continuing tendency to conduct the overwhelming majority of its trade with partners from capitalist countries. This has not always been the case. Before Shanghai was granted its "preferential" status in 1990 there was little foreign investment in the city. The Shanghai authorities, aware of their own competitive slump, instigated policies to "streamline" the entry of foreign capital and their success in capturing it has been the greatest influence shaping the new financial center. The availability of this new capital has allowed the Shanghai authorities tremendous scope to renovate, upgrade and build anew in their quest to make Shanghai a global city.

Capitalizing on its industrial base, well-trained workforce and relatively good infrastructure, Shanghai was successful in attracting industrial joint ventures to the Pudong New Area. Tax holidays and reduced taxation periods focused on attracting Sino-foreign joint ventures, cooperative enterprises and wholly overseas-funded manufacturing businesses. Overseas-invested businesses enjoy a five-year property tax holiday on new properties built by them or purchased in the Pudong New Area, providing that they also occupy the property. To encourage business operations to invest in the Pudong in the early years of the project, overseas-invested businesses established before 1996 would receive exemption from import duties and taxes. Further, to promote technology transfer, industries inviting foreign investment and involving technology transfer are exempted from import duties and import-related VAT (Value Added Taxation) on equipment imported for their own use as part of the total investment. With these incentives in place, Pudong developed quickly. The preferential policies provide added incentive for investors to locate their developments in the Pudong. This is particularly true for international investors who are increasingly displaying a preference for Lujiazui and the Bund, which now provide the addresses for many of Shanghai's most influential companies.

The cacophony of form in the city

Shanghai is an enormously complex urban environment. Three players define the form of the city – the investors in property, both local and foreign, local governments, who control the use of land in Shanghai and lastly various state enterprises (see Wu Wei 1994). Competition between local governments to attract investors and the desire for state enterprises to profit from land holdings under their control created a situation of intense competition leading to a boom in construction reflected in the landscape of the city. The landscape of Shanghai resembles the urban equivalent of a wheatfield with towers springing from the earth in every direction. As part of the creation of Special Economic Zones, China established urban land use rights reforms in 1988. Although the socialist "market" economy has enabled the establishment of a real estate market, the complicated competition between local governments and state enterprises has created a very strange kind of land gradient within Shanghai. The nature of the "land-lease" system (in principle the same as exists in Hong Kong) in combination with the control of local government, exacerbated by state owned enterprises and the government's speculative capacities, has created a land market which does not necessarily follow investment logics familiar to North American or European situations.

There is no private ownership of land in Shanghai. Ownership is maintained by the state, however development rights are transferred to other parties. The Municipal Land Administration (MLA) represents the state in matters of land control in

6.5 View toward Puxi side of the Huangpu. Photograph taken from the observation floor of the Pearl Television Tower. Obvious is the complexity of the urban form of the city.

the city, but the local governments negotiate the sale of the land-lease and determine the conditions and length of the lease. Lease terms vary; however these are typically seventy years for residential and fifty for non-residential uses. As with many other things in China this emerging market has generated its own peculiarities. Indeed, there is often no relationship between "market" demand and the construction of new space in the city. This is not to say that the leasing habits of commercial operations are random. On the contrary, international firms in particular locate themselves as close to the Bund as possible or in the new Lujiazui district. However, the relationship between market demand and the location of new construction is not always clear. Part of this can be attributed to local government mayors who in their four-year terms want to leave a legacy (Zhao Wan Liang 2000). This means that each mayor wants to

construct as much as he can, as a sign of how successful his tenure has been. Although this has changed in the last few years it was certainly the case in the early years of land reform in Shanghai, which coincided with the availability of easy capital.

This decentralized land control means that it is very difficult to adhere to a city-wide plan. This, obviously, was not always the case. In the days of state socialism there was a tighter relationship between economic planning and physical planning. The role of the city as a primary industrial engine in the Chinese economy was rather simpler and therefore easier to manage with Shanghai having a rather defined and limited role to perform. The transition from this relatively narrow agenda to one, which is opportunistic, broader and more difficult to define, occurred in a remark-

6.6 Street scene in Puxi. Shanghai's streets are filled with urban vitality.

ably short period of time and the land organization and control systems of the government have lagged behind the pace of development in the city.

The Shanghai context

The city of Shanghai, located along the Huangpu River, is the largest city in China and one of the largest in the world with a population of some 14 million people and is composed of ten rural districts and ten city districts. Since the opening of China and the transition to a socialist market economy, Shanghai has mushroomed. There are currently 4000 buildings over 24 stories in the city with another 1700 either under construction or waiting for planning approval (Zhao Wan Liang 2000). The city is divided into East Shanghai (the Pudong) and West Shanghai (Puxi), with the Huangpu River acting as the divide. Puxi is the old part of the city, a great arc on the west side of the Huanpu River fronted by the famous Bund. The Pudong is the new Shanghai, with the Oriental Pearl Television Tower sitting in front of new highrise office towers. The heart of the old city is located a few blocks west of the Bund around Nanjing Road and Yunan East Road. The cultural center of the city is located around Renmin (People's) Square, the temple of the city god and Yu Yuan Garden. Situated in the Jiangsu province, the city sits on the alluvial plain of the Yangtze River and the name Shanghai, literally translates as "upriver to the sea."

Shanghai began as a fishing village some 700 years ago during the Tang and Song dynasties. Even 150 years ago it was subordinate in size and influence to other cities such as Suzhou and Hanzhou. Its location, at the confluence of the Yangtze and Huangpu Rivers, led to it becoming a commercial shipping port and as international trade increased during the Ming Dynasty (1368–1644), Shanghai became a major town in

southeast China. For hundreds of years, the emperors of China actively isolated the middle kingdom from the rest of the world. Although China had some international trade contacts, they decreed that China was totally self-sufficient and simply did not need nor want outside contact. The end of China's isolation came with the Opium Wars and the Treaty of Nanking in 1842. Its rise to world financial center in the early part of the twentieth century is directly related to its role as a treaty port.

After the First Opium War, China ceded Hong Kong to the British and five other cities were opened up to Western trade, namely Guangzhou, Xiamen, Fuzhou, Ningpo and Shanghai. By the turn of the century, there were around fifty such foreign enclaves, the most important being Shanghai. Under the Treaty of Nanking, Shanghai became an international business center. Other foreign concessions joined the British including the French (1847), the Americans (1863) and the Japanese (1895). In the "international settlement," foreigners were allowed to establish their own laws and use their own security forces. By 1853, Shanghai was the busiest Chinese port and had a population of some fifty thousand. By the turn of the century, its population had grown to one million people.

Until the 1930s, Shanghai enjoyed the coexistence and incorporation of different cultures with the different regional Chinese cultures. The introduction of foreign capital and the rise of national industry and commerce accelerated the development of the city and its economy, making Shanghai a major economic and cultural metropolis in the early part of the twentieth century. After the People's Revolution of 1949 Chinese control was reimposed over all of the city. As Rimmington notes, the new regime, while prepared to make use of the city's industrial and commercial know how as a model of development across the

6.7 The Huangpu River, historically the eastern edge of the city, is now the seam between Puxi and Pudong.

6.8 The Bund expresses the grandeur of Shanghai as an international trading port (copyright Doug Cogger 2002).

country, rejected all remnants of colonialism and consumerism. This, combined with a focus on rural development, meant that much of the pre-revolution development in the city came to an end (Rimmington 1998: 65).

Under Chinese control, Shanghai became an industrial powerhouse and the economic engine for all of China. In Mao's time (1950–76) Shanghai sent thirteen times more revenue to the central government than the amount it received for the city budget. In fact, as late as 1984, Shanghai still gave more than 85 percent of its budgetary revenue to Beijing (White and Cheng Li 1998). Figures from 1982 suggest that Shanghai produced eleven times the level of gross domestic product per capita than all of China combined (Meier 1982). During the early part of the 1980s, however, Shanghai's position as industrial power-

house began to slide. It desperately needed to upgrade its technological capacity in order to remain competitive and to achieve this the central government in Beijing designated Shanghai as a "special economic zone" in 1984. This allowed the city to be a "recipient for capital investment and technology transfer from developed nations" (Berry and McGreal 1999: 46).

Now open 2 TNCs

Opening doors in a global world

Shanghai faced three major challenges in the period of open reform in the 1990s. The revenue sent to Beijing had left Shanghai with little money to update urban infrastructure and because of this Shanghai was in desperate need of new road construction, better transportation, improved water supply, housing and an improvement in the environmental quality of the rivers. In addition,

6.9 View within Lujiazui looking toward the high-rise core.

Shanghai was desperate for new investment, especially in the Pudong area.

In response to this, the city started an aggressive remaking of itself. Capital was created through the "transfer of land use rights," which became the prime source of raising money in the late 1980s. Land rents replaced extractions from state firms as the primary means of municipal capital generation for urban construction. Revenue generated in this way was equivalent to 60 percent of Shanghai's total fixed investment for 1993 (White and Li 1998). In addition in the late 1980s, Shanghai borrowed US$1.4 billion dollars, with approval from Beijing, for urban construction projects such as the Shanghai metro and the new Yangpu Bridge (Zhang Hui Min 1999).

Since 1990, Shanghai has undergone unprecedented, rapid and large-scale development. The transition from planned economy to socialist market economy and from the free use of land to the paid use of land has required an appropriate adjustment of the city's layout and function. In line with this, the Shanghai Municipal People's Government obtained the approval of Beijing to open and develop the Pudong area in the early 1990s. In addition to development in the Pudong, the historic city center in Puxi was also a major focus of renewal efforts in what became a major redevelopment for the entire city. The municipal government established five main considerations for the redevelopment of Shanghai, based upon transportation infrastructure, a multi-centered city layout, the renovation of industrial areas, urban housing and a series of ecological projects. These plans include the construction of 400 miles of expressway around Shanghai and in addition, as part of a comprehensive transportation policy, six miles of new transit line are to be constructed every year (Zhang Hui Min 1999). With the opening of the Pudong area, the relationship between the city and the Huangpu River changed.

The Huangpu was no longer the eastern edge of the city and instead became the center and focus of a newly imagined city. It now exists as the join between Puxi and Pudong, the old and new Shanghai and major efforts are underway to redevelop the land holdings along both sides of its banks (see Marshall 2001).

Lujiazui – dreaming of a Chinese city for the twenty-first century

The dream of creating a new Shanghai on the opposite bank of the Huangpu River started with planners at the Shanghai Urban Planning and Design Institute in the early years of the "open door" policy. Prior to this, dating back to the early 1970s, this side of the Huangpu River was imagined as a riverside park. The idea of an extension of the city into Pudong dates to the beginning of the 1980s (Shanghai Lujiazui 2001c: 40). The 1986 Shanghai master plan shows strong indication of this possibility and it was about this time that detailed planning of the area of Lujiazui got underway. There were in fact two early schemes dating to 1986 and 1987 for the extension of the old city center across the river (Shanghai Lujiazui 2001c: 40).

In 1990, the Shanghai Lujiazui Finance and Trade Zone Development Company was established by the municipal government to develop Lujiazui. At the same time the mayor of Shanghai, Zhu Rongji (now Premier of China), started to articulate his vision for what Shanghai and Lujiazui should be. It seems apparent that Zhu realized that if Lujiazui was to be successful, and if Shanghai were to become an international city, that the project must engage itself into a global sphere of influence. From the start this project was not going to be thought about only in local terms.

During 1990 and 1991 four design schemes were produced for the area. Unhappy with the progress

6.10 The dream of Lujiazui – to present a global face to the world.

of the planning and the lack of exposure for Luji-azui, Zhu Rongji sought the assistance of the Institut d'Aménagement et d'Urbanisme de la Région Île de France in Paris to help develop the scheme and to acquire international exposure. Although the Institut d'Aménagement et d'Urbanisme de la Région Île de France had been advising the central government since the middle of the 1980s, the move on the part of Zhu Rongji was radical for its time. For almost forty years China was closed to the rest of the world and actively resisted the influence of foreigners. Zhu Rongji however openly sought the advice of foreigners and in 1991, a delegation of Shanghai officials, including Mayor Zhu, visited a number of international cities. In Paris the delegation studied the French experience of the *Grand Projects* and developed an instant attraction to the *La Défense* project. The scale and exuberance of *La Défense* impressed the Shanghai delegation. Zhu and his delegation realized that if Lujiazui was to become a global center of finance it would have to be marketed as such. This would require that an element of spectacle had to develop around the project. To guarantee that there would be international attention generated around the project an agreement was made to utilize French resources to organize an international architectural competition for Lujiazui (for a detailed account of the politics of development in Lujiazui see Olds 2001).

Four international firms were asked to participate in the project along with one Chinese team. The international teams were Richard Rogers from the UK, Massimiliano Fuksas from Italy, Toyo Ito from Japan and Dominique Perrault from France. The Chinese team was a collaborative effort between the Shanghai Urban Planning and Design Institute and faculty from Tongji University. The brief given to the design teams was simply phenomenal. It called for a total of almost 4 million square meters of development, divided as follows;

Office	2,650,000
Apartments	300,000
Hotels	500,000
Conference Center	250,000
Retail	120,000
Cultural Center	10,000
Service Facilities	3000
Total	3,833,000

Source: Shanghai Lujiazui Ltd (2001a)

The competition was a remarkable and rare opportunity for designers to engage in a project whose scale demanded a complete idea for what a city should be. In this sense the design proposals provide a tremendous insight into design thinking and its relationship to the city and the development of urbanity. Of particular interest is how these schemes dealt with the dual agendas of satisfying of both the urbanistic and global ambitions.

The scheme that is perhaps best known is the Richard Rogers scheme. In part this may be true because of the clarity and seductive formalism of the project. Rogers' scheme, far more than any of the others, can be appreciated as a singular object, although the scheme is certainly not one. Because of this, the project can be easily comprehended. Rogers proposed a large central open space around which the project was articulated into six satellite sub-centers, each with a population of 80,000 (total population 480,000 people). The plan is circular in shape and envisioned as an integrated framework of public space and transportation systems. The project was tied to a larger transportation infrastructure plan, which aimed to reduce the dependence on vehicular traffic within and to and from the project. The transportation systems within the proposal included rail, tram, bus, cycle and pedestrian routes. Each district focused around a transportation interchange and each was positioned within a ten-minute walk from the central green space of the project. The

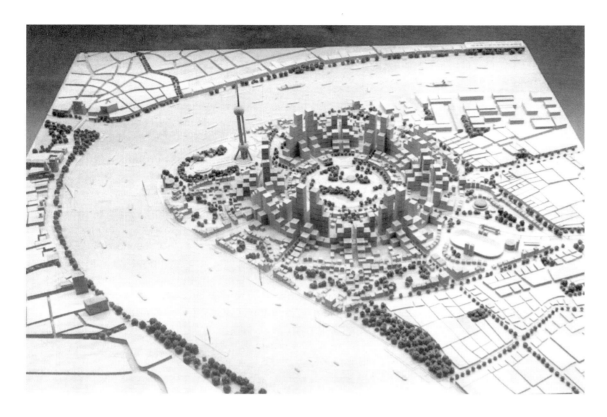

6.11 Richard Rogers' proposal for Lujiazui (copyright Shanghai Lujiazui Ltd.).

massing of the project allows views to the water-front from deep within the site, creating strong links to a re-imagined Huangpu River and producing a ring of high-rise buildings around the central void, which steps back to allow light into the central space. Housing was arrayed on the outside of the ring, in close proximity to the surrounding river-park, hospitals, schools and community facilities with commercial programs centered on the transportation interchanges. The program for the project was more varied than what the brief called for with the aim of generating an intense and dense urban environment of inter-action between people.

In the articulation of the program and the arrange-ment of the elements within the scheme it appears clear that the project is premised on the idea that the physical container of the city should aim to support the social sphere of life around which communities might cluster. In addition, it seems clear that the project takes a position of not deter-mining what the nature of that community inter-action might be but that interaction in and of itself is a good thing and an essential aspect to any urban proposition.

Dominique Perrault's proposal seems to include this same sensibility but was more explicit with regard to the global component of the program. Perrault attempted to create a dual project, one which gave the Shanghai authorities what they wanted in terms of an expression of global corpor-ate representation and yet simultaneously attemp-ted to fabricate a community zone through a peculiar and deliberately random interior arrange-ment. Perrault's global component involved a wall of skyscrapers in a 90-degree quadrant along the

6.12 Dominique Perrault's proposal for Lujiazui (copyright Shanghai Lujiazui Ltd.).

Huangpu, facing the Bund. This is the "foundational act" of the new city. This wall of towers set up two different conditions – on the riverside an urban park and on the other a smaller grain of mixed-use development. His idea was to create massive office towers, 300 meters tall, and by concentrating the required program here, release the rest of the site for a lower scale urban environment centered on a central park space. This park, surrounded by residential districts, would then become the center of the community. The arrangement of this smaller grain fabric is reminiscent of the apparent randomness that can be found in the older residential districts in Puxi and the scheme incorporates some of the existing traces (roads, buildings and property lines) that were to be found on the site.

Perrault's scheme is based on the idea that the focus for all urban development should be the building of neighborhoods. In the plan drawings of the scheme it is evident that Perrault imagined his proposal within a much larger structure of neighborhoods. This can be seen, for example, on the edges of the plans, which clearly show the project surrounded by smaller scale development parcels extending beyond the edges of the paper. The global city is then arrayed on the edge, defining the view from the older city on the other side of the river. In this way Perrault's project is the reciprocal of the North American central city, where high-rise office towers dominate the center, and the neighborhoods diffuse away from the core.

6.13 Massimiliano Fuksas' proposal for Lujiazui (copyright Shanghai Lujiazui Ltd.).

Massimiliano Fuksas' scheme is almost the inverse of Perrault's. Fuksas proposed a dense core surrounded by a ring of less dense development. The scheme attempted to be contextual to a tradition of Chinese city making and proposed an elliptically inscribed grid, bisected by a linear parkway, inspired by ancient Chinese city plans. The block structures and the road network define a grid of blocks inscribed within an elliptical ring road. The form of the scheme, however, is typical of the North American model. At the center of the scheme sits a cluster of high-rise development, which fractures and reduces in scale as one moves away from the center.

Toyo Ito's proposal involved a functional circulation system that was organized on two levels. The top level included pedestrian circulation while the lower level included, a subway and vehicular traffic circulation. The scheme drew on Ito's fascination with digital realms and attempted to create a garden of microchips where the network of new technologies and the basic flow of nature would begin to overlap and work together (see Hanru and Obrist 1997). Developing this notion Ito presented a "bar-code" of five bands of mixed development between which bands of parks would serve as the social containers of this new urban landscape. The elements that constitute Ito's composition, if taken singularly, appear banal. Rather, the interest is made in the relationships between these pieces and in the physical and programmatic tensions elucidated through their adjacencies. Ito's scheme, more than the other international competitors, struggled with the imageability of the new financial center in that its intellectual construction was less about form and more about program. In the Ito scheme form was

6.14 Toyo Ito's proposal for Lujiazui (copyright Shanghai Lujiazui Ltd.).

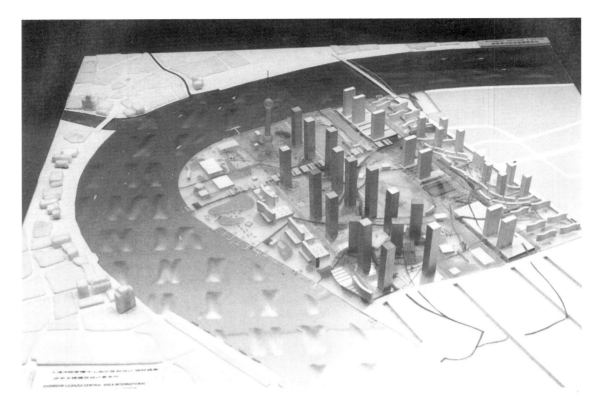

6.14 Toyo Ito's proposal for Lujiazui (copyright Shanghai Lujiazui Ltd.).

the result of a collage of these various layers. When one looks at the model, however, and one imagines that the surrounding areas of the project have been constructed, the image presented by the project becomes more diffuse. The diffuse nature of the scheme's image would be at odds with the idea that Lujiazui would present a strong and coherent image that could be marketed in the global market place.

Two interesting aspects are present in all of the international schemes, which reflect a contemporary western view of the city and are in marked contrast to the realized project. The first is the idea that cities are better if they are mixed and programmatically complicated. Reminiscent of a new traditionalism these projects seek to deny the singularity of a corporate environment, which is both in marked contrast to the stated ambition of the

brief, and also the eventual constructed outcome. Also in all of the schemes there is an absence of land use zoning, which would demarcate in plan a series of singular and separate use areas. Instead of this, all of the international competition entries include notions of vertical and horizontal mixing embedded into the structure of the schemes. In addition, there is a belief expressed in the schemes in the idea that the public realm as a space of coming together is a focus for community interaction. It is in the public realm that the inhabitants of these schemes would manifest an urban culture, in the great tradition of London, New York, Paris or even old Shanghai. The executed project in comparison lacks this sense of an urban public realm because of the dominance of commercial space and the articulation of the public open space in relation to it. The promise of Lujiazui, as expressed in the various competition entries, has not been developed in the constructed project. The result is unfortunately a collection of high-rise towers and an amorphous open space lacking any capacity to support urban culture. Further, this is exacerbated by the fact that to access the Lujiazui Central Park (and this was a shock for the author) one has to pay!

A major aspect of all of the international schemes is the reduction of the motor vehicle as plan generator. Block structures are articulated in response to ideas about the public realm and community making, which are centered on the priority of pedestrian circulation. The case of the Richard Rogers scheme in particular emphasizes both an ecological motivation as well as a community making aspiration to reduce the reliance of vehicular transportation. In this scheme a reduction in motor vehicle use both preserves energy and

forces individuals to engage in an environment of communicative action through face-to-face interaction, unattainable if they were to sequester themselves into a motor vehicle.

The scheme that was ultimately "judged" the winner was from the Chinese team. This team elaborated on the traffic and zoning analysis already executed by the municipal government and their entry did not differ significantly from previous plans already developed by the Shanghai Urban Planning and Design Institute. One must remember that this competition provided the first opportunity for Chinese officials to engage with foreign designers and there was an inevitable distrust of the foreigners' ability to adequately understand the specific requirements of the Chinese context. Further, being one of the first engagements with foreigners it may have proved difficult

6.15 Shanghai Urban Planning and Design Institute proposal for Lujiazui (copyright Shanghai Lujiazui Ltd.).

to completely accept the Western aspects of the international schemes. The Chinese team ultimately won because of their superior understanding of the local environment. Their scheme was deemed to be politically more acceptable and it was technically easier to implement quickly.

The original Chinese scheme involved a strong development axis, which split the site into two halves. These halves were then subdivided and a loose clustering of high-rise and super high-rise buildings were arrayed. The apparent informal positioning of the massing of the project speaks to a lack of directedness in the minds of the projects creators. Absent also from the original scheme was an open space around which the scheme could focus. The only open space existed along the edge to the Huangpu River but its lack of articulation suggests that it was only thought of as a residual space. The original Chinese scheme paid far more attention to some of the contextual and residual elements on and around the site than any of the foreign schemes, so the Chinese scheme could be immediately implemented. However, it fundamentally was a scheme that did nothing more than accommodate floor area. The lack of urbanistic intention in the scheme was more than oversight. It suggests, rather a deliberate denial of urbanity. The agenda of the global project and the agenda for a rich urbanity seem incompatible in this scheme.

In May of 1992 the original invitations were issued and in November, the five schemes were presented to the "Committee of Experts." While none of the foreign schemes were chosen as a "winning" scheme for the competition, the Shanghai Urban Planning and Design Institute did adopt some loosely derived ideas from the four international entries and incorporated these derivations into their own vision. In the end, the location of existing infrastructure and the existence of several already leased sites informed a very prag-

matic plan. These were considerations that none of the international entries addressed, nor could they be expected to fully appreciate the context.

In January of 1993 the Shanghai Pudong New Area Administration was established. The design for the project underwent further elaboration from February to March of that same year. The working group from the Shanghai Urban Planning and Design Institute developed three comparative design schemes. The first proposal loosely reflects some of the components of the Richard Rogers scheme combined with the general arrangement of the Shanghai scheme. This new proposal tried to make the road networks and building orientations fit with the existing context. The second new proposal maintained the development spine of the Shanghai scheme and made adjustments to the transportation provisions of the context reflecting new developments that were occurring on and around the site. The third scheme attempted to "absorb" the best of the international schemes and included "the very strong urban images with the super high-rise towers, the arc-shaped high rise belt, green spaces oriented in an axial arrangement, the central open space and the riverside park" (Shanghai Lujiazui 2001c: 42). It was this scheme, which was ultimately chosen for design development.

From March to May of 1993 the third scheme was further developed to include several ideas derived from the international entries. The first was to incorporate a park into the project and to define this space with a ring of tall office towers. This format was derived from the schemes of Rogers and Perrault. The second was the development of a distinctive skyline to create an image that could be appreciated from the Bund. This was certainly an integral aspect of Zhu Rongji's formula for Lujiazui. The third was a greater acknowledgment of an orientation, which sets up an axis that, in plan at least, extends from the Bund through to the Zhuyuan Commercial and Trade Zone and ends in the Pudong Central Park. The fourth was the development of a wall of high-rise office towers, which would sit in an arc and define the edge of the entire Lujiazui area. This wall of high-rise in effect would act as the gateway to the Pudong New Area in much the same way as the Bund heralds Puxi. Such modifications were only minor amendments to the original Shanghai Urban Planning and Design Institute plan and ultimately were adopted in such a casual manner that their ori-

ginal motivation and relevance were lost. From late May to early August the master plan was finalized.

The final form of the project arranges the riverfront green space, the central park and a green belt as the central spine of the project from which everything else is then arranged. The form of the central park was changed from Rogers circle to reflect a more "organic" shape (Shanghai Lujiazui 2001c: 45). It was also increased in size to 16 hectares. A cluster of central buildings surrounds the park. The

6.16 View from the Pearl Television Tower looking into the Central Park of Lujiazui.

6.17 View from the corner of Central Park, Lujiazui.

high-rise zone and the southern and eastern development zones then encircle this central cluster. The arc-shaped high-rise zone was moved to the historic Lannidu and Beihutang Roads, to reflect the form of the river bay and to form the mirror of the Bund. The Oriental Pearl Television Tower became a figural element in the composition of this arc. The arc is composed of eighteen high-rise buildings totaling 1.4 million square meters of commercial space (approximately 15 million square feet). In order to form the edge with a sense of enclosure and rhythm, the heights of the high-rise buildings are between 160 and 200 meters (520 to 660 feet). The site of the eighty-eight-story Jinmao Tower was moved eastward and two other super high-rise projects were introduced to create a cluster of three towers in the center of the project. These towers will be between 360 and 400 meters tall (1180 and 1300 feet).

There are altogether twenty-five buildings in the core areas, which include the central park zone, the high-rise building zone and symbolic buildings in the eastern and southeastern entrances to the project. The total floor area of these buildings is 2.5 million square meters, which accounts for approximately 60 percent of the total floor area of the project (approximately 27 million square feet or about 5.6 World Trade Centers), with an average floor area ratio of 5.2 (Shanghai Lujiazui 2001c: 42). The final scheme for Lujiazui, approved by the municipal government in 1994, permitted sixty-nine buildings with a total of 4.2 million square meters of space.

The utopianism present in Tokyo Rainbow Town, MM21 or Muang Thong Thani is not present in the articulation of the plan in Lujiazui. Instead its form tells us very little about how the Chinese planners imagine an ideal city to be, except that it be predominantly commercial and extremely large. The size of the project seems to outweigh and overcome any other consideration. The project is not imbued with notions of community. Indeed the open areas of the project are largely unarticulated spaces that exist between curious high-rise structures.

This lack of urbanistic position is evident at two scales. It is evident at the scale of the entire project in the sense that the form of Lujiazui lacks an identifiable structure. It is also evident at the scale of the street. The issue here is a contradiction between the idea of the block as a definer of space and the idea of towers situated in space. In Lujiazui towers sit in proximity to each other without creating relationships between each other. The result is a kind of vacuous pedestrian realm with little attention paid to the pedestrian scale of the project. This is particularly evident in the pedestrian crossings over expansive roadways. While Lujiazui certainly is not bustling with automobile activity there will come a time when these crossings will produce a major conflict between cars and people. This, combined with the Shanghaiese failure to give way to pedestrians, will ultimately lead to tragic results. The issue seems to reduce to the difference between roads and streets. A road is a transportation infrastructure used to provide vehicular access to development projects. Streets, on the other hand, offer a far richer and complicated zone. They are the public realm, where communities come together in the space of the city. They are spaces of interaction for people. Cities around the world have struggled with how to incorporate towers and streets, with limited success. If there were one element that the Shanghai authorities should have taken from the international schemes, it should have been a commitment to the creation of a public realm in Lujiazui. This unfortunately did not occur.

Lujiazui – building a Chinese city for the twenty-first century

The Pudong New Area project is ten years old. In the first five years of construction, priority was given to building road links, telecommunications facilities and the energy systems. The Yangpu and Nanpu bridges were built into the longest and third longest cable-stayed bridges in the world. In the second five years, 100 billion yuan (US$12 billion) was spent on building an airport, a telecommunications hub and a deep-water port. The Pudong International Airport, Waigaoqiao Port Bonded Zone, Pudong Information Hub, the No. 2 subway line, External Ring Road, East China Sea Natural Gas Transportation System, Sewerage Treatment Plant and the International Conference Center were all completed during this period. As the largest infrastructure project in Shanghai, the Pudong International Airport was built at a cost of 13.3 billion yuan (US$1.6 billion). The airport has the capacity to handle 20 million passengers and

750,000 tons of cargo a year. However, of all the elements constructed in Lujiazui, three stand out as encapsulating the global image factor – the Oriental Pearl Broadcasting and Television Tower, the Shanghai World Finance Tower and the Jin Mao (Golden Trade) Tower.

The Oriental Pearl Broadcasting and Television Tower is situated at the tip of Lujiazui. The height of the tower is 468 meters, which makes it the tallest structure in Asia and the third tallest in the world. The tower is supported on three columns each with a diameter of 9 meters. The eleven steel-structured round balls (including the space cabin, upper ball, lower ball, five ball-like sky hotels in the middle and three decorative small balls at the bottom) are thought of as eleven shining pearls embedded on

6.18 View from the Huangpu River at the high-rise core of office complexes.

6.19 View from Jin Mao Tower toward Oriental Pearl Tower. The Bund and Suzhou Creek can be seen on the other side of the Huangpu River.

6.20 View from Jin Mao Tower looking down upon Central Park, Lujiazui.

the body of the tower. The tower sits in a park and the project aims to evoke the idea of a series of pearls dropping down on to a Jade plate, two precious materials in Chinese culture. The project includes five sightseeing floors, one revolving restaurant for four hundred people, 20,000 square meters of retail space, twenty-five deluxe guestrooms (inside one of the balls), and six high-speed lifts inside the tube of the tower. The Oriental Pearl Tower has become the new symbol of Shanghai and appears in countless postcards and promotions for the city.

The Shanghai World Finance Tower (Shi Mao) is, at time of writing, unbuilt. The project, designed by Kohn Pederson Fox, is proposed to be 460 meters tall, which would make it the world's tallest building. The tower resembles an enormous blade, its stark simplicity in contrast to the visual confusion of the rest of the city. At the top of the blade is inscribed a 50-meter diameter circular opening. The project includes retail in the lower floors, offices in the middle and is topped by a hotel. The project will stand a staggering ninety-five floors above ground and include 240,000 square meters of floor space. The project's developers, Mori Corporation in Japan, are recovering from their own domestic and international financial problems wrought by the Asian Economic Crisis and although the project is still alive its construction date is yet to be determined.

Jin Mao, designed by Skidmore Owings and Merrill, is located immediately adjacent to the Shi Mao project. The design of this project deliberately evokes the ancient pagoda forms of Chinese traditional construction. Jin Mao is the tallest building in China, standing at 420 meters. The project includes 278,000 square meters of office, hotel and retail. The developer of Jin Mao was the China Shanghai Foreign Trade Center, which is a state-owned company. The building incorporates intelligent systems at many levels. Of particular interest is the use of advanced communication systems to lure international tenants to the project.

The current situation

In 1997, new supply of commercial space in Shanghai amounted to 2 million square meters, a growth of 35 percent over the previous year. In 1999, office vacancy rates averaged more than 40 percent in Puxi (total stock 2.65 million square meters) and 70 percent in Pudong (1.22 million square meters). Simply, there is a massive oversupply of office space in Shanghai. What is interesting, however, is that in the case of the state owned enterprises, at least, this oversupply is not necessarily a problem. In the case of Lujiazui, the construction of the artifact as a symbol of progress outweighs the need for high occupancy rates. In simple terms, for the Shanghai authorities it was more important to have the project built than to have it occupied. If the project were truly "market" driven, there would be very little to point to. While this sounds simplistic it responds to the need for a symbol of the city's aspirations to be a global capital. Image, in Lujiazui's case at least, is everything.

Despite a regional slowdown induced by the Asia Economic Crisis the Pudong New Area has continued to accelerate its functional development while it continued to build up its infrastructure. In 1997, the new area achieved a total value-added 60.822 billion yuan, an increase of 18.3 percent over the same period of the previous year. Its total industrial output reached 134.901 billion yuan, a growth of 18.4 percent. Fixed asset investment in the new area totaled 47.829 billion yuan, a rise of 28.2 percent. Also in 1997, the new area's export totaled US$3.755 billion, an increase of 16.9 percent. A total of 615 directly foreign-funded projects were initiated in the Pudong with a total contracted overseas investment of US$1.8 billion (Shanghai Lujiazui 2001a). Such indicators show

6.21 View within Central Park, Lujiazui. Gardeners take a break from tending this empty landscape.

the inertia of the Chinese economy to world financial crisis.

In Lujiazui a total of 158 buildings have been completed to date. The Shanghai Stock Exchange, the Shanghai Property Rights Exchange, the China Talents Market (Shanghai), the Shanghai Real Estate Trade Center and the Shanghai Grain and Edible Oil Exchange have already moved into the new buildings.

Preferential policies given to overseas investors in Pudong New Area remain unchanged and the government has indicated there will be more incentives for investment in priority industries of Pudong, such as lower land prices for target industries. Shanghai's planners have added two more tunnels to the city's blueprint for dealing with cross-river traffic congestion. With the additions, a total of three new tunnels and another bridge over the Huangpu River should be ready by 2005. A

35 km-long super-speed magnetic levitation (maglev) rail will be constructed to link Pudong International Airport and the Longyang Metro Station. Express trains running at speeds of over 505 km per hour will facilitate the seven-minute journey. Officials estimate that the bulk of the airport's 200,000 annual commuters will take advantage of the rail line.

Lujiazui represents the new China. Within it lie the ambitions of an entire nation. It also represents a tremendous experiment in urbanization on a scale never before witnessed. Here we see evidence both of an instant urbanity, seemingly growing overnight, and of a new kind of urban condition the likes of which we are only just coming to terms with. The absence of urbanistic intention in the project is both curious and troubling, an issue for concern for all those that believe that cities are the containers of life and an issue that will be taken up again in the concluding chapter.

7.1 View of the model of the West Zone of Zhongguancun
(copyright Tsinghua Urban Planning and Design Institute).

7 The Silicon Valley of China

Zhongguancun Science and Technology Park, Beijing

This chapter was written with the special assistance by Zhong Ge of Tsinghua University.

The 21st century, characterized by knowledge-based economy, is now approaching us. The competition of 21st century will be a competition in science and technology and in recruiting talented people and a competition in seizing the commanding elevation in the knowledge-based economy.

Liu Qi, Mayor of Beijing

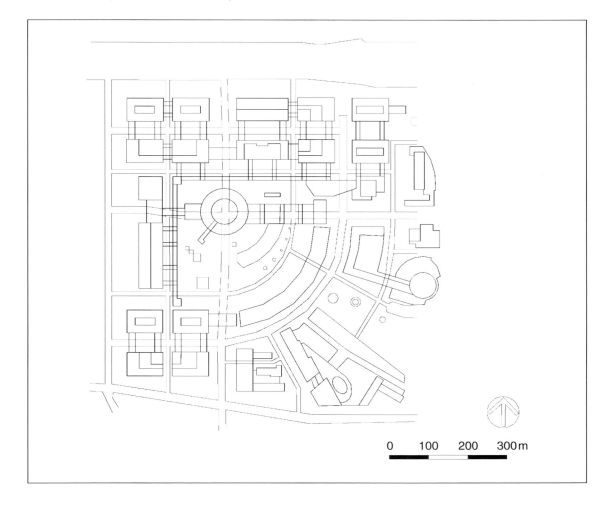

Map of West Zone of Zhongguancun, Beijing.

China will look to Zhongguancun in the 21st century as it did to the South China open city of Shenzen in the 1980s and Shanghai's new Pudong area in the 1990s.

People' Daily Newspaper

Positioning the image of the city in a scientific manner and building a grand landmark symbolizing the strategy to make China a great power in the 21st century.

Promotional webpage for Zhongguancun

In the competitive global economy many countries are developing science and technology parks in attempts to establish advantage. Malaysia has made an ambitious commitment through its own Multimedia Super Corridor (Chapter 10), Hong Kong aims to be a high-tech hub with its Cyberport Information Technology Park and Silicon Harbour and Singapore too has its own Singapore One development. In China there are several new science and technology parks including the Guanzhong New and High Technology Industrial Development Zone in Shaanxi Province, the Guangzhou Science Town and the Hangzhou High-Tech Software Park. The Zhongguancun Science and Technology Park is the first and biggest national science park in China, established in 1988. Located in northwest Beijing, it covers approximately 75 square kilometers. Inside Zhongguancun more than 6000 hi-tech enterprises in the fields of information technology, biology, medicine and others have their offices and large multinational information technology (IT) corporations such as IBM, Motorola, Microsoft, Lucent, Hewlett-Packard, and Epson have their research and development institutes there. Prominent universities and colleges, such as Tsinghua University and Beijing University are also located within the area of Zhongguancun. More and more companies are moving into the park, attracted by its hi-tech business development environment and preferential tax treatment.

Until recently Beijing was not a city associated with the explosive urban growth in China. Indeed, unlike Shenzen, Guanzhou, or Shanghai, Beijing's modern development has been slower. This may at first seem curious since Beijing is the political capital of the country. Despite the fact that all of China is administered from Beijing, the city itself was not part of the initial foray into socialist market development. This was deliberate however as this great experiment was first tested in other places. Recently this policy has changed and Beijing is now rapidly and aggressively pursuing a path of development and expansion. An integral aspect of Beijing's repositioning efforts is its embrace of science and technology and an essential part of the city's efforts is the Zhongguancun Science and Technology Park.

Beijing is known for the fact that at its center lies the Forbidden City, the great imperial palace of the Ming dynasty. This remarkable artifact encapsulates the five Confucian virtues of humanity, sense of duty, wisdom, reliability and ceremonial propriety. While the Forbidden City will forever be embedded in the center of Beijing, the city is currently in a remarkable moment of rebuilding itself. The center of this remarkable city represents its history; however its edges are where its new identity will be made. It is here that Beijing seeks to claim a territory in the global economy, as a premier science and technology node. There are more than seventy universities and colleges in the city and a total of almost sixty percent of the Chinese Science Academy and 650,000 scientists and engineers are located there (Yang and Li 2000: 152).

Zhongguancun Science and Technology Park (ZGC) is a comprehensive global project, which aims to transform the economy of Beijing from one based on industry to advanced technologies. For forty years the city has been largely isolated from the rest of the world. However in the wave of the new economy, Beijing is targeting her future toward a more open and international city aiming to be a pre-eminent international political, cultural, and tourist center as well as an important contributor to the national economy. Further, as capital of China, it sees an increasing role for itself as a city of influence in the Asia Pacific region.

The West Zone of Zhongguancun is the first phase of the project with more than one million square meters of above ground floor area. As the initial phase, the West Zone is also the administrative and research and development center, the high technology center and the cultural and commercial service center for the entire Zhongguancun Science and Technology Park. The master plan of the West Zone, carried out by the Tsinghua Urban Planning and Design Institute, demonstrates the application of current urban design concepts in the Chinese context and provides us with an insight into the specifics of contemporary Chinese thinking on urban form. Influenced by urban design theories from abroad, the design integrates modern concepts with notions of traditional Chinese urban philosophy. The West Zone may well prove to be a pivotal project in the development of urban thinking in China.

Beijing – capital of open door China

Twenty years of economic reform, especially the rapid economic growth of the last decade, have had a significant impact on the socio-economic landscape of Chinese society. It has also led to inevitable and profound political and ideological transformations. In Beijing, this has led to the construction of new parts of the city, including areas of new housing and a series of large-scale urban projects. Principal among these are three large-scale undertakings that all attempt to reposition the city as a node in the global sphere. These projects are the new Central Business District (CBD) to the east of the old city at Chaoyangmen, the new Olympic center in the north of the city and Zhongguancun Science and Technology Park in the northwest.

Beijing is the political and cultural center of China and has been so for more than eight hundred years. Situated at the northern end of the North China Plain, the city was established at the intersection of trade routes connecting northeast China, Mongolia, and central China about two thousand years ago. It was the site of several dynastic capitals before the establishment of the Yuan Dynasty by Kubilai Khan in 1271. As such the city encapsulates a historical record of Chinese urban philosophy dating from the thirteenth century and one that continues to influence contemporary city making in Beijing.

Originally called Dadu, it was a completely designed city, which adhered strictly to a traditional Chinese philosophy of capital city construction. The city had three walls to differentiate the outer city, the imperial city and the palatial city, which are all rectangular in shape. Traditional elements and topological principles still influence contemporary city making in Beijing. Fundamentally, the "courtyard" continues to be the prototype for all living environments. This space can be found in almost all the Chinese traditional building types, including houses, temples, public institutions, monuments, and even the emperor's palace. The "wall" also plays an instrumental role in Chinese cities. The city itself can be thought of as a large "courtyard house" surrounded by the city wall. The street has always held an important function in Chinese urban situations as the principal urban space of the city and the chessboard street pattern, typical of traditional Chinese urban environments, provided a myriad of public spaces to support urban life. Lastly, Chinese cities (especially capital cities) are the result of special philosophies based on ideas of the cosmos (for a full explanation of Chinese urban philosophy refer to Sit (1995)).

Immediately after the People's Revolution in 1949 Beijing began a major restructuring of itself. In the 1956 General Plan of Beijing, the nature of the city was defined as:

> our country's political center, cultural center and science and art center. At the same time it should, and must be a major industrial city.
>
> (Sit 1995: 86)

Guided by the slogan "Learn everything from the Soviet Union," the key objective of Beijing's urban construction during this period was rapid industrialization with priority given to the development of heavy industry. Physically this meant a brutal insertion of industrial facilities without heed to issues of appropriate use, scale, adjacency or environmental control. It was not uncommon, for example, to find facilities for heavy industry inserted into small-scale residential neighborhoods. As a result, the urban fabric of the city became dominated by industry and inevitably the city suffered a host of environmental consequences in terms of noise, congestion, as well as air, soil and water pollution.

The focus on the industrial sector, along with problems in the control of growth, led to a series of urban problems in the 1970s. The physical growth of the city was not well structured. Its population growth was difficult to control; developable land was in short supply and a general scarcity of water and electricity became endemic (Sit 1995: 170). These problems not only made the city a less than desirable place to live; they also reduced the productive capacity of the industrial sector. Through the 1970s, and well into the 1980s, Beijing planners went through a process of rethinking the industrial focus of physical and economic planning. This can be seen as early as the Comprehensive General Plan of 1982, where the idea that Beijing should be "the political and cultural center of the nation" was once again promoted.

Unlike previous plans, the 1982 plan explicitly aimed to place Beijing at the center of China's dealings with foreign countries with a reduced emphasis on it being an industrial city. This led to a new economic strategy where Beijing should develop advanced technology-intensive industries, which would take advantage of the intellectual resources of the city, provide highly paid employment and significantly diminish the environmental degradation of heavy industry. In addition, the 1982 General Plan promoted a substantial development in commercial and service industries to act as supports to this new science and technology focus. At the same time, energy intensive and polluting industries were targeted for significant reform.

While industry remained the mainstay of the economy this new agenda for planning transformed industrial operations structurally to what became known as the "five small and two high" model (small consumption in energy, water, material, land and transport, and high in added-value and technology). With this appreciation of different types of high-tech industrial operations, the new pillars of the industrial sector in Beijing were to be operations that were described as clean – car manufacturing and electronics, aerospace and superconductor industries. This position has guided subsequent planning in the city. Following this the first high-tech companies began to locate into the Zhongguancun area and in 1988 the Haidan Experimental Zone was established which was the precursor to the ZGC.

The General Plan of 1992, which is the most recent and current plan, promotes the tertiary sector as the mainstay of the urban economy. This strategy includes a comprehensive development of the tourism, finance, insurance, and real estate sectors. Under this strategy recent development in Beijing has been centered on a number of principal areas of development – the Zhongguancun Science and Technology Park development, the new Central Business District (CBD) and the facilities for the 2008 Olympic Games (including sports and entertainment facilities, a World Trade Center complex, a conventional center, office buildings, hotels and apartments in an area of approximately 1600 hectares).

The emergence of Zhongguancun Science and Technology Park

Today, the aim of planners in Beijing is to make the city the best in the world, "in social order and morality, in culture, technology and education, in cleanliness and hygiene, and lastly in economic prosperity, convenience and stability" (Tsinghua 2000). This rather ambitious aim became the inspiration for all planning in Beijing in the 1990s and created a number of peculiar results where planners became excessively exuberant in the pursuit of this vision. For example, it led to the provision of overly wide roads and over-generous green and open space. Everything, it seems, had to be bigger and better than anywhere else to ensure Beijing's position as the most important city in China. This strategy provides the government with physical elements that display the importance of the city. This is important because it displays physical evidence of the government's urban ambitions. This is also a major component for projects such as Zhongguancun Science and Technology Park that aim to claim an important role in both the national and international spotlight.

An indication of just how important this is in the ZGC is the fact that the Beijing Municipal Government and the national government's Department of Science and Technology worked together to develop a proposal for the ZGC, highlighting the project's importance to both local and national

government agendas. The application to establish ZGC passed the national government on June 5, 1999. This application proposed that the ZGC would be a national science and technology and creative model based within an environment of beauty, with modern facilities, convenient traffic and advanced information systems. In addition the ZGC should be a base for scientific research closely allied to market conditions and a center for high-technology human resource education. Besides being a world-class science park, the ZGC will be a high-technology enterprise incubation facility. In many respects the creation of the ZGC is not unlike the establishment of the Shenzhen Economic Special Zone or the Pudong New District in Shanghai. Certainly the ZGC will be as important to China's emerging engagement with the world. From this perspective, the foundation of ZGC is not only an economic development zone but also a vehicle for changing the economic position of Beijing.

The ZGC project includes a total area of 374 square kilometers (145 square miles). This area includes the Central Science and Technology Creation Zone (75 square kilometers) toward the south of the ZGC and the High-tech Industry Development Zone (280 square kilometers) toward the north. The Central Science and Technology Creation Zone includes a core region and two-development axis, which run along urban arterial streets. The core region, covering some ten square kilometers, comprises the Chinese Science Academy, Tsinghua University, Beijing University and the West Zone of Zhongguancun. This core region is an urban infill development located amongst dense urban fabric. Bai Yi Road is the main spine of the core region running north to south, along the side of the science business center in the West Zone of Zhongguancun. The High-tech Industry Development Zone comprises several clusters focusing on different industry developments, including an information industry

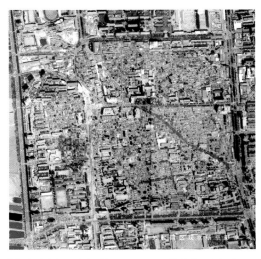

7.2 Aerial view of the Zhongguancun site in its original condition (copyright Tsinghua Urban Planning and Design Institute).

cluster, a biological engineering research and development cluster, a new material development cluster and a group of residential districts.

The ZGC also includes four small science parks situated around the fringe of Beijing. They are Fengtai Park located in the south of the city, Changping Park located in the north, Electric City Science Park in the northeast and the Yizhuang Science Park located in the Yizhuang Economic Development Zone in the southeast of Beijing. The five sub-parks, as they are known, have their own administrations, which fall under the auspices of the Zhongguancun Administration Committee (ZAC). These separate committees are responsible for making development plans, registration and administration of high-tech enterprises, administration of the special construction fund and the construction of modern service systems.

The Beijing Science and Technology Park Construction Company (BSCC) is the organization responsible for the construction of the ZGC. It is a large stock company whose stocks are controlled by the municipal government. The BSCC focuses all of its activities on land development, infrastructure construction and real estate development within the ZGC. The ZGC is a "first-class" land development project. In China such a designation refers to the consolidation of rural land or older urban districts into single land parcels to facilitate the removal and relocation of original residents, land clearing, large project planning, infrastructure construction, environmental and accessory facility improvement, project auction, and comprehensive services for single building development. The BSCC is currently developing the West Zone of ZGC, the Zhongguancun Software Park, the Bio-Science Park, and the Xi-er-qi Residential District.

West Zone of Zhongguancun

The West Zone is the administrative, financial and research center of the entire Zhongguancun Science and Technology Park. It will be a showcase of new technological and material developments and will be the market place for Chinese technological innovations. In addition the West Zone will be the cultural and commercial service center for the ZGC. It is a 52-hectare land parcel, with Bai Yi Road passing along its eastern side and Beijing's Fourth Ring Road passing just to the north of the site. The BSCC was entrusted by the Beijing Municipal Government to conduct primary land development in the West Zone and to auction the land for development.

The site for the project was a bustling fabric of traditional courtyard houses and active commercial streets. This is reminiscent of some of the larger urban renewal projects in the United States from the 1950s and 1960s in that all the original residents and small local enterprises had to be relocated. This demolition included the headquarters of Haidian District government, the court of the Haidian District and the Broadcasting Bureau. However, despite the clean slate approach to development on the site there is an attempt to maintain a trace of the original site in the new project by incorporating a diagonal street, which bisects the plan from the northwest to the southeast. Originally, this was a historic path that the emperors of the Qing dynasty moved along on their way to the Summer Palace and in more recent times became a small pedestrian street full of commercial and community activities. While such disregard for historical fabric may be shocking, it certainly expresses both the political importance of the project and an unbridled optimism in the future by the Chinese planners.

The urban renewal quality of the project is evident also in the acceptance by the community of their fate. This might also be seen as the relative weakness of the community to voice opposition to these types of relocation activities. By the end of 2000, all of the original residents had been moved to other housing districts and site preparation was complete. In 2001 (at the time of writing), the infrastructure is under construction and about 500,000 square meters of building construction has begun. While construction continues, the BSCC is involved with promotion activities, which operate at various levels – international, regional and domestic and attaches great importance on the idea of international technological and economic cooperation.

The project aims to participate actively in international exchange and take full advantage of various sources of international capital to develop its hi-tech industry. By the end of 1999, there were more than 1100 wholly foreign funded, joint venture or sino-foreign enterprises, which accounts for about 20 percent of the total enterprises in the project. The investment by foreign-funded business has accumulated to US$3.26 billion (Zhongguancun Administration Commission (ZGC) 2001). In order to encourage the development of hi-tech enterprises in the park, the central government has instigated a series of "preferential" policies. These include fixing the income tax rate for foreign-funded hi-tech enterprises to 15 percent, with the added incentive that if export output reaches above 40 percent of the gross output, that the income tax be further reduced to 10 percent. In addition, income tax will be exempted for the first three years from the date of registration and will be reduced to between 5 percent and 8 percent for the following three years, depending on output.

Designing the Chinese Silicon Valley

The West Zone design competition opened in August of 1999 with a deadline set for October 8,

1999, a design period of less than two months. There were twelve competitive design proposals from China, Britain and America, with the winner of the competition being the Urban Planning and Design Institute of Tsinghua University. The design team for the project included twenty people, led by the chief designer Zhi Yin, the president of the Institute and also Vice Dean of the School of Architecture at Tsinghua. Interestingly, Zhi Yin had just returned from a study trip to the United States prior to the competition and among other things spent time studying Silicon Valley. After some further development the Beijing Municipal Planning Commission approved the West Zone plan in April 2000.

The design for the West Zone aims for a "world-class environmentally sustainable development," which incorporates "a unique Chinese character and socialized services" (ZGC 2001). However, what this means in terms of sustainable development is unclear. The project does not, for example, articulate a higher level of urban sustainability nor undertake to adopt higher performance standards for energy consumption, waste generation, or non-polluting materials. In this regard the project adopts the rhetoric of a global project as a facility to create an image of itself for both domestic and international consumption, which may be at odds with the reality of the executed project. However, there is some utilization of passive technology through natural ventilation and passive sunlight inclusion in the design.

Formally the plan divides the project into four blocks surrounding a central green space. The large building complexes such as the Finance and Information Center, the Science and Technology Convention and Exhibition Center and the Comprehensive Administration Center are located in Block 4, which is the largest of the four blocks. The technology and trade building complexes are distributed in an "L" shape in the other three

7.3 Land use plan of the existing site (copyright Tsinghua Urban Planning and Design Institute).

7.4 Artist's impression of the urban environment of the West Zone (copyright Tsinghua Urban Planning and Design Institute).

blocks. Various supporting facilities will be located within the project, distributed throughout the first and second floors. The four large building complexes have a height of 80 to 120 meters (260 to 400 feet), and the heights of other buildings range from 50 to 70 meters (164 to 230 feet). The buildings are arranged such that there is a gradual increase in the height of buildings from the west to the east of the project.

The West Zone accommodates various types of programs, such as trade, finance, information, administration, exhibition, entertainment, cultural activities, and green areas. In terms of the buildings, approximately 65 percent will be allocated for trade activities, 20 percent for finance and information, 5 percent will be for administration facilities, and 10 percent for the supporting services, which will include commercial and industrial services and also entertainment facilities (Tsinghua 2001). Approximately 50 percent of the site is green space. This includes a series of

green spaces that exist at many levels within the project. Other green spaces exist around the project linking between the project and its context. Between the buildings, pedestrian networks and "public sitting rooms" are arranged to create spaces for community interaction. The project also incorporates a series of roof gardens, which are linked with a dual level transportation system. Pedestrian movement is facilitated through an elevated network of bridges that link the various buildings together and separate cars from people. The project incorporates multiple levels of public space, not unlike that which occurs in parts of Hong Kong. The aim here is to intentionally complicate the urban environment of the project.

Despite the project's intentionality the environment of the West Zone reflects little of Chinese traditions of garden or landscape design except, perhaps for the inclusion of water. This central green space does demonstrate the designers' ambitions that a naturalized environment should be a central focus.

7.5 Artist's impression of the urban environment of the West Zone (copyright Tsinghua Urban Planning and Design Institute).

This space is interesting because there is no concept of public green space in Chinese landscape tradition. Rather, landscaped green space exists either as small-scale private gardens or large-scale natural environments in Chinese tradition. The highest landscape achievement being the design of private gardens such as the imperial gardens and mansion gardens. From the Chinese perspective, public landscapes exist as the natural scenic mountains and rivers much admired by poets, intellectuals and artists. As such landscape architecture (in the modern Western perspective) has a very short history in China.

While it may be difficult to draw conclusions from traditional landscape practice in the project, the design utilizes two aspects of traditional Chinese city plans – the wall and the courtyard. The arrangement of the project around the perimeter of the site defines a very strong and identifiable edge, reminiscent of the great walls of the Imperial

Palace. These walls are arranged to create a series of courtyards within the project. These public sitting rooms are a constant element in Chinese architecture and can be found in the emperor's palace as well as ordinary residential buildings. In these ways the project acknowledges a strong historical connection to city space making in Beijing. This connection is very different from the situation of the Lujiazui project, which denies any historical connection to city space making in Shanghai. In comparison these projects speak to a fundamental difference in the utilization of symbolic architectural representation.

While it may be argued that both projects aim for the creation of an identity that expresses the idea of a global city, there is a fundamental difference in the use of symbolic representation between the two. While Lujiazui deliberately eschews a traditional city-making legacy, the West Zone embraces it. This embrace is certainly not in a literal fashion. Rather it is used metaphorically in the development of the massing and formal arrangement of the architecture. This gives a very different reading to each global project. In the case of Lujiazui the project symbolically abandons any familiarity and embraces a new language of global capital. In the West Zone, however, evidence of traditional Chinese elements establishes a tension between the global and the local. The project attempts to reinforce its localness by deliberately representing essences of "Chineseness." Further, there is an acknowledgment that this essence has value in the global market place to establish a signature identity.

Certainly in terms of global image making the West Zone has to be the symbol of Beijing's new high-tech economy. Beyond the sheer landmark presence of this enormous project other factors were also developed to present this character. This included such things as the incorporation and marketing of the use of advanced construction materials and new building technologies in the fabrication of the buildings. Other design elements such as the use of a large projection screen and

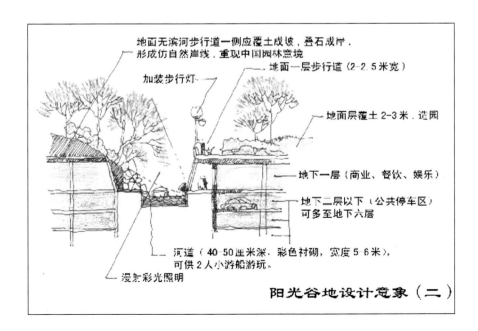

7.6 Design sketch of Sun Valley, displaying the treatment of landscape over the basement parking (copyright Tsinghua Urban Planning and Design Institute).

7.7 Artist's impression of the urban environment of the West Zone (copyright Tsinghua Urban Planning and Design Institute).

the use of a particular architectural aesthetic, often described as "high-tech," further contribute to the manufacturing of a global image for the project.

On Chinese Silicon Valleys

The design for the West Zone reflects a certain pedigree within the history of modern architecture, reminiscent of some of the megastructure images produced in the 1960s by people such as Hans Hollein with his "Aircraft Carrier City" or the fantastical projects of Archigram or later the "Exodus" project by Rem Koolhaas. Each of these projects represents architecture's attempt to contain all of the functions of the city and to express this in a containerized form. In such a project the architecture is elevated in scale to become the city. It becomes separate and self-sufficient, no longer relying on the host to support its existence. This

transition connects deeply with the designer's ego for at this moment the architectural project becomes self-referential, a closed system, which negates the need for any understanding of the context in which the project resides. In this way the project is no longer a part of the city. The West Zone can also be thought of as an urban project with these city pretensions. While the issue of Chinese symbolism may be seen as an attempt to reinforce the specifics of the local the singular object nature of the project works against this reading and clearly separates it from the surrounding context. This is further exacerbated by road widenings around the edges of project, which isolate it further. The West Zone is therefore removed from its immediate context by both its massive scale and the lack of permeability of the surrounding edges, instead sitting like some enormous ship on the outskirts of the city.

7.8 Artist's impression of the urban environment of the West Zone (copyright Tsinghua Urban Planning and Design Institute).

In this regard the West Zone follows the same logic as other global urban projects in its presentation as a separate and defined entity. The West Zone of ZGC follows this by attempting to represent all of China's Silicon Valley ambition in a singular architectural project. China is certainly not alone in dealing with representational issues and Silicon Valley ambitions. Among other things, all of these projects grapple with this issue of architectural representation. It is interesting, however, that Silicon Valley itself is impossible to reduce to singular architectural representations. It is the ultimate postmodern expression of formless energy and vitality, an anti iconic but incredibly powerful space. There is nothing that one can point to as that which represents the symbol of Silicon Valley. Indeed in architectural terms the buildings in the valley, for the most part, are banal containers. The lack of such representation is at odds with the agenda of the global urban project, which relies on the ability to present itself in the global market place through various forms of global media. This poses a major issue for projects such as the ZGC, where there is a deliberate attempt to not only represent but also to signify the success of Silicon Valley. The goal for the global urban project is to manufacture a powerful and unique image and to garnish reputation through association not with Silicon Valley itself, but with the idea of success that Silicon Valley emanates. Time will tell if the ZGC will live up to the task.

7.9 Artist's impression of the urban environment of the West Zone (copyright Tsinghua Urban Planning and Design Institute).

Vietnam

Hanoi and Ho Chi Minh

8.1 Artist's impression of Saigon South new financial
district (copyright 2001, 2002 – Phu My Hung Corporation).

8 *Doi Moi* and the Ascending Dragons of Vietnam

Hanoi North and Saigon South

For countries such as Vietnam, the global economy offers tremendous attraction by offering the promise of access to global sources of human and financial capital. The goal then is to tap into these sources to create wealth. In the case of Vietnam and other poor countries the challenge is how to do this from a very primitive base. Vietnam is the second most populous country in South East Asia after Indonesia with a population of almost 78 million people. It is also the poorest. In a region of tiger economies, Vietnam stands out as one that has not made the same gains as other countries in the region. Decades of war, communist economic policies and trade embargoes have created enormous impediments to economic growth and development. Vietnam lacks basic infrastructure to support the kind of successes experienced by other countries in their courtship with the global economy, a socialist country which has only recently followed China's lead and attempted to integrate itself economically with the rest of the world. This integration however has been thwarted by chronic inefficiencies. The country is now attempting to address this with a series of aggressive economic and political reforms, aimed at developing sustained economic momentum in Vietnam. The Vietnamese efforts at reform and economic sustainability include the provision of much needed infrastructure including the construction of new urban projects. Hanoi North and Saigon South are two such urban developments. Their story sheds light on the challenges countries face in dealing with the volatility of the global economy.

Two factors in particular can be blamed for the country's comparatively poor economic performance, which the Vietnamese authorities are currently targeting. The first is that unlike China, Vietnam has struggled to create an atmosphere conducive to global investment. This has impeded Vietnam's position in the competitive market. The second is that it is starting its economic development from a much poorer position than China did at the beginning of its "open door" policies. It does, however, have ambitious plans for itself and recent efforts toward ASEAN and WTO compliance show this commitment. Indeed the ratification of the Bilateral Trade Agreement (BTA) with the United States by the country's National Assembly in November 2001 is an enormous step forward in this direction.

The creation of large-scale development projects is one manifestation of a country attempting to accelerate its access to global wealth. These projects represent the physical form of Vietnam's version of the "open door" policy, or *doi moi*. Hanoi North and Saigon South represent two of the largest *doi moi* projects. Located in the historic capitals of the north and the south they also represent the differences that persist between these two situations. Hanoi, in the north, is the center of the socialist government and the northern project represents the struggle that socialists have faced in coming to terms with the new open economy. Things move at a sluggish pace in Hanoi and the project has failed thus far to materialize. Ho Chi Minh City (formerly Saigon), in the south, by comparison is the more vibrant of the two cities and continues its role as the commercial center of Vietnam. In the *doi moi* Vietnam, Ho Chi Minh City has been better able to embrace the capitalist system and take advantage of it to secure economic rewards. The success of the southern project shows this.

The Hanoi North Project, in the cultural and political capital of the country, is one project that epitomizes the ambitions of *doi moi*. Covering an area of some 7600 hectares, the project aimed to produce a new city on the banks of the Hong Song (Red River). A collaborative development effort between Korean developers and the Vietnamese government it employed designers from the United States, The Netherlands and Japan in

the making of its plan. The story of its production and demise is one that captures the new age of architectural production in the global world.

The Saigon South project, by comparison is a successful undertaking, responsible for a tremendous improvement in Ho Chi Minh City. The winner of numerous urban design awards, this project has weathered the difficult investment climate of *doi moi* Vietnam and continues to move toward completion. Its success is due to differences in the nature of these cities in their abilities to engage with and understand the global economy and also to the ability of their international developers to engage with and understand their Vietnamese partners. In the tale of these two cities we witness

8.2 A village market in the Mekong Delta in southern Vietnam (copyright Maurice Roers).

both the differences in modern Vietnam and the role of urban projects in the global economy.

Vietnam

Vietnam lies on a peninsula bordered by China, Laos and Cambodia. The country is organized in forty-four sections administered directly by the central government including the cities of Hanoi, Ho Chi Minh, Can Tho and Hai Phong, forty provinces and one special zone called Ving Tau-Ba Ria. Vietnam existed as a series of independent entities since early in the history of the South East Asian region. Its recent history is well known to most people. A former French colony it was invaded by the Japanese in World War II and after prolonged conflict became two countries in 1954. In the new South, President Ngo Dinh Diem used strong United States backing to create an authoritarian regime that suppressed all opposition but could not eradicate the Northern-supplied Communist Viet Cong. The ensuing tensions ultimately leading to war, which was won by the North despite military intervention. On July 2, 1976 the Socialist Republic of Vietnam was officially proclaimed.

After the war, Vietnam faced tremendous obstacles. Millions of people in the north and south had been killed and millions were displaced from their homes. The country's infrastructure was destroyed or badly damaged by bombing. Ethnic tensions developed between Chinese merchants and the Vietnamese. The Chinese merchants in the south actively resisted the collectivization of their economic interests and many were forced to flee the country, straining tensions between Vietnam and China. As Sino-Vietnamese relations soured Vietnam became increasingly isolated from the rest of the world. It came to rely heavily on trade and other assistance from the Soviet Union. Continuing military conflicts with Cambodia, which culminated in a Vietnamese invasion of

Cambodia in December 1978, continued to strain the Vietnamese economy. The United States and most other Western countries imposed a trade embargo. The economic and political isolation of the Vietnamese government meant that it struggled to develop the country's economy, the government lacked resources to repair wartime damage and there were significant problems in unifying the country under the socialist economic model.

In recent decades Vietnam has sought to change both its economic position and its relationships with the outside world. In 1986 the government of Vietnam announced a new perestroika type of economic policy. Called *doi moi*, it aimed at opening up the Vietnamese economy after decades of isolation. With three-quarters of its exports generated by agricultural production or crude oil extraction, Vietnam realized that its future lay in rapidly developing its industrial sector. In order to do so the Vietnamese would rely on developing joint ventures with foreign enterprises and *doi moi* aimed to attract foreign investment into the country.

In the years following the announcement of *doi moi*, urban areas in Vietnam have undergone tremendous changes. In many respects the changes that have occurred in Ho Chi Minh and Hanoi parallel those of cities in China. In pre *doi moi* Vietnam the government played a central role in controlling and planning the economy. There were restrictions on investment and on the population, which meant that development was held under very close control by the authorities. The government worked to create an egalitarian society free from the inequalities induced by capitalism. Property was brought under state control and strict restrictions were in place on its use. As in China prior to the open door policies, state sponsored industrial operations formed the basis of the national economy.

In post *doi moi* Vietnam the revision of these old ways has been a slow and painful process. It has struggled to develop an institutional structure that would support change. It has, for example been slower to accommodate the influx of foreign capital than the Chinese at the same stage of their open door policies. For many years Vietnam's economy was closed. It therefore had a non-convertible currency. Its banking system was primitive and it had no stock market. The result of these difficulties has been to create, until very recently, an unstable investment climate in post *doi moi* Vietnam. Foreign investors, at first keen on making quick returns, soon abandoned investing in Vietnam because of the combined uncertainty of the investment climate and the instability generally felt in the region because of the Asia Economic Crisis.

Contemporary Ho Chi Minh City and Hanoi display the results of this instability with half-constructed buildings displaying the remains of developer's ambitions. The idea that Vietnam would become the next "tiger" economy in Asia has not come to fruition, as quickly as some investors would have liked. Aware of these difficulties however the government has worked hard to create a climate conducive to foreign investment. In response, the government aims to license foreign direct investment projects worth US$12 billion over the next five years and increase the FDI sector's share in the country's GDP to 15 percent (Asia Times 2001a). Foreign investors will be encouraged to join in developing export-oriented products, processing and servicing industries, applied information technology, biotechnology, oil and gas exploration, electronics and telecommunications. This reversal has likewise meant that some of the real estate projects that had stalled are undergoing a revival. In Ho Chi Minh City, for example, this included several signature projects including the former Marriott Hotel, which opened as The Legend Hotel in September 2001. In addition

foreign investors will be encouraged to invest in projects designed to create the necessary infrastructure for Vietnam's future – the two projects examined in this chapter are examples.

Doi moi and the new Vietnam

Vietnam's economic growth has most greatly been hampered by the country's lack of infrastructure. From 1954 to 1975 Vietnam was divided into north and south. These operated as two separate economic models. The North Vietnamese government followed other socialist models and promoted heavy industry and the collectivization of agricultural production. This economy was very inefficient but aid from the former Soviet Union masked these deficiencies. The southern economy was largely based on free enterprise and was supported with aid from the United States. After the reunification of the country however, the northern economic system became the model for the whole country. The burden of the war effort combined with economic isolation and inefficient management strained the economy and hampered development of the country's infrastructure. As a result it did not develop an efficient and productive industrial sector and even today agriculture is still the most important economic sector in Vietnam, making up 27 percent of the nation's GDP and employing 70 percent of the population (http://www.vnn.vn/english/news/business/1-5-1.html).

The Vietnamese government instituted an open door policy in 1986 aimed at revitalizing the economy through a program of economic reforms called *doi moi*. Accelerated by the collapse of the Soviet Union, Vietnam's chief political and financial supporter, *doi moi* is a reform program aimed at encouraging foreign investment. The intention, not unlike the Chinese experiment, is to change from a centrally planned socialist economy to a "market economy with socialist direction," or what has become known as market socialism. However,

8.3 A new office building under construction in Ho Chi Minh City. Such sites were common in the early years of *doi moi*.

8.4 Slums along a tributary of the Saigon River in Ho Chi Minh City (copyright Maurice Roers).

8.5 View of a residential district south-west of Ho Chi Minh City's downtown core (copyright Maurice Roers).

doi moi does not involve a rapid opening of Vietnam's borders to the outside world. Instead it favors gradualism and conservatism over radical change, with economic restructuring to come before privatization. With the lifting of the US economic embargo in 1994 in combination with *doi moi* initiatives, the country continues to grow under this system of free trade.

Economic growth was 9.3 percent in 1996, 8.2 percent in 1997, and 5.8 percent in 1998, showing a drop related to the regional economic slump (see Social Watch 2001). In 1999, economic growth was 4.8 percent and for 2000 it was 6.8 percent (Economist Intelligence Unit 2001). While it is evident that there was a general decline in economic growth, Vietnam suffered less than other countries due to the Asian crisis. Its economy, being less integrated into the global flows of capital, was also less exposed. Certainly compared with its ASEAN neighbors, Vietnam weathered the Asian crisis quite well (see Kokko 1998).

The government agency responsible for coordinating foreign investment is the Ministry of Planning and Investment (MPI), formed in 1996 following the merger of the State Committee for Cooperation and Investment (SCCI) and the State Planning Committee (SPC). Foreign investment licenses are issued by the MPI. However authorization can be delegated to the provincial and urban People's Committees and to the management boards of Industrial Zones (IZs) for certain categories and sizes of projects. Currently sixteen provinces and ten Export Processing Zones (EPZs) have this authority (Ministry of Planning and Investment 2001). The Foreign Investment Law provides a range of tax incentives in order to encourage investment in exporting industries, in certain industrial sectors, in disadvantaged and other selected areas and to encourage the reinvestment of profits. The new Foreign Investment Law simplifies and, in theory at least, speeds up the procedure for the issue of a foreign investment license.

The majority of this foreign investment is located in three "growth triangles" – the Hanoi-Hai Phong-Hai Long triangle in the north of the country, the Hue-Da Nang-Quang Ngai triangle in the center of the country and the Ho Chi Minh City-Bien Hoa-Vung Tau triangle in the south. The Vietnamese government has developed industrial zones to offer investors an easy entry route into Vietnam. These comprise fully serviced industrial sites with existing factories built to a "good" standard which are available for lease. The management boards of some IZs are also authorized by the government to grant foreign investment licenses and thus provide a "one-stop shop" service to investors. Special tax incentives are also available to investors based in IZs. In order to encourage investment in the production of exports, in 1991 the government developed the planning of a number of EPZs, modeled to a large extent on those in Taiwan. In 1993 it issued the additional statute on IZs in order to overcome difficulties in infrastructure and to encourage further foreign investment, particularly from small and medium sized enterprises.

Despite some success in attracting foreign investment to these areas, there is a growing concern about the waste produced by these facilities. Around 300 industrial plants in Vietnam's key southern economic zones pump out an estimated 200 tonnes of fumes every day and release 200,000 cubic meters of waste water into the Saigon-Dong Nai river system, resulting in the pollution of water resources, including subterranean water (Asia Times Online 2000). This is one of the unrecognized aspects of *doi moi* development in Vietnam. Vietnam's technological catch up and quest for development has also unearthed some negative characteristics. The Vietnamese, however, are not blind to these problems. In 1999

8.6 The Long Bien Bridge in Hanoi over the Red River (copyright Maurice Roers).

the Asia Development Bank approved a US$70 million loan to improve drainage and sewerage and lessen flooding problems in three of the most densely populated districts in Ho Chi Minh City, benefiting around 240,000 people. The solid waste management components will serve the whole of HCMC and its estimated population of 7 million (Asia Development Bank 2001). To appreciate *doi moi* development in Vietnam one must appreciate that there is still a significant difference between Hanoi in the north and Ho Chi Minh City in the south.

Thang Long – Ha Noi

Hanoi is the capital of the Socialist Republic of Vietnam. Situated in the Red River delta, the center of the Northern plain area, Hanoi has been the capital of the Vietnam feudal state since 1010 AD. Nine hundred and ninety years ago King

Ly Thai To decided to move the capital to this part of northern Vietnam, where, legend has it, a dragon was seen flying heavenwards (hence Hanoi's ancient name, Thang Long or Ascending Dragon). Hanoi, therefore, is one of the most ancient cities in South East Asia. The literal translation of *he nei* means "in the river" and every monsoon season, from May through to September, areas of the city are inundated with water. The city is criss-crossed with drainage channels and levées, aimed at controlling the flooding. Poorly coordinated urban development however has exacerbated the flooding problem in the city placing increased pressure on the city's drainage system. The city is well positioned regionally. It is connected by highway to the rest of the country and has good connections to the ports of Hai Phong and Ha Long City. It has an international airport at Noi Bai, to the north and a proposed airport at Mieu Mon to the south of the city.

8.8 Street scene in Hanoi showing the state of the building fabric in the old city (copyright Maurice Roers).

The focus for the city is still the Old City, the famous "36 streets and wards" of Hanoi. For many centuries this site has been a commercial township. However because of a devastating fire in the 1870s, most of the building fabric of the Old City only dates to the late nineteenth century. The traditional fabric of the Old City consists of one- and two-story "long houses" similar to those found in parts of China. The layout of the Old City, actually about eighty crooked roads, was modified and expanded by the French in the 1880s, in an effort to make the plan more efficient. The nineteenth-century city persists in Hanoi as a result of the lack of urban development in the closed period. However this period also saw a lack of investment in the city, which resulted in the city's physical environment suffering from neglect. The freezing of the city in time is reminiscent of the situation in Havana (see Marshall 2001). Similar to Havana, Hanoi has also been the subject of extensive preservation efforts by groups such as UNESCO (see Logan 1995). These efforts aim to preserve the historic fabric, which is under tremendous pressure from new development interests. Part of the intention of the Hanoi North project was to create sites where new development would be allowed in an effort to diminish development pressure and preserve the Old City.

Hanoi displays a history of international exposure in its built form. The best example is the French Quarter, which lies southeast of the Old City. The French influence in Hanoi is evident in the form of much of the architecture in the city and in particular some of the streets. Among them is Trang Tien Street, which forms the edge between the Old City and the French Quarter. Reminiscent of Parisian boulevards, Trang Tien Street is a wide tree-lined street, which still displays its colonial villas and public buildings. Similar to Shanghai's Bund, the

8.9 Ho Chi Minh's mausoleum in Hanoi with a line of visitors waiting to pay their respects (copyright Maurice Roers).

French Quarter displays a rich architectural legacy of colonial occupation. It was this legacy that the government sought to promote as an attraction to lure foreign corporations to Hanoi in the early days of *doi moi* by offering these villas as offices for foreign companies.

Hanoi also displays evidence of the close relationship the Vietnamese had with the former Soviet Union. This is obvious in the Soviet inspired housing estates that encircle the southern parts of the city, constructed to provide housing for workers employed in state enterprises. These are not dissimilar to those found in parts of China. The Soviets were also engaged by the government of Hanoi to produce a master plan for the city. This plan, known as the Leningrad Plan, proposed a new city center on the south and west banks of West Lake.

Map of Tu Liem District, Hanoi.

Radial boulevards, formalized green "leisure spaces" and high-rise public buildings character-ized the plan but due to Vietnam's economic posi-tion, it was never realized. There are, however, some parts of the city that clearly display a Soviet influence, principal among them is Ba Dinh Square, the site of the National Assembly and Ho Chi Minh's Athenian acropolis inspired mausoleum.

There is ample evidence of *doi moi* in the fabric of the city. In the established areas of town new developments stand in stark contrast to the older and smaller fabric of the city. Diminishing investor interest due to a lack of confidence in the new Vietnam and the Asia crisis however, stalled several of these projects. There were several large-scale urban developments outside of the city that capture the spirit of *doi moi*. One of these was the 400-hectare Citra West Lake City, to be developed by the Ciputra Group from Indonesia in the Phu Thuong Ward of the city. The Ciputra Group was one of Indonesia's largest property and real estate companies, involved in the development of a number of prime projects and estates throughout Indonesia. The Citra West Lake project focused on a golf course with surrounding hotel and conven-tion facilities, office buildings and luxury housing. The project was to be filled with expatriate workers in an environment far beyond the economic reach of most Vietnamese. The project did not move beyond the design phase however, as Ciputra became one of many casualties of the Asian Economic Crisis. The demise of Ciputra was typical of many developers in the region who were at the mercy of rapid devaluation in the Indonesian Rupiah and spiraling interest rates (http://www.ciputra.com/invest/fistate98/fistat1.htm accessed July 23, 2001).

Hanoi North

The clearest expression of the *doi moi* city in Hanoi, however is the Hanoi North Project. In 1996 the Korean developer Daewoo, one of the largest foreign investors in Vietnam prior to their own financial problems, engaged the American firm of Bechtel to perform an urban planning assessment for a 7500-hectare project to the north of Hanoi. This project was one of the most ambitious of any proposed in the Asia Pacific Rim. The main site for the project, some 6800 hectares, was on the northern bank of the Song Hong (Red River). Here a new city was to be constructed. The rest of the project, some 760 hectares was south of Song Hong adjacent to Tay Ho (West Lake) in the Tu Liem District. Strategically located at the head of the Hanoi-Hai Phong-Hai Long growth triangle, the Hanoi North Project aimed to be the economic and technological center of the region. It was a *doi moi* project, which aimed to thrust Hanoi into the twenty-first century.

Daewoo's vision was an elaboration of Hanoi's master plan but at a scale many times greater than that envisioned by Hanoi's planners. Three principles were adopted from the Hanoi Plan and were to act as the foundation of the project – the development of infrastructure, the promotion of industrial operations and controlled urban growth. The Daewoo vision expanded on this idea and proposed a major urban center on the other side of Song Hong. It seems obvious that Daewoo's vision was inspired to great degree by the success of Liujiazui in Shanghai, another example of a city that created a new downtown on the other side of a river. In many respects the fundamentals of Daewoo's proposal are within the language of *doi moi* and aimed at developing globally competitive industries based upon an intelligent infrastructure.

In this global engagement Daewoo would fill the role of international partner to the Hanoi govern-ment, coordinating global investors and managing global alliances. This would give the project a level of global credibility in the international market

8.10 Views of Tu Liem model, part of the Hanoi North Project produced by Nikken Sekkei (copyright Daewoo Engineering and Construction Co., Korea).

place. Daewoo is a global entity involved in imports and exports of more than 3500 products with 165 nations (see http://www.dwc.co.kr). The company's extensive global information network allows it to access the latest and most complete information concerning trade expansion, commercial transactions and marketing opportunities. Further the company provides a range of services that includes financing, technology, facilities, and production processes in such diverse areas as resource development and plant export. The Hanoi North Project was Vietnam's ticket to the wealth of the global economy and as such Daewoo were given tremendous scope by the Hanoi authorities.

Daewoo engaged Bechtel who were responsible for the initial planning and in broad terms articulated the major elements of the project. Other design consultants were then engaged in the making of the vision for the project – Bechtel, Skidmore Owings and Merrill (United States) and the Office for Metropolitan Architecture (Netherlands) worked on districts north of Song Hong (Red River). Nikken Sekkei (Japan) worked on the Tu Liem District, south of Song Hong.

On the north side of the river the project centered on the creation of a new central business district (over 3.5 million square meters of commercial space) covering an area of some 200 hectares. Around this a series of residential commercial and industrial districts would be located. On the south side of the river, in Tu Liem, the project called for a mixed residential component and because of its adjacency to the Ho Tay waterfront, luxury hotel and commercial development. If built, Hanoi North was to become the future of Hanoi, one day surpassing the existing center.

The Ministry of Construction forecast that by the year 2020, the population of Hanoi would be 2.5 million people (Vietnam government 2000). This would be an increase of half a million people over the current population. Being the largest development project in Hanoi, the designers assumed that it would attract between 20 and 30 percent of this growth in population. This would give the project an assumed population of at least 750,000 people with a gross land density of approximately 100 square meters per person as identified in the Hanoi master plan. One of the major concerns for the plan was that it would order the spontaneous growth that occurs around Hanoi and which the Hanoi planners seem unable to control. Part of the problem in Hanoi is that in the government's desire to attract rapid growth it has allowed projects that do not conform to the master plan, which further exacerbates pressures on inefficient infrastructure. As a result, much of the initial planning for the Daewoo project concentrated on developing the most efficient infrastructure layouts which would expand Hanoi's existing potential as well as create new potential in the project.

The individual projects by the design teams vary in both form and content. Nikken Sekkei's scheme is a good example of the challenges faced by designers in articulating global urban projects. Nikken Sekkei's Tu Liem scheme aimed to create a center for international business, commerce, culture and recreation, incorporating world-class office space, hotels and entertainment facilities (Nikken Sekkei 1997). Tu Liem was conceived as an independent project within the larger Hanoi North Project. It was to be a global city providing international standards, accommodating a residential population of 80,000 people. The designers articulated a physical plan, which aimed to be specific to its site, provide for the most efficient use of land, maximize the potential of the site and provide a strong identifiable image. In itself the Tu Liem proposal is a massive new development covering a total of 640 hectares and in many respects it is a microcosm of the larger project.

Acknowledging the "global" nature of the undertaking the designers of Tu Liem were influenced by several features of Singapore, which for them and for the Hanoi authorities represent the model global city in the Asia Pacific Rim. They adopted from the Singapore model the strong iconography of towers to give a sense of global identity to the project. In addition they proposed high quality public spaces and a comprehensive greening program, which included public space along the edge of the lake, reminiscent of Marine Parade in Singapore. The plan for Tu Liem includes a waterfront zone, where luxury hotels sit on the water's edge, a Central Business District zone and several residential zones. A *Park Mall* runs across the site separating the project into a northern and a southern half. Each of these halves is further divided

into a series of residential areas, which focus upon central community facilities.

The open space of the Tu Liem proposal is made up of several elements. The primary open space is the *Park Mall*, conceived of as a cultural gathering space. This space was to have museums and entertainment areas. The presence of the existing canals is utilized as a layer of pedestrian movement through the city. These tracks through Tu Liem were to include pedestrian and bike paths and running trails. Importantly the canals and water network were also provided to operate as storm water retention during the wet season. The designers positioned a linear parkway in front of the commercial developments, which would include recreation areas and marinas. The design also used a green edge around the project to create a separation between the housing areas and the expressways.

8.11 Artist's depiction of the shore line of Tu Liem. Here designers aimed to present a global image to attract global investors (copyright Daewoo Engineering and Construction Co., Korea).

The proposal includes four types of housing; low density housing at thirty units per hectare is located in groups near open spaces; medium density low-rise housing at 100 per hectare is located in clusters around community facilities and close to the expressways; medium density high-rise housing, also at 100 units per hectare is located at the periphery of the development; and, high density housing at 250 units per hectare is located adjacent to the *Park Mall*. These densities establish an average density of 121 persons per hectare, which is a little higher than the 100 per hectare of the Hanoi master plan.

One of the issues that the scheme raises is how designers ground their design intentions. The site for Tu Liem is a series of agricultural land holdings criss-crossed by a series of canals. The designers struggled with the fact that there existed very little "context" around which to structure their ideas. The articulation of the plan, however, attempts to respond at some level to the context. The canals

8.12 Artist's depiction of medium density low-rise housing produced by Nikken Sekkei (copyright Daewoo Engineering and Construction Co., Korea).

were used to create a series of water bodies that bisect the site. These in turn articulated a series of green spaces around which community programs were arrayed forming the focus for the residential neighborhoods. The articulation of the larger idea builds from this constructed context, an attempt to ground the scheme into the site and to establish a continuum of some sort of legacy in this newly imaged place.

The scheme for Tu Liem raises many issues for thinking about the role of design in the global urban projects. If one accepts the notion that urban design is a critical activity engaged in the evaluation of the contemporary city and the simultaneous representation of a new and better city then the issue for situations such as Tu Liem seem to be about, at least initially, the context to be critiqued. Given the nature of the site at Tu Liem there was little existing urban condition to critique. This then suggests that Hanoi itself might be the starting point for such a critical exploration. This critique might take any number of forms. It might, for example begin with the randomness with which large new developments are inserted into the smaller historic fabric of the city. It might also begin with typological and morphological analysis of the built fabric of Hanoi. Neither of these seems to have acted as the starting point for thinking about what should occur on the site. There is, however, another context, which has not been addressed yet and that one is the context of the global city itself.

The context of the global city is not a real context in the sense of a place, although there certainly appears to be a strong understanding of this context in terms of built form in the Tu Liem scheme. The closest example of a built place that resembles the ideal global city is Singapore. It contains all of the ingredients that are coveted by countries like Vietnam. It is hugely successful and tremendously wealthy and this is expressed both

in the clustering of its downtown office towers and also in the extreme neatness of its streetscapes. Not only is Singapore a success; it is also a symbol of how a backward nation can capitalize on opportunities offered in the global economy and rise to become a global financial center of some importance. It should be no surprise that countries such as Vietnam, who after all aim for the same transformation, look to it as some kind of nirvana. The issue for designers at Tu Liem then was how to produce a better form of this nirvana.

So despite the persistence of the canals that cross the site, the local context was mostly ignored in the scheme for Tu Liem. Instead the designers embarked on an excursion in how to make a new kind of Singapore, but one that was even more efficient. The starting point then became the road system. In a manner similar to that which we have already observed in Tokyo Rainbow Town and Minato Mirai 21, the designers first set out the most efficient roadway system for the site. Just as with Zhongguancun, the scheme operates in isolation to its surroundings. Despite connections to regional highways the circulation for the project is completely internalized, thus eliminating the need to rely on the rest of Hanoi to make the project work. Once the road system was "solved" in these terms the resulting parcels were then programmed.

The programming of uses involved the arrangement of green, commercial, cultural, recreation and residential spaces to satisfy the demands outlined by the Bechtel master plan. In undertaking this exercise issues of the appropriateness of urban form and use were addressed. This ultimately seems to come down to a balance between the global and local dimensions of the project, between "Singaporeanness" and "Hanoiness" in both form and use. In terms of form there are obviously certain moments within the overall structure of the project that demanded particular global responses. These might be termed the "picture postcard" opportunities that would proclaim the global image of Tu Liem. The obvious locations for this kind of expression are along the waterfront and the design renderings prepared by Nikken Sekkei explore this aspect of the project. These considerations, along with the given of the canal locations, informed the arrangement of uses within the scheme. The global city of high-rise office towers and hotels would be close to the water and the residential components arrayed around them.

The Tu Liem scheme also raises issues of the inevitable moral obligations of the designers in the global urban projects. The global city of high-rise office and hotel developments is far out of reach for the majority of people in Hanoi. While this may be beyond the scope of design's authority, it is a fact. The designers then become instruments in the propagation of a dominant urbanism, one that is certainly much wanted by the Vietnamese government. And while I am not going to suggest

a way out of this problem it certainly bears thinking about in the global domain of architectural practice. We will return to this issue in Chapter 11.

With the Asia Economic Crisis, Daewoo's plans for the Hanoi New Town dissolved. Enmeshed in their financial difficulties Daewoo pulled out of the project in 1997. The project represents both a manifestation of "blind faith in Asia miracle" and the cruel reality of the Asian Economic Crisis. Despite the fact that the project failed to develop beyond its initial imaginings, it remains an important moment in the history of city making, not for the idea encapsulated in its urban form, rather for the extraordinary idea that cities could be developed at this scale today.

Ho Chi Minh City and Saigon South

In comparison to Hanoi North, Saigon South is a very real project and is currently under construction. Many of the ambitions for these projects are

8.13 Artist's depiction of park and pond in the Cultural and Recreational Parkway of Saigon South, produced by Skidmore Owings and Merrill (copyright 2001, 2002 – Phu My Hung Corporation).

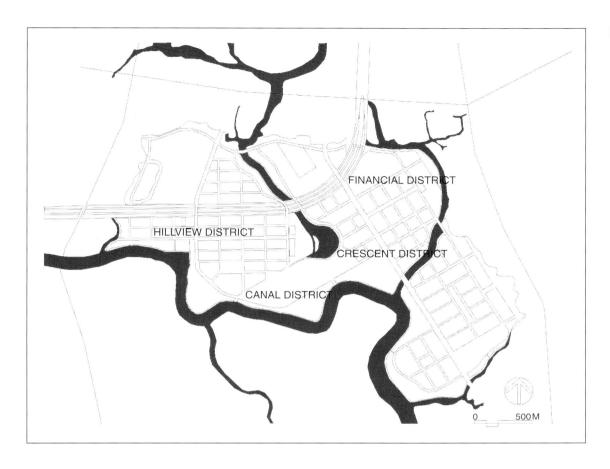

FINANCIAL DISTRICT

HILLVIEW DISTRICT

CRESCENT DISTRICT

CANAL DISTRICT

0   500 M

exactly the same but the demise of Hanoi North and the success of Saigon South are the results of differences in the development climates that exist in these two cities.

Ho Chi Minh City (HCMC), although not the political capital of Vietnam, is the nation's largest city and is critically important for *doi moi*. HCMC achieved considerably more success than Hanoi in its economic development in the 1990s and is aiming at further development in the next decade. The city lies between the Mekong River Delta and eastern Nam Bo (South Vietnam proper). Originally named Saigon, the city was renamed in 1975, after the victory of the Socialist Republic. The city has a population of approximately 7 million people, although officially this figure is 5.25 million. The administrative area of the city, covering some 2000 square kilometers, is criss-crossed by hundreds of rivers and canals and the largest of these is the Saigon River, which winds its way through the city. The urban area of Ho Chi Minh City covers approximately 140 square kilometers and includes fourteen districts and counties. The remainder of the administrative area is classified as rural comprising eight sub-districts with ninety-eight communes. This rural classification is somewhat ambiguous however as there is a significant amount of unregulated and spontaneous construction in the city.

The city is strategically located at the junction of land, rail and water transport. It has two main railroad stations and several major highway connections to Cambodia and other parts of Vietnam. The port of Saigon is an inland river port, actually 50 kilometers from the sea, able to accommodate large tonnage ships. Tan Son Nhat International Airport is located seven kilometers to the north of the city center. Investment in HCMC is promoted by the Department of Planning and Investment (DPI), which works under the leadership of the HCMC's People Committee. Its role is to attract and implement inward investment projects. DPI describes itself as a "one stop shop" where would be investors can obtain information about the type of investment, which is encouraged by the government, the most appropriate form of that investment as well as a range of specific projects. The Ho Chi Minh City People's Council Chairman Huynh Dam, states that HCMC's economy now contributes 20 percent of the national GDP, 40 percent of total exports, 30 percent of the nation's industrial production, and 30 percent of the government's budget revenue (Asia Times 2001b). As a result, Ho Chi Minh City is the center of Vietnam's economic revival.

In its draft five-year socio-economic development plan for 2001–5 the city has the objective of:

achieving sustainable growth at 10 percent per annum, to focus on production and service sectors, to develop technical and social infrastructure and to improve economic management mechanisms to be ready for globalization and regional integration.

(World Bank 2001: 107)

Key objectives of this plan are the planning for infrastructure development to improve the transportation system, water supply, water

8.14 Typical view of Ho Chi Minh City (copyright Maurice Roers).

drainage, housing and environmental protection. To achieve these ends the Ho Chi Minh City People's Committee is involved in a strategic partnership with a group of global donors. These donors assist in "overall strategy formulation and in the implementation of the priorities for investment and institutional strengthening" (World Bank 2001: 107). A total of eleven global donors are involved in various capacities with what is known as the Official Development Assistance Partnership (ODAP). The main global participants of the program are The World Bank (WB), the United Nations Development Program (UNDP/UNCHS), the Asia Development Bank (ADB) and the Japan Bank for International Cooperation (JBIC).

The vision for Ho Chi Minh City involves the development of a multi-nodal urban structure. The pressing overcrowding and over extension of infrastructure is to be addressed through the expansion of the city, of which Saigon South is critical, as well as the rehabilitation of the existing fourteen urban districts. In addition there is a vision to develop an extensive transportation system within this urban structure, which would connect the inner city with outer lying areas through various traffic modes. This vision does include an environmental agenda and a major part of Ho Chi Minh's planning vision is to develop appropriate infrastructure to address environmental pollution. This calls for the relocation of industrial facilities to planned estates and the rehabilitation of the canal and drainage systems. The ADB loan mentioned previously is a major component of this rehabilitation. Another goal of the government is to provide socio-economic infrastructure (i.e. schools, hospitals, culture and sport facilities) and the supply of affordable housing. To do this the government finances and in addition to loans actively seeks to attract global investors. These investors include the property sector and

several high profile real estate developments have been built.

Ho Chi Minh City's planners have wrestled for many years with the direction in which the city should expand. The city has previously expanded north and west. Further expansion in these directions, however would have been difficult given the location of the airport and the city's water supply to the north and the over extension of infrastructure to the west. The idea of extending the city south dates back to the 1920s. The city's increasing importance led the French to consider areas for future expansion but the direction of this expansion has always been subject to controversy. Only in 1998, however, did the Ministry of Construction announce that this direction would be south. Prior to this it seemed obvious that the city would expand east, across the Saigon River in a fashion similar to that proposed in Hanoi.

The east, or northeast, was favored because of the relatively high elevation of the land, a precious commodity in low-lying urban areas prone to flooding. In addition, the east also contains an important transportation junction, the National Highway 1A intersection with National Highway 51 to Bien Hoa and Vung Tau. While the east has excellent potential, several large-scale urban projects have failed to move forward. The proposed city center in An Phu for example, a joint venture between Hong Kong City Horse Development Company and Ho Chi Minh's Urban Development Services Company would have been one of the largest urban developments in Vietnam. It did not materialize for a number of reasons, among them political uncertainties and bureaucratic inefficiencies (see Nien Newspaper 1998). Another reason has been the authority's hesitancy on how and where to cross the Saigon River. These uncertainties have elevated the importance of the south as a viable direction for the expansion of the city. In the early 1990s, the decision was made to explore

8.15 Typical mixed use of development with retail on the ground floor and residential above (copyright Maurice Roers).

the potential of expanding the city to the south. Although there was abundant land close to the city center to the south it had remained undeveloped because the infrastructure necessary to open it up had not been constructed. However, the success of projects such as the Tan Thuan Export Processing Zone (TTZ) was evidence that development in the south is viable.

The TTZ is the first and most successful export-processing zone in Vietnam. The 300-hectare site covers an entire peninsula of District 7 adjacent to the HCMC Port Area. It is a joint venture development between the Central Trading Development Group (CT&D) and Tan Thuan Industrial Promotion Corporation (TTIPC). CT&D is the foreign half of the joint venture, being from Taiwan. The Ho Chi Minh City People's Committee (HCMCPC) set up the TTIPC. The joint venture, known as the Tan Thuan Corporation (TTC) was set up in 1991. Since the beginning of 1993, over 153 tenants have invested more than US$638 million in industrial operations that range from food processing to semiconductors (Francey 2001). The project has gained an international reputation being voted the best EPZ in Asia by the Economist Intelligence Unit and by Euromoney Corporate Location Magazine (Central Trading and Development Group (CT&D) 2001). In addition TTC was the first EPZ development and management corporation to acquire certification. It is also the first EPZ in Vietnam to become a member of the World Export Processing Zone Association (WEPZA). The other joint venture between CT&D and TTIPC is the Phu My Hung Corporation licensed in 1993 and responsible for the development of Saigon South.

CT&D's role in the joint ventures is very similar to Daewoo's role in Hanoi North. CT&D was established in 1989 in Taiwan to develop trade and investment opportunities in the Asia Pacific Rim. The company's interests in Vietnam include: the

Phu My Hung Corporation (originator and developer of Saigon South), the Hiep Phuoc Power Station, which provides almost 10 percent of electricity in Vietnam, and the Tan Thuan EPZ. CT&D is one of the largest single foreign investors in Vietnam with a total capital investment of US$650 million (Francey 2001). Not surprisingly, CT&D maintains a close working relationship with the government of Vietnam and the People's Committee of Ho Chi Minh City. CT&D is an example of a successful global operator that has been able to bring its global perspective and resources to the Vietnamese situation. The company's engagement in Vietnam started in 1989 when it investigated the possibility of investing in several emerging countries for large-scale development projects. The choice of Vietnam was the result of careful assessment of such possibilities. At this time CT&D outlined its plans for development projects in HCMC and the application and documents for license were submitted on October 1, 1992. On May 19, 1993, the Phu My Hung Corporation license was granted and at the same time permission was given by the Vietnamese authorities to develop Saigon South (Francey 2001).

CT&D has been successful in Vietnam where many others have failed. According to Daniel Francey of the Phu My Hung Corporation, several reasons can explain this success. When CT&D decided to invest, its management saw parallels to Taiwan in the 1970s, a situation they could immediately relate to. CT&D brought to Vietnam individuals with experience in developing the first EPZs in Taiwan, which served to build the essential foundations for the Tan Thuan EPZ. Second Francey notes that all of CT&D's projects are strategically located in the south of HCMC, just 10 minutes from the city center. CT&D has developed a proven track record with the Vietnamese authorities and all of its projects contribute to the city's economic growth. In addition, CT&D has been prudent in the phasing of its investments, allowing

8.16 Aerial view of Saigon South circa 1995 with the development boundary shown (copyright 2001, 2002 – Phu My Hung Corporation).

8.17 Close up view of the site for the Saigon South New City Center circa 1997. In the distance at the top of the image the older downtown core of Ho Chi Minh City can be seen (copyright 2001, 2002 – Phu My Hung Corporation).

better expenditure allocation when necessary. Perhaps the most important factor, however, is the choice of a good partner with excellent relations to government officials.

Saigon South master plan

At the time that Phu My Hung's license was granted in 1993, CT&D organized an international design competition. In all about forty firms responded, of which seven were shortlisted for a detailed proposal presentation. Skidmore Owings and Merrill (SOM) made the strongest impression on CT&D with their vision for Saigon South (Francey 2001). The SOM master plan for the project, dated May 1994, creates a string of development parcels connected by a highway spine.

This spine was later constructed as the Saigon South Parkway. The focus of the development is the New City Center located at the eastern end of the string. Other developments on the string include University Place, a high tech center and several merchandise centers. Detail design continued through to 1996. The scheme developed under SOM's supervision and included the work of Koetter Kim and Associates, Boston and Kenzo Tange Associates, Tokyo.

The major elements of the plan were set by the SOM master plan, which has continued to guide development and provide the directedness of the project. The seam between the new development and the existing fabric of Ho Chi Minh City's Districts 4 and 5 is a Cultural and Recreational

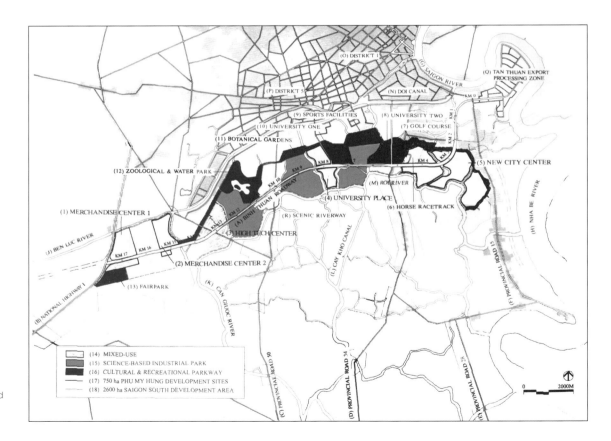

8.18 Saigon South master plan produced by Skidmore Owings and Merrill, LLP showing the spine of the proposed Saigon South Parkway (copyright 2001, 2002 – Phu My Hung Corporation).

Parkway, which includes sports facilities, a zoo, a botanical garden, a water park and two university campuses. Images of this parkway, produced by the design teams, display a lush and well-maintained environment not unlike Fredrick Law Olmstead's Jamaica Way with its Pond in Boston. The images certainly contain elements of this kind of romantic nineteenth-century urban situation. Although produced to promote the designer's ideas, it should not be confused with the reality of the project. The objective of these images, rather, is to create an atmosphere for the project. The design guidelines for the project, however, allow for more varied interpretations and this is one of the major strengths of the SOM led effort in that it is not prescriptive but defines a general arrangement of possibilities.

On the southern side of the development a Nature Conservancy extends the length of the project, which separates the project from development that might extend beyond it and provides needed

overflows to protect against tidal floods due to *tsunami*. The project's spine is the Saigon South Parkway, a 17-kilometer long, 120-meter wide expressway (ten lanes). This road is the first major East–West connection in Ho Chi Minh City and allows direct connection between the existing downtown area in District 1 to the New City Center in Saigon South (District 7). The parkway includes some ten bridges that cross a variety of rivers and channels.

The New City Center is the main focus of the Saigon South Project. It comprises the Financial District, the Crescent District, the Canal District, the Medical Campus, the Hillview District, the Recreation District and the South Side District. The Financial District is the banking and finance center of the project. Here a new stock exchange and currency trading facilities are to be constructed. Here too will be located convention and conference facilities. Artists' renditions of the Financial Center bear close resemblance to views along

8.19 View of the Hillview District January circa 2002 (copyright 2001, 2002 – Phu My Hung Corporation).

8.20 View of Hillview District from across the golf course circa 2000 (copyright 2001, 2002 – Phu My Hung Corporation).

Shenton Way in Singapore and one would assume that this is wholly deliberate. Singapore has become the Asian city to be emulated by many for its global cache, as was also the case with Tu Liem.

The Crescent District is a continuation of the commercial area. The Southern Cross Building is completed and several others are either under construction or committed. The Canal District, inspired by San Antonio's Canal District, will have specialty retail, boutiques, cafés and restaurants. The Medical Campus has the new International Finance Corporation funded Franco-Vietnamese hospital and will also have a nursing school. Residential districts are located in the Hillview and Recreation Districts. These districts have high quality housing, including the 354-apartment Hung Vuong Apartments and the 99-villa Phu Gia Villa Project. These apartments appeal to the emerging middle class in HCMC and sales have

been brisk. The South Side District houses the New City Center's schools. These include the Saigon South People's Founded School, the Saigon South International School, the Taipei School, the Japanese School and the Korean School. Other education projects include the RMIT International University (RIUV) and the HEPZA Technical College.

The RIUV project will be developed on a 17-hectare area of a 62-hectare site in Saigon South. The project sponsor is RMIT University (RMIT), an Australian university based in Melbourne. Since the 1990s, RMIT has been involved with joint programs and local partnerships with universities in Hong Kong, Malaysia, Japan, Thailand, Vietnam and other Asian countries. RMIT Vietnam (RIUV) will be the first university wholly owned and operated by RMIT outside Australia and the first wholly owned foreign-owned university in Vietnam. RMIT envisions that the completion of the full campus of

8.21 View of Hillview District and Saigon South Parkway circa 2001 (copyright 2001, 2002 – Phu My Hung Corporation).

RMIT Vietnam could take about twelve years, by the end of which total student enrolment could grow up to 13,000 with the first phase of the construction completed in 2003. The project cost is estimated at US$33.8 million and is being financed by the International Finance Corporation (IFC) of the World Bank and the Asian Development ment Bank.

The project will alleviate the acute shortage of colleges and universities in Vietnam. Only one out of six applicants can enter a college in Vietnam at present. In addition, Vietnam has a huge shortage of people with foreign language, business management, computer and other technical skills. The project, by providing degree programs, and short-term foreign language and professional training adapted to the market needs, will make a significant contribution to the development of human capital in *doi moi* Vietnam. It will also make it possible for thousands of Vietnamese students, who do not have the financial means to study abroad, to receive Western-style university education in Vietnam.

The layout of the New Center displays a well worked out plan composed of two interlocked grids rotated in response to the presence of existing watercourses and the Saigon South Parkway. This produces a shift in the plan, which is accommodated without sacrifice to block form or roadway infrastructure. This rotation also creates an interest in the plan of the city and integrates it into the marsh areas surrounding the project. Land parcels in Ho Chi Minh City are traditionally 4 by 20 meters. This forces all houses to be built as row housing. One of the greatest advantages of the parcel size in Saigon South is that they allow for a

8.22 View of My Hung Villas (copyright 2001, 2002 – Phu My Hung Corporation).

variety of different building typologies. This allows for the utmost in flexibility in the project and given the long time span needed to bring the project to fruition allows for change to be absorbed seamlessly.

The success of the project in economic terms can be gauged by the amount of development that has located within it. The success of the project in terms of its urbanism is far more difficult to gauge. One often worries about issues of cultural sensitivity and appropriateness. One might ask if the design for Saigon South promotes an appropriate Vietnamese expression of urban form. This issue is moot for two reasons. On the one hand the Vietnamese urban tradition would not allow the scale of projects necessary to promote the economic model of *doi moi* Vietnam. On the other, what does

exist is for the most part a residual legacy of French colonialism or Soviet inspired rationalist inefficiency.

This raises a series of interesting questions for designers. In the absence of an appropriate urban tradition, what trajectory should one pursue? What is important to appreciate in the Saigon South Plan is that the designers have outlaid an infrastructure that might support a variety of different outcomes. One should not read too much into the imagery presented in the sketches. Rather, the level of control proposed in design terms does not dismiss the possibility that new and locally inspired urban outcomes might find root and ultimately create an entirely different imagery. This is the ultimate success of Saigon South and the value that it brings to Ho Chi Minh City.

8.23 View of Saigon South Parkway (copyright 2001, 2002 – Phu My Hung Corporation).

On ascending dragons

Vietnam currently enjoys an excellent position in the region, outperforming its neighbors in terms of economic growth. The country is politically stable and the government is willing to make necessary changes, easing regulations and procedures for foreign investment, in their desire to be a global player. Hanoi North and Saigon South are two very different attempts to provide global infrastructure to support these ambitions. While Hanoi struggles to emerge, Saigon South is moving ahead with accelerated pace. Streets are being paved and new infrastructure is being provided to accommodate new building projects, including the signature Gateway Building, which started construction in January of 2002 for completion in January of 2003. Phu My Hung Corporation is certainly extremely confident in the future of Vietnam and of their project.

These projects show us the vagaries of urban development in the realm of global projects. Despite the fact that both projects can be described in similar terms and indeed share common ambitions, such ingredients alone do not make for successful urban projects, global or otherwise. What is clear is that such projects rely to a great extent on the political and social contexts of their host locations and the limits of design. There is often a misconception by designers that if the scheme is good enough in design terms then it will be successful in other terms as well. Clearly this is not enough.

Hanoi North and Saigon South make clear that design has a role to play but that role must be couched in larger understandings of the politics of urban development. This is an often-neglected aspect of urban design but one that is central to its agency and success. In a global architectural

8.24 Artist's impression of Scenic Riverway, Saigon South (copyright 2001, 2002 – Phu My Hung Corporation).

8.25 View of the Vietnamese landscape between Hanoi and Hai Phong (copyright Maurice Roers).

practice the issues of politics are more complicated and difficult to comprehend. The lack of understanding of the specifics of the local reduces the capacity of the ideas presented in the schemes and results in the propagation of simplistic proposals or architectural cliché. If architecture is to have a role to play in defining the physical settings of the global economy then locality and its peculiarities must be elevated to an equal position in the agenda of design. Only in this way will design find relevance and meaning in the production of city spaces in a global world.

8.26 My An Apartments in the Hillview District of Saigon South (copyright Phu My Hung).

Singapore

9.1 View of the Singapore Urban Redevelopment
Authorities' model of the city showing both the existing
downtown and the New Downtown.

9 New Downtown – Ideas for the City of Tomorrow

Singapore's New Central Business District

Imagine an oasis of palms, ponds and pavilions. Imagine space age like glass and steel buildings set amongst this lush landscape. Imagine thousands of brainy people from all over the world conducting research and concocting cutting age technological innovations in their cubicles in these buildings. Imagine them breaking off for lunch at a funky restaurant in that oasis. Imagine them sipping their café latte and exchanging ideas, creating "synergy," even striking deals. Imagine no further.

Sumiko Tan
home-work-play

We want to position Singapore as a key city in the Asian renaissance of the 21st century and a cultural center in the globalised world. The idea is to be one of the top cities in the world to live, work and play in, where there is an environment conducive to creative and knowledge-based industries and talent.
Renaissance Report – Ministry of Information and the Arts, Singapore Government

Situated adjacent to the present Central Business District of Singapore sits an expanse of flat undeveloped land, the result of twenty years' worth of reclamation activity. Almost completely

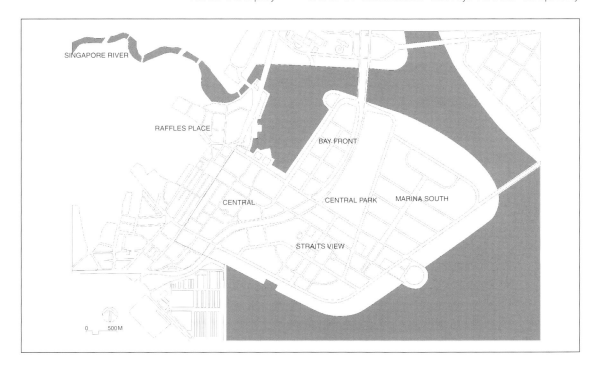

Map of New Downtown, Singapore.

unoccupied at this time, Singaporean planners envision that one day this 372 hectare area will be home to a new city. This new city will be the crowning achievement of Singapore as a great urban experiment, a trophy to the idea that cities can be completely controlled and fashioned in response to utopian concepts of idealized social situations. The New Downtown represents the ultimate fulfillment of the idea that Singapore is a global city. First proposed in the 1980s, the New Downtown was incorporated into Singapore's 1991 Concept Plan, the document that articulates the physical direction of the island state. Since then the vision for this new city on the bay has developed in both scope and detail.

The scale of the New Downtown will completely recast the image of the city. The New Downtown would more than double the size of the existing downtown core of the city. Envisioned at a time of tremendous confidence in the future of the island republic and in planning's ability to mould that future, the New Downtown encapsulates the spirit of the Asian development miracle and represents the ultimate vision that Singapore seeks for itself – the physical manifestation of the "tropical city of excellence."

This tropical city of excellence is a remarkably small country being only 682 square kilometers in area (Singapore Department of Statistics 2001). It is an island that has been growing. In 1967, prior to massive land-fill operations, it was only 587 square kilometers. Government estimates project that the island will grow to a maximum of only 743 square kilometers. Singapore would physically fit in the United States 14,000 times. The island is 42 km long east–west and 23 kilometers wide north–south. The size of the place means that land is a precious commodity and its use is highly

9.2 View of the skyline of downtown Singapore, the site of the New Downtown is immediately to the left of this image.

regulated. The planning and zoning controls of the Urban Redevelopment Authority (URA) are extensive. The URA is Singapore's national planning authority, a statutory board under the Ministry of National Development. This Ministry is responsible for Singapore's physical development through long-term land use planning, public housing, public works, urban redevelopment, parks and recreation and other aspects of physical development. Every square meter of land on the island has been allocated in accordance with a grand vision for what Singapore should become.

The tropical city of excellence

Singapore is unique in the sense that more than any other city it displays the result of government entrepreneurship, control and facilitation. The physical environment of Singapore is a precise reflection of its government's political, social, cultural and economic visions. It is the physical reflection of a great experiment led by the vision of one man Lee Kuan Yew – to build an ideal society in the midst of tropical Asia. This vision pervades every aspect of life in Singapore, from business, to lifestyle, to freedom of the press, to the form of the physical city.

Although small it is one of the most ethnically diverse locations in the Pacific Rim. Its population is made up of Chinese 77 percent, Malay 14 percent, Indian 7.6 percent, a small amount of other kinds of people (1.4 percent), which includes the expatriate population. The Chinese populations come from different parts of China. They are predominantly Hokkien (local term for the Fujianese), with the next largest group coming from Teochew heritage (local name for the Chaozhouese) and then much smaller groups of Cantonese, Hakka and Hianese. This results in a

9.3 View from Raffles Place toward Orchard Road giving a good impression of the density and scale of the city.

9.4 The environment of Singapore expresses the transformation from colonial trading post to global city.

heterogeneous cultural landscape and a variety of different dialects and customs. Once British control was relinquished this posed many significant issues for Singapore in the early years of its independence. Unlike other nations in the Pacific Rim, Singaporeans lacked a common ethnic bond that would solidify their foundation as a nation. Indeed the journey to independence was not an easy one in Singapore. Singapore's history however is a microcosm of global development.

Singapore is one of the best examples of the impact of globalization on urban form. It was a world port for over a century and developed a thriving trade culture. During the 1960s, Singapore started on a rapid and aggressive path toward industrialization and the nation's development since independence has been phenomenal. Under the direction of Lee Kwan Yew Singapore seemed very aware of its position in the world and its potential. Its industrialization was from the start aimed toward global markets and is today one of the leading "little dragons" in South East Asia.

Singapore and its integration into the global economy

The tropical city of excellence is a concept that has propelled Singapore from colonial backwater to global city. It is the central theme behind all planning and development on the island and represents a desire to make Singapore a city of international standard in South East Asia. From the moment of separation from Malaysia in 1965, the Singapore government has worked toward this end. Through economic policy, infrastructure planning and social policy, the government has "laboured to transform the city state into a linchpin of the new global capitalism" (Beng 1993: 105). As Yuan and Choo have asserted, Singapore's potential as an international business center was increasingly recognized, and major governmental decisions were taken to support this by creating

needed infrastructure (Yuan and Choo 1995: 91). Planning and urban design played an important role in this provision.

The city state has an efficient transportation system and telecommunications network, modern and efficient airport and sea terminals, efficient business environments and a highly developed public housing system, all of which act to strengthen the city state's global competitiveness. In addition, Singapore aims to become an intelligent island and its Tech2000 plan aims to make it a place where information technology improves the quality of living, of work, of home and play (see Choo 1997). The Global Competitiveness Report for 2000 ranks Singapore second in the world for growth competitiveness, a measure of the potential of the country, and ninth overall for current competitiveness (see Porter 2000: 192).

The phasing of Singapore's integration into the global economy can be observed in the changes in its economic structure. Over the past three decades, manufacturing, financial and business services have become the two most important categories of economic activity. These changes enabled the city state to create a more developed, diversified and globally integrated economy. In both its exports and imports, Singapore's trade is moving toward technology-intensive and human capital-intensive commodities. The government of Singapore is well versed in the issues of competitive advantage and has accepted the influence of globalization as yet another necessary aspect of the contemporary situation in which they find themselves.

The government's response to globalization can be seen in the development of a number of programs developed by the Singapore Economic Development Board. These include M2000 (Manufacturing 2000) and IBH2000 (International Business Hub 2000). Reflecting the success of these programs, and others like them, key statistics show that the number of foreign-controlled companies present in Singapore increased by 82.6 percent to 11,243 between 1983 and 1993, whilst the net foreign equity investment increased by Sing$19,535.9 million dollars during the same time period (Singapore Department of Statistics 1996a). Between 1986 and 1996, the total number of air passenger arrivals into Singapore increased from 4,446,000 to 11,587,000 (Singapore Department of Statistics 1997). These figures reflect the increasing global integration of both the economy and society in Singapore.

It is not surprising that the republic has developed an international presence as a major commercial and financial center as well as a significant location for the regional headquarters of major multinational corporations. This is because Singapore plays a critical strategic role in linking the world to the vast markets in the Asia Pacific region. It also facilitates the complementary growth of cities in the region by providing a convenient opening to the vast capital, resources and professional experiences in the international community (Yuan and Choo 1995: 90). Clearly, Singapore's role in the network of global cities is illustrated by its twin global and regional functions, both as a key business center and a key center for high value manufactured goods. The emergence of Singapore as a global city is reflected in the physical form of the city, in particular in the emerging vision for the New Downtown.

Designing a new city on the bay

The New Downtown provides us with an interesting example of how Singaporean's see the future of the city. Its form depicts the unencumbered representation of a Singaporean utopia. Designed to be a self-contained city within a city it will ultimately accommodate the corporate headquarters of multinational financial institutions, 5-star hotels,

luxury retail complexes and high quality housing. Singapore, of course, is located about one degree north of the Equator and its climate is a major influence on how Singaporeans view themselves. Much of the planning and promotional material produced by the Urban Redevelopment Authority contains explicit reference to the idea of a modern tropical city. In terms of the New Downtown this raises the question of the compatibility of the idea of a modern high-rise city with a tropical city.

The site of the New Downtown sits adjacent to the southern area of the existing Downtown Core, which is south of the Singapore River. This seam is a three-kilometer long stretch of commercial office buildings that run from the Tanjong Pagar subway station to Raffles Place along Shenton Way. From this seam a series of perpendicular roads extend across the new landscape, connecting to the existing urban fabric at Church Street, Cross Street and Maxwell Road. The Ayer Rajah Expressway continues around the coast forming a new coastal expressway and the outer edge of the new development. The New Downtown is divided into four areas – Central, Bayfront, Straits View and Marina South. Each of these areas is designed to have centers, around which larger-scale developments would occur. There are several aspects of the plan that are worth discussing.

One of the most obvious differences between the plan for the New Downtown and the fabric of the older part of the city is the tremendous increase in the scale of the development. This increase occurs in terms of the size of the block pattern, the size and scale of the open space and the size of the developments themselves. The existing downtown area of Raffles Place supports some of the largest and tallest buildings in Singapore. Yet the size of the proposed development in the New Downtown would dwarf the buildings in the existing core. One only has to examine the Urban

9.5 View of the high-rise office towers in Raffles Place, sitting along the edge of the Singapore River – symbols of global financial control.

9.6 View of the Singapore model showing the extent of the reclamation site and the scale of New Downtown in comparison with the rest of the city.

Redevelopment Authority model to appreciate that the New Downtown expands the scale of urban development in Singapore. The image presented here is of a city many times denser and taller than the existing one. This is curious on several levels.

The increase in scale is curious for both the amount of space projected into the New Downtown and also for the nature of that space. If one were to make conclusions about the nature of commercial space in the future by looking at the design of the New Downtown, then one might conclude that commercial office buildings will expand in both height and also in floor plate in the coming decades. While there is ample evidence of recent tall building in other parts of the Asia Pacific Rim, Lujiazui being a notable case, there are some that suggest that this form of building is no longer appropriate for the requirements of contemporary

corporations and that new kinds of office environments are appearing (see Duffy 1997).

Duffy makes the point that given changes in the way corporations work the older office building models will no longer be valid. Such possibilities could prove fatal for the New Downtown, not only because of the tremendous amount of new office space proposed but also for the nature of such space. If we think back fifty years and recall the nature of American downtowns, they were very different places than they are today, in no small part by the insertion of massive amounts of commercial office space. No one could have foreseen that office environments would manifest in the way that they did. If we think forward now, to a time fifty years in the future, one wonders what innovations in commercial space may have on the form of cities. The New Downtown raises the idea of

whether it is even possible to conceive of downtowns in the future.

In their quest to imagine what a modern tropical city might look like the Singaporean planners suggest that this vision closely resembles New York. This is both disappointing but also somewhat inevitable. In examining Hanoi North and Saigon South I noted that Singapore is the example par excellence for the Asian global city. The Singaporean planners, likewise, seem to hold New York as the model par excellence of the global city. Indeed more specifically Battery Park City seems to have been the only urban model emulated. One of the greatest challenges for urban design is to find appropriate models from which to base urban design propositions. This is complicated today because many historically derived models are no longer relevant to the

reality of the global city. The issue for the New Downtown is how much of the model should be carried forward and to what extent should the model be reformulated, revised or dismissed.

The New Downtown lacks any sense of difference that might suggest what a "tropical" city might be and how this might be different from New York. Instead of a new way of thinking about the city the Singapore planners, relying on a Lynchian vocabulary of urban language, describe seven elements to the urban design of the project. These elements are urban pattern, pedestrian network, vehicular access, streetscape, building form, open space and roofscape. While each of these elements can be adequately described individually, the relationship between them is less obvious and how this might inform a new "tropical" conception of the city is likewise obscure.

The plan of the New Downtown is compositional in nature, derived from Beaux Arts ideas of axial arrangement and symmetry. The elements of "urban design" that govern its creation seem weak and superfluous to the overall object quality of the project. This object quality represents a need to read the project as a complete whole. Nevertheless, the size of the project would mean that this completeness would never actually be a reality. The time taken to build the project would mean that it would always have an "in process" character. As such the spaces that define the project would have to have a coherency in and of themselves to support this sense of incompleteness. However, the spaces within the project lack any sense of interest, nor articulation in and of themselves. The New Downtown does not provide us with a new way to think about nor appreciate urban spaces. Neither does it establish a new urbanity that might suggest possibilities for the future of urban design. Rather it relies on a conventional urban design methodology of form making where geometry and massing define the arrangement. This is problematic because it relies on a complete construction of the project in order to be evaluated, which would never occur.

The existing downtown, centered in Raffles Place, is typical of most North American downtowns in that it is active during day and dormant by night. Super high-rise office buildings designed by I.M. Pei, Kenzo Tange and Kisho Kurokowa cluster together on the banks of the Singapore River. During the day these projects absorb thousands of office workers who all leave and return to their homes at six o'clock at night. Besides the expatriate and tourist bars of Boat Quay it is an area in Singapore that epitomizes the banality of modern cities. The URA planners recognize this and in conjunction with the drive for vitality expressed in the 2001 Concept Plan, the New Downtown is imagined as an active zone during the day and night. The zoning of the new project allows for res-

idential and cultural uses but the scale of the spaces for communal occupation seem too large. This is certainly the portrayal one sees in the planning imagery presented by the Urban Redevelopment Authority.

The vision for the New Downtown is described in a number of URA promotional documents. Of particular interest is the document entitled "New Downtown – Ideas for the City of Tomorrow," published in August of 1996. The document describes the vision of the New Downtown as:

An efficient and gracious city, integrating efficient transportation, quality infrastructure and beautiful environment. The New Downtown will offer a variety of living and working environments. It will be well-served by public transport. Pedestrians will also be able to move about easily in all weather comfort, separated from the vehicles.
(Urban Redevelopment Authority 1996)

The document aims to provide a sense of the quality and character of the New Downtown. It is replete with images of other "world cities" and Battery Park in New York City features heavily in the image gallery. It is clear from these images that the planners are seeking a highly cultivated environment. It is a vision that displays a complete order, where the architecture is controlled and ordered. The landscape too is polite and trimmed, where Boston Common is provided as an example of living next to nature. There are two types of open space in the plan for the New Downtown. The first is a 400-meter wide waterside parkway that surrounds the entire project. The second is a green area reminiscent of Central Park. However, the imagery of these spaces is overtly North American. Other cities feature in these scenes as well. For example street scenes from Barcelona are placed adjacent to images of the Grande Arche in La Defense. Besides the association of places

9.8 Close up view of the New Downtown model showing the scale of the new development.

with a particular kind of urban success, however, it remains unclear what the intention of these images is. Where one expects specific description one finds instead only vague assertions.

In addition to photographs of other places there are a series of fantastic perspectives, printed on silver paper. This sequence of images portrays a series of spaces within the New Downtown. They display an ultra modern city reminiscent of some of the megaproject images of Battery Park City from the 1960s. Pedestrians appear to scamper at the base of huge office towers and enormous civic buildings. Automobiles have been removed from the pedestrian realm leaving untold acres of pedestrian plazas. Commercial architectural styling, represented by the latest fashion in commercial high-rise architecture, defines the character of masses of high-rise buildings. All of these towers sit on top of what can only be assumed,

given the dimensions shown, to be large retail podiums.

The interiors of these retail spaces are also depicted in a series of interior perspectives that suggest the imagined spaces of metabolist projects from the 1960s. Huge atriums rising eight stories in the air appear to disappear over the horizon, suggesting that these interior spaces continue for thousands of meters. It is within these drawings that the enormity of the planning problem sinks home. They, more than any other aspect of the document, raise the issue of how one adequately represents the city of the future. More specifically in Singapore's case, how does one think about the urban form of a tropical city and how might this be different from a city at 42 degrees north latitude. It certainly appears that the design of New Downtown does not respond to its tropical setting, and rather appropriates its urban

9.9 View of Lower Manhattan. Given the impression of the New Downtown model, it appears likely that these will be the kind of streets produced in Singapore.

imagery from other world cities in other climatic zones.

Designing and building a global nation

Singapore's development is a story in integration with the emerging global economy. It was a little fishing village in 1819 when Sir Stamford Raffles came ashore at the mouth of the Singapore River to establish an East India Company trading post on this tiny island at the tip of the Malay Peninsula. Singapore has always enjoyed a strategic position at the juncture of trade routes from Europe to China. During the nineteenth century, trade in the region was hotly contested as the British, Dutch, Spanish and Portuguese developed an intense commercial rivalry. This rivalry led to territorial arguments as each nation vied for larger shares of regional trade. The Treaty of London in 1824 put an end to this friction, carving up South East Asia to colonial rule. Under the treaty, the Dutch ceded all their interests in India to Britain. On the Malay Peninsula they withdrew their objections to the occupation of Singapore and withdrew from Malacca. The British, in return, ceded Bencoolen and Sumatra to the Dutch. It was also in 1824 that Britain signed a treaty with Sultan Hussein of Riau-Johore and the Temenggong of Johore to cede Singapore to Britain forever.

After World War I, Britain's dominance in South East Asia waned. The emerging Pacific Rim began to change the role of the colonial powers in Asia as Japan, America and Australia began to define greater roles in the region. Through most of the first part of the twentieth century Singapore continued to act as a major trade center in South East Asia, a situation that remained unchanged until the Japanese invasion of Singapore in 1942. In 1945, British sovereignty was once again imposed on Singapore. The city was overcrowded. Poverty was common and essential infrastructure had either been ignored or damaged.

In 1946, Singapore established its own administration, separate from the Malay Peninsula. The creation of an independent administration was the first move toward self-government. The postwar constitution granted limited local representation. However, 1946 through to 1958 was a time of political discontent and social upheaval. This upheaval was leveled at two fronts. On the first the local population became increasingly discontent with their colonial masters. The other was the rising influence of Communist influence in Singapore and the prolonged warfare waged in Malaya by Communist guerillas. In 1958, after years of difficult negotiation, a new constitution was set in place that gave Singapore self-government. In 1959 the People's Action Party (PAP) were elected to power. The early 1960s were a time of deep unrest for the emerging nation. Malaysia was formed on 16 September 1963, and consisted of the Federation of Malaya, Singapore, Sarawak and North Borneo (now Sabah). The merger proved to be short lived. Singapore separated from the rest of Malaysia in August 1965, and became a sovereign, democratic and independent nation. On 22 December 1965, it became a republic, with Yusof bin Ishak as its first President.

As soon as Singapore gained independence a massive industrialization program was launched. The basis for this industrialization strategy was outlined in the United Nations' Proposed Industrialization Programme of 1961 headed by Albert Winsemius, a Dutch economist. Singapore attacked its industrial development along many fronts. It immediately sought to improve the infrastructure of ports and transportation networks. It sought to develop industrial estates with the extension of the Jurong Industrial Estate and the creation of smaller estates in Kallang Park, Tanjong Rhu, Bukit Timah, Tiong Bahru and Tanglin Halt. It also sought to attract foreign investment. The PAP set up the Economic Development Board and charged it with guiding Singapore's industrial development. The aim was to turn Singapore into an export-oriented, labor-intensive industrial hub in South East Asia.

In addition to the attraction of investment, the Singapore government created a series of agencies to manage the economic and physical growth of the island to ensure that both fiscal and social agendas were met. The Housing and Development Board (HDB), the Jurong Town Corporation (JTC), the Port of Singapore Authority (PSA), the Singapore Tourist and Promotion Board (STPB), the Public Utilities Board (PUB), the Economic Development Board (EDB), the Development Bank of Singapore (DBS) and the Monetary Authority of Singapore (MAS) are examples of these state enterprises, all of who came into existence in the first five years of independence.

Making the space of the city

Long before the emergence of the New Downtown, Singapore initiated a series of major urban transformations. The 1960s were a period of massive and unprecedented change in Singapore's urban landscape, social structures and economy. As part of this massive industrialization strategy, the island of Singapore began to change. The Jurong Industrial Estate on the southwest corner of the island, for example, was situated on a massive swamp, which required filling and stabilization. The eastern coastline of the island also changed radically with the Bedok reclamation, which created almost 400 hectares of new land. In addition to the creation of industrial estates, the government sought to redress living space in the city. The government initiated a massive urban renewal program. The main

9.10 Images of Singapore shophouses in Tanjong Pagar. To the bottom of the image one can see several rooftops of renovated shophouses.

objectives of the program were slum clearance, revitalization of the city center, improved housing and urban infrastructure.

In conjunction with the massive investment in industrial development and infrastructure, the form of the city was further influenced by the construction of housing estates, by the Housing Development Board (HDB) over large areas of the island. Beginning in the 1960s, the urban renewal program and the HDB housing estates began to mould the fabric of the city and bring the physical form of the city into line with the ambitions of the Singapore government to make the city a modern and efficient metropolis.

The planning for this vision was framed by two United Nations planning initiatives. The first UN plan of 1962 proposed by Erik Lorange, the Norwegian architect, set out the basis for the urban renewal of the city center. The second UN plan of 1963, by Otto Koenigsberger, Charles Abrams and Susumi Kobe established the idea of the ring concept, which was incorporated into the 1971 Concept Plan and guided the development of Singapore up to the 1990s. The ring concept involved the idea of a ring of satellite towns encircling a large green space in the center of the island, which was to be among other things a water catchment area. Along with housing, there was also a major provision of office, retail and hotel space. From 1961 to 1970, Singapore increased the amount of non-residential space in the central business district by a factor of 8.5.

One of the consequences of urban renewal in Singapore was the destruction of large areas of shophouses. The oversupply of commercial space in the 1980s, along with a growing realization of tourist potential in a historic Singapore, resulted in a change in development policy in the central area, which led to the preservation of the remaining shophouses in the historic areas in Chinatown, Tanjong Pagar and Boat Quay.

9.11 The Housing Development Board apartment blocks cover the entire island and more than any other form of building define the landscape of the city.

Toward a thriving world-class city

In less than two generations, Singapore transformed itself from a congested colonial port into a modern and efficient island state, which boasts world-class infrastructure. The Concept Plan has played an important role in this transformation. Since 1971, the Concept Plan has been in place to guide long-term and strategic direction for physical development. The plan is reviewed once every ten years to keep up with changing world trends and Singapore's aspirations.

The beginning of the 1990s brought with it both renewed growth and a major review of planning in Singapore. In 1991, a new Concept Plan was released by the URA which included a series of targets to be reviewed in 2000, 2010 and the year X. Year X was an unknown date when the population of Singapore would be 4 million people, at that time the projected ideal size for the Republic. In reality the target of 4 million was reached in 2000.

The New Downtown was not the only major urban design initiative introduced in 1991. In addition, the 1991 Concept Plan aimed at strengthening a series of subcenters around the island. In addition, a series of information based high technology areas were proposed in recognition of the continuing need to upgrade Singapore's competitive position. In the new plan the central area was to continue to act as the heart of the city, however its dominance was to be reduced through the development of these regional centers. This new concept was a departure from the "ring" idea and instead proposed a "constellation" pattern for development in the island. However, this seems at odds with the New Downtown proposal. The investment needed to make the New Downtown would be enormous. The idea that one would diffuse investment throughout the island and at the same time concentrate on the development of such a massive core suggests that Singapore's planners may have over estimated the amount of growth possible.

The 2001 Concept Plan is being prepared based on the population scenario of 5.5 million people living in Singapore by 2050. Because of this, one of the major considerations of the new plan is that Singapore will have enough housing and recreation space to accommodate this population. It aims to provide both an environment of "quality living" while acknowledging that there must be sufficient space for industry, business and other needs. In terms of housing this inevitably means the provision of higher density housing. The 2001 population density is 5885 persons per square kilometer, which would increase to 7400 persons per square kilometer, still considerably less than current figures for Shanghai (approximately 12,600 per km^2) and equivalent to current figures for Hong Kong (7100 per km^2). In line with the renewed emphasis on urban vitality, the Central Area is once again a major focus for residential development. Under the 2001 Concept Plan the Central Area will see a doubling of population. The New Downtown plays a significant role in the 2001 Concept Plan, both as a new place to live and also as a new location for urban vitality.

The success of this vision, however, will be dependent upon the growth of the republic over the coming decades. The rate of construction of the New Downtown will be difficult to determine for a number of reasons. Between 1970 and just prior to the Asian Economic Crisis in the late 1990s, Singapore increased its total rentable office space from less than 100,000 square meters to a little over 5 million square meters. Since then production of new commercial space has naturally been slower. In 2001 the stock of completed office space increased by 9000 m^2 to 6146 million m^2 (nett) as at the end of the first quarter of 2001. The

9.12 For the majority of the population the HDB estates define the experience of urban life.

9.13 Also built on reclaimed land in Marina Bay is the John Portman designed Marina Mandarin Development.

vacancy rate of office space fell 0.9 of a percentage point to 10.4 percent as at the end of the first quarter of 2001 (URA 2001). This suggests that indeed there is demand for more commercial space on the island, but certainly not at the scale required for the joint development of the core and satellites centers.

The phenomenal growth in office space over the last forty years was driven by a tremendous increase in office employment through the success of Singapore's finance and business activities. The sharp slowdown in the Singapore economy in more recent years has diminished the demand for this type of space. This downturn can be attributed to three key factors. The deepening recessions in 1998 in most parts of Asia led to a slump in Singapore's external demand. Erosion of Singapore's cost competitiveness as a result of the sharp depreciation in the regional currencies exacerbated the decline of exports. Finally, the global over-capacity in the electronics industry contributed to the decline in the manufacturing sector. Although Singapore ranks highly in the Global Competitiveness Survey, the Singapore economy completely lost the phenomenal momen-

9.14 View of the New Downtown model giving an indication of the major open space in the development.

tum of the early part of the 1990s and has entered a new phase of development activity. Given this, one wonders if the island city is no longer going to record the impressive growth figures it did in the 1960s and 1970s. As it approaches developed nation status and as its capacity for growth becomes smaller, the island must make a transition to a mature phase of development. This period is one of transition in Singapore, complicated by the after effects of the Asian economic crisis.

During the tremendous growth phase over the past forty years, Singapore produced on average of 150,000 square meters of commercial space per year, in a period of rapid growth in office employment. The master plan for the New Downtown includes a total of 3 million square meters of commercial office space in the Bayfront Area alone. Assuming that Singapore restricted devel-

opment just to this part of New Downtown area (which does not represent all of the office space in the New Downtown), it would take twenty years to develop the project at this crude average and would require that commercial office space was not built anywhere else on the island. With the development of regional centers this seems highly unlikely. Further, this crude average covers all types of office space. The New Downtown will only accommodate Grade A high technology space suitable for multinational headquarters buildings, further reducing market capacity. The time period of twenty years is likely to be expanded for the reason that continuing advances in communication technologies and changes in the way workplaces are being defined, the demand for Grade A office space may reduce. It therefore seems highly unlikely that this dual satellite and core development policy will lead to the development of the New Downtown. Despite this the Singapore

9.15 View of Central Park in New York City. Clearly this image informed the making of the New Downtown.

planners present the project with unallied conviction.

The New Downtown raises many questions with regards to the appropriateness of contemporary urban form in the global sphere. It is, undeniably, the unencumbered expression of the glory of the city state. It is the ultimate conclusion of forty years of physical planning in Singapore and can be seen both as an expression of hope for the future and a summary of the history of planning in the independent state. It is forward looking in the sheer enormity of the vision – a new city on the bay and a summary in that all planning in Singapore ultimately leads to this conclusion – an expression of Singapore's vision for what a tropical city of excellence might look like.

9.16 View of the New Downtown.

Malaysia

Kuala Lumpur

10.1 View of the Petronas Twin Towers in Kuala Lumpur.
The manufacturing of a global image to present Malaysia to
the world.

10 The Making of a Malaysian Capital

Putrajaya and the Multimedia Super Corridor, Kuala Lumpur

Malaysia welcomes the advent of the Information Age with its promise of a new world order where information, ideas, people, goods and services move across borders in the most cost-effective and liberal ways.

http://www.mdc.com.my

The Multimedia Super Corridor (MSC) is a giant test-bed for experimenting with not only multimedia technology, but also, and more importantly, the evolution of a new way of life in the unfolding age of information and knowledge. The MSC is, therefore, "Malaysia's gift to the world," a creation that welcomes the involvement of the global community in sharing the useful lessons of multimedia development.

The Honorable Dato Seri
Dr. Mahathir bin Mohamad
Prime Minister of Malaysia

Malaysia's Multimedia Super Corridor (MSC) is an integrated environment with ambitions to be the perfect global multimedia context. It is a project that encapsulates the ambition of an entire nation in its attempt to fully integrate with the global economy and reap the rewards that such integration will bring. It is the direct result of the Malaysian government's attempts to secure a profitable and productive future in the next century. The MSC is a "corridor" of development covering an area 15 kilometers wide and 50 kilometers long. It starts at the Kuala Lumpur City Center (KLCC), the site of the world's tallest build-

ing, and continues south to the site of the region's largest international airport, the Kuala Lumpur International Airport (KLIA).

The MSC is a massive infrastructure project designed to provide a state of the art information based environment capable of securing competitive advantage over other such science cities in the region. Its competition include Hong Kong's Cyberport Information Technology Park and Silicon Harbour, Singapore's Singapore One development and the new West Zone of Zhongguancun in Beijing. In the minds of MSC's creators information will be the new currency in the twenty-first century. The control of information distribution and indeed its content will be the emerging competitive battleground for city governments in the decades ahead. The MSC includes two of the world's first "Smart Cities," Putrajaya, the new seat of government and administrative capital of Malaysia and Cyberjaya, an intelligent city with multimedia industries and operational headquarters for multinationals wishing to direct their worldwide manufacturing and trading activities using multimedia technology. The Malaysian government aims to fashion Kuala Lumpur into an important decision and control node in the new economy of the twenty-first century.

This chapter examines the context of the MSC and Kuala Lumpur and will explore in detail the design and development of Putrajaya. Putrajaya is one of the most important components of the MSC. In total the project covers an area of 14,700 hectares. This area is made up of a number of sub-areas including the Putrajaya Commercial Precinct, which covers approximately 7500 hectares and will accommodate a population of 240,000 people and another site, covering 2790 hectares, which will be a residential development with an estimated population of 80,000 people. The core area of the project encompasses 4390 hectares and will be examined in greater detail. The core accommodates government functions, business and cultural facilities. It will employ 79,000 government employees and 59,000 private sector employees (Mahathir 1998: 35). Prior to the start of construction, however the site was a collection of state lands, rubber and palm oil plantations and Malay Reserve areas. From this Putrajaya will develop to be the second city of Kuala Lumpur.

Kuala Lumpur or literally "muddy confluence" is the capital of Malaysia. It takes its name from the confluence of the rivers Gombak and Klang. It is a city whose development history displays the phys-

ical effects of the Asian economic miracle. A decade prior to the Asian economic crisis the Malaysian economy was renowned for its incredible economic growth achieved through aggressive economic strategies and showcased by bold infrastructure and construction projects. The relationship between urban policy and economic policy is very clear in the Malaysian context with the Malaysian government recognizing that the city is an important piece of global infrastructure and through its manipulation they have attempted to facilitate economic policies addressed toward issues of global competition.

Many of the physical changes occurring in the fabric of the city of Kuala Lumpur are in direct response to globalization policy initiatives from the national government. These policies led to the development of certain kinds of building projects. The focus of activity within Kuala Lumpur has changed with the recent completion of KLCC as economic activity, people and traffic circulation

10.2 View across Putrajaya Lake. On top of the hill in the distance is the palatial residence of Malaysia's Prime Minister (copyright Anand Krishnan 2002).

have shifted away from Jalan Bukit Bintang to the new node. New projects in and around Kuala Lumpur are now providing spaces where new city forms are being tested. The development of projects such as the Multimedia Super Corridor, Putrajaya, Cyberjaya, the Petronas Twin Towers (the tallest buildings in the world), Kuala Lumpur City Center, Kuala Lumpur International Airport (the largest in the region), Kuala Lumpur Linear City (the longest building in the world), the environmentally controversial Bakun Dam, the Kedah Reclamation, the Northern International Airport, the bridge to Sumatra and the New Johor to Singapore Bridge all represent Malaysia's expression of itself in built form and are the physical outcome of Prime Minister Mahathir Mohamad's Wawasan 2020 Plan.

Malaysian progress and Wawasan 2020

Wawasan 2020 (Vision 2020) is a national government initiative that aims to move Malaysia to developed nation status by the year 2020. Wawasan 2020 is a comprehensive series of policy goals that seek to double Malaysia's real gross domestic product every ten years between 1990 and 2020. The economic objective is to secure the establishment of a competitive, diversified and balanced economy with a mature and widely based industrial sector, a modern and mature agriculture sector and an efficient and productive services sector in an economy that is technologically proficient.

In Malaysia there is a strong sense of identity and a constant attempt to reinforce a Malaysianness in every endeavor. The Prime Minister of Malaysia is explicit that Malaysia should not follow the path of other countries. The Malaysian model of a developed economy is envisaged as different from other developed economies. In his paper entitled *Malaysia: The Way Forward*, presented to the Malaysian Business Council in 1991, Prime Minister Mahathir Mohamad described the development model for Malaysia:

> Without being a duplicate of any of them [meaning other developed nations], we can still be developed. We would be a developed country in our own mould. Malaysia should not be developed only in the economic sense. It must be a nation that is fully developed along all dimensions: economically, politically, socially, spiritually, psychologically and culturally. By the year 2020, Malaysia can be a united nation, with a confident Malaysian society, infused by strong moral and ethical values, living in a society that is democratic, liberal and tolerant, caring, economically just and equitable, progressive and prosperous and in full possession of an economy that is competitive, dynamic, robust and resilient.
>
> (Mahathir 1991)

Projects such as Putrajaya are representative of an attempt to express both this ambition and actualize it. These projects also reflect aspects of larger changes in the Malaysian economy and society. Malaysia's economy has been quite literally transformed within the last decade, moving rapidly away from a low technology commodity based environment to one where manufacturing and the service sectors are employing higher and more sophisticated technology. Rapid industrialization, coupled with a shift toward more capital-intensive production, has changed human resources development in Malaysia with an emerging social mobility. Currently, the country is facing a shortage of trained people, particularly in the fields of engineering and management. Despite these deficiencies, the ambitions of Wawasan 2020's authors remain.

Developing Wawasan 2020 in 1991 the economic planners in Malaysia predicted that the GDP

10.3 Petronas Twin Towers, Kuala Lumpur.

should be about eight times larger by the year 2020 than it was in 1990. To achieve this the Malaysian economy needs to grow by an average of about 7 percent (in real terms) annually over thirty years (ISIS 2001). To fuel this growth, the Malaysian government embarked on a tremendous construction plan. This was locally referred to as Mahathir's Megaprojects. Economic analysts and other observers have expressed skepticism over the economic justification for the megaprojects and also in the reality of 7 percent growth over a thirty-year time period. However, despite the skepticism the sheer number of such projects and scale of the government's vision are impressive (opposition to such projects can be seen on web sites such as http://www.freemalaysia.com).

The Asian economic crisis has delayed or stopped most of these large-scale construction projects. In addition, the crisis put a major brake on Malaysia's advancement to developed nation status and proved to be a setback to the dream of Vision 2020. Compounding the already serious problem of the economy, Malaysia is currently subject to political turmoil unprecedented in its intensity since 1969. However, despite the present difficulties, the period from 1959 to 1997 was one of meteoric growth.

Multimedia Super Corridor

Based within decades "miracle" growth emerged the idea of creating megaprojects in order to do two things for Malaysia. The first would be to construct an infrastructure capable of attracting, keeping and fostering global control and capital. The aim simply was to build a city attractive to international operations in order that they locate there. The second was to simultaneously express the stature of the Malaysian nation by building the best, the tallest and the longest in the world. The MSC is the largest and most ambitious of these initiatives.

The Multimedia Super Corridor (MSC) is the nucleus of Malaysia's strategic vision for its new economy. The US$10 billion MSC is Malaysia's futuristic multimedia zone, aiming to accommodate the world's top information technology companies. In line with its vision the MSC houses a world class IT network consisting of a high speed and cost competitive telecommunication infrastructure offered to MSC designated companies (Cyberjaya 2001). The MSC is in actuality a zone within which a series of large scale urban and infrastructure projects can be found.

The northern focus of the MSC is the Kuala Lumpur City Centre (KLCC), a 40-hectare development in the heart of the city on the site of the former Selangor Turf Club. The first phase of KLCC included the construction of the Petronas Twin Towers project designed by Cesar Pelli, which provides an additional 385,000 square meters of office space to the city center. The eighty-eight-story towers were completed in 1997. They are the tallest buildings in the world at 1483 feet (451.9 m) tall. This makes them 33 feet taller than Chicago's Sears Tower. The towers incorporate geometric elements from Islamic architecture. The floor plan of each tower is composed of two rotated squares inscribed by a series of circles. The architecture of the towers encapsulates the spirit of the Malaysian nation, aiming to express unity, harmony, stability and rationality. These are important principles of Islam and appear as themes in many speeches of Dr. Mahathir (see Mahathir 1998).

Images of these towers now dominate all of Malaysia's publicity material from tourist maps to government web sites. While one can question the need for such tall buildings, particularly in light of September 11, their iconography remains tremendously important for marketing Malaysia on the global stage. Not only does the project draw international attention to Kuala Lumpur it also represents the idea that Malaysia is just as good, if not better, than any other "developed" nation. It is a symbol of Malaysian accomplishment and marks an arrival of a new level of development.

Other projects proposed with the MSC include the now defunct, Kuala Lumpur LinearCity (KLLC), a linear collection of eight development packages that were to occupy the banks and more interestingly 12 kilometers of air rights over the Klang River, which winds its way through the center of the city. It was to have included the longest building in the world, aptly named Giga World. The best way to describe Giga World would be to imagine a 2-kilometer long tube suspended on arches winding along the path of the river. If one were able to cut a section through this tube one would find fourteen levels. On the top four levels of the tube one would encounter "River Walk," a themed simulation echoing the actual river experience that exists some ten stories below, which was to include authentic Venetian paddleboats (see Marshall 1999).

Cyberjaya (Cyber City) is another of the principal projects within the MSC. The Cyberjaya Flagship Zone covers an area of 2894 hectares and is being developed as a self-contained intelligent city. It aims to be the ideal business and living environment for knowledge-economy enterprises. Developed by Setia Haruman Sdn Bhd, as the master developer, it is strategically positioned and accessible via a network of highways. It is approximately 30 minutes from the KLCC and 20 minutes from the International Airport (Cyberjaya 2001). Cyberjaya boasts an advanced City Command Center (CCC), which is the "brain" of the city. The CCC integrates systems and subsystems within the city and provides value-added services for the residents within a citywide community network, which provides interactive broadband services and fast internet access. The project has an array of marketing material targeted toward the global investor. (Readers should visit http://cyberjaya-msc.com/av/ where project fly-throughs allow a view of the development.) The audio-visual material from the promotional website displays an urban form reminiscent of low-density American business parks. Buildings appear casually arrayed amongst lush tropical vegetation. Curving and winding roads appear to cut track marks over this landscape.

The project that best exemplifies the characteristics of the Malaysian megaprojects however, is the New Federal Administrative Center of Putrajaya, conceived as a deliberate expression of confidence for a postcolonial country at the dawn of the new economy on the verge of reaping informational age returns. Where the Petronas Towers represent Malaysia's efforts to encapsulate its beliefs and ambitions into the form of a single project, Putrajaya represents an attempt to capture and express these same ambitions in the making of urban form. In Putrajaya we find clear evidence of how the Malaysian government thinks about and produces global urban form within the competitive sphere of the global economy.

Economic planning, global competition and Malaysian megaprojects

The vision behind the Malaysian economy and the creation of the Malaysian megaprojects comes from the Economic Planning Unit (EPU) of the Prime Minister's Department, responsible for formulating policies and strategies for medium and long-term economic development with the overriding objective of achieving national unity (see http://www.epu.jpm.my/). The EPU guides the economic direction of the government through a series of strategic plans. To understand how economic planning manifests large-scale urban developments one has to understand something of the EPU's strategies. The most relevant to this discussion are the Second Outline Perspective Plan (1990s) and the Third Outline Perspective

10.4 View across Kuala Lumpur toward the Dataran Merdeka (formerly the Selangor Club Padang), once the focal point, and cricket green, of the British colonial presence in Malaysia.

Plan (2001–10). Both have contributed greatly to the shift in Malaysia's investment from a labor-based economy to an information-based economy.

The Second Outline Perspective Plan (OPP2), operational from 1991 to 2000 provided the platform for the implementation of the National Development Policy (NDP). This broad economic development framework strengthened Malaysia's position as a modern industrial-based economy and as a result brought significant economic and social progress. The NDP aimed at striking an optimum balance between the goals of economic growth and equity, with the ultimate intention of eliminating social, economic and regional inequalities. During the OPP2 period, Malaysia witnessed the strengthening of its manufacturing base, both in terms of its contribution to growth as well as composition of industries. The services sector was expanded in size and improved in qualitative terms with the changes in the economy.

Malaysia's economic performance over the last decades has been characterized by a high growth rate attained in an environment of low inflation and low unemployment (World Bank 1993). However, in 1997–8 the Malaysian economy suffered as a result of the Asian economic crisis. The full impact was felt in 1998, causing a severe contraction in the Malaysian economy. During the Third Outline Perspective Plan (OPP3) period (from 2001 to 2010), the government's efforts will focus on raising the resilience and international competitiveness of the economy to a new and higher threshold. Some of this will involve developing a resistance to the impact of globalization through the reinforcement of Malaysian identity and insulation of the Malaysian economy from external influence. This will be necessary if Malaysia is to have any chance of achieving the status of a fully developed country as envisaged in Wawasan

2020. The Malaysian government hopes that this will allow the country to take advantage of the opportunities that will arise with globalization and to reduce the disadvantages. In order to do this the government is aiming to secure competitive advantage in the next century by turning Malaysia into the information-processing center of South East Asia.

Malaysia is placing great faith in the promise of the knowledge economy. If it is able to successfully develop a knowledge infrastructure it hopes that this will strengthen Malaysia's capability to innovate, to create new knowledge and expertise, which can then be exported. Currently Malaysia is importing this knowledge and expertise; however there is a constant drive toward knowledge transfer. This was also part of the contractual agreements between the foreign contractors and the developers of KLCC. Part of these agreements required a formal training and information exchange between the foreigners and the locals engaged with the project. In addition, the knowledge-based economy will complement and accelerate the change from an input-driven to a productivity-driven growth strategy, a major policy thrust initiated under the Seventh Malaysia Plan.

Several initiatives have already commenced to facilitate the development of a knowledge-based economy. The Malaysian government has emphasized investment in the areas of science and technology, research and development, infrastructure and financing to position itself prominently in the global map of knowledge-based economies. This is where Dr. Mahathir's goal of Malaysia deciding its own destiny will be made.

Malaysia's engagement with the global sphere exposes the complexity and duality of national identity under the forces of globalization. Mention has already been made that in much of the globalization literature there is an interest in the flattening of social and cultural difference through the process of globalization. What is interesting about Malaysia's engagement with globalization is that it is one of both immersion and resistance. Malaysia is simultaneously pursuing greater connections to global markets, indeed proposing that it will become a key node in the global economy, while at the same time asserting independence through the definition of Malaysian identity and self-determinacy. The history of Malaysia can be seen as a process of a gradual emergence of Malaysian identity through a conscious search for its definition. Projects such as the MSC and Putrajaya must be understood in light of this duality. It is important to understand some of this history to appreciate Malaysia's emerging nationalism and how this is tied into the symbolic representation of projects such as the Petronas Twin Towers at KLCC or Putrajaya.

Malaysia and its rise to tiger status

Malaysia has been engaged in international exchanges for over 700 years. The modern story of Malaysia starts with the introduction of Islam to the Malay Peninsula in the 1400s, over two hundred years before the first Europeans arrived. The peninsula has been influenced by several European powers, first the Portuguese and then the Dutch in the 1600s. The British, who arrived at the end of the eighteenth century, soon included what was then Malaya into their expanding empire. In 1880 Kuala Lumpur was made the base for British operations in the region and in 1896 it became the capital of the Federated Malay States. The early economy of the Federated States was based on the extraction of tin and the cultivation of rubber plantations. These activities attracted large numbers of Chinese and Indians who worked as

10.5 View across Kuala Lumpur toward the Maybank Building.

laborers on railroads, as rubber tappers or administrative workers. Eventually this influx changed the ethnic balance of the country. Once the new immigrant pattern was established the Chinese began to dominate the management of the economy, creating tensions between them and the Malays.

After World War II, the British regained control of Malaya after losing it to the Japanese. Upon their return the British were faced with many segments of local population who actively rebelled against the imposition of colonial rule. In 1948, the Communist Party of Malaya began a guerrilla war against the colonial government, beginning twelve years of political and social unrest known as "The emergency." The British struggled to suppress the insurgents; however the unrest spread and although the Communists were ultimately defeated, other groups such as United Malays' National Organization (UMNO) and the Malayan Chinese Association (MCA) were able to negotiate greater political representation. On August 31, 1957, the Federation of Malaya achieved independence (Merdeka) and Tunku Abdul Rahman became Malaysia's first Prime Minister. The Federation of Malaya was composed of Malaya (now Peninsular Malaysia), Singapore, Sarawak and Sabah. In August 1965 Singapore seceded from the federation and became an independent republic. Malaysia is actually composed of two non-contiguous regions; West Malaysia, which includes the Malay Peninsula and East Malaysia on the island of Borneo. Kuala Lumpur, the capital of the country, is situated in West Malaysia.

Upon independence Malaysia struggled to bring together a series of diverse ethnic groups and to develop its own sense of self, separate from the identity and role it played under colonial control. The history of Malaysia since that time has been one of developing economic success and working toward the presentation of a unified national iden-

tity. The country's staggering economic growth laid the foundation for this presentation. Initially the government was forced to concentrate on economic issues, social improvement and political stability. As the country matured and economic and social gains were made, the government moved to claim an international presence through the development of a Malaysian identity. This can be seen in Malaysia's growing involvement in regional affairs and in the crafting of a carefully presented international image. One aspect of this is the construction of architectural symbols. All nations construct buildings that represent their nationhood. Malaysia is no different. However, it must be understood that years of planning preceded their construction.

Soon after independence, the first of many Malaysian Plans, the economic direction policies for the country, were initiated. Each plan operates for five years before it is reviewed and replaced by a subsequent plan. When the First Malaysian Plan (1966–70) started, the agricultural sector accounted for 31.5 percent of the country's GDP. In this early plan, agriculture was seen as an engine for economic growth. This gradually changed as the country started to develop its industrial position. By the Third Malaysian Plan (1976–80), agriculture's share of the GDP had declined to 27 percent (Mahathir 1998: 18). The agricultural sector was and is still of major importance to the Malaysian economy. Malaysia is one of the world's leading producers of palm oil. However the government realized that in order to stake a claim in the global economy the country would have to diminish its reliance on agriculture and improve its industrial position.

The country's drive toward industrialization has had tremendous consequences on the urbanization in the country. Principal among these has been a migration into the cities as people moved off the land. The majority of this population was

Malay, who moved from low-paid agricultural jobs to find new employment in the cities. During this process there developed a significant income disparity between the Malays and the Chinese, producing tremendous political and social conflict culminating in race riots in 1967. To address these disparities the Malaysian government developed a series of policies to address both racial heterogeneity and also the association of ethnicity and economic functions. These had tremendous consequences for Malaysia's industrial development.

The introduction of the New Economic Policy (NEP) in 1971, an affirmative action program aimed at improving the relative positions of the economically disadvantaged Malay community, stressed the growth of labor intensive resource-based (processing of rubber, tin, palm oil, etc.) and non-resource based manufacturing. In this sense Malaysia's postcolonial industrialization story is different from Singapore and partially explains the relative differences between the countries. Malaysia concentrated on the development of labor-intensive industries and while this may have produced slower economic growth it was politically expedient in providing jobs for the Malay population. Since the 1980s this emphasis has gradually changed, as the Malaysian government has attempted to shift the basis of the economy to make it more competitive.

Once the foundations were established, Malaysia aggressively pursued both an adjustment in economic direction and the construction of large-scale urban projects. Indeed the two were seen as one and the same. Through the provision of new spaces in the city, new economic activities could be fostered and in addition these new projects provided Malaysia with an opportunity to construct symbols of Malaysia's progress. The greatest

10.6 View of the Central Business District of Kuala Lumpur.

177

symbol of them all is the New Federal Administrative District, Putrajaya.

Putrajaya – flagship of a nation

The idea of developing a New Federal Administrative District dates from the end of the 1980s. Aware of the pressures brought on by growth and traffic congestion in Kuala Lumpur, the Economic Planning Unit of the Prime Minister's Office began thinking about developing a new administrative center away from the old core to both improve the urban environment and to sustain Kuala Lumpur as a premier business center. While the new town development of Sha Alam was perhaps the more obvious choice for the new center, it was considered too remote from Kuala Lumpur and the already planned international airport. Subsequently other sites were also evaluated. These included a proposal for the new center developed by Kenzo Tange on a site in the Genting Highlands but this idea was considered too expensive

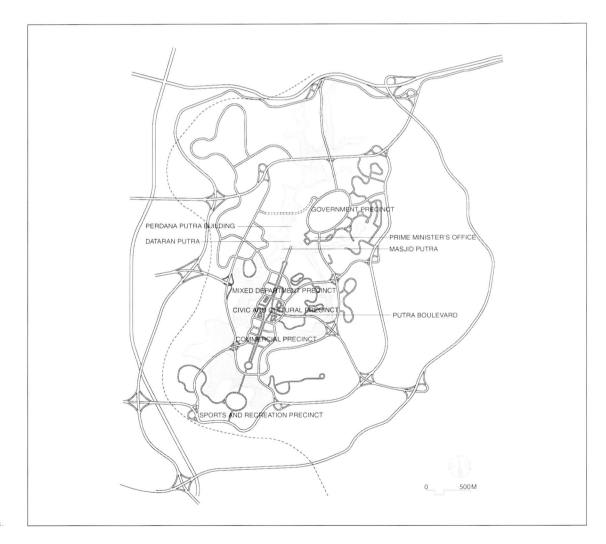

Map of Putrajaya, Malaysia.

and its location was politically unacceptable because it was determined that the new center needed to be within the boundaries of the State of Selangor. After studying several alternative sites, the government decided, in June of 1993, to locate the Federal Government Administrative Center to Perang Besar in Selangor because of its adjacency to the site of the proposed International Airport. Although at that time the MSC concept was still in its infancy (see Mahathir 1998: 34), there was always the idea that this new administrative center would be a critical component of it.

In 1995, Putrajaya Holdings Sdn. Bhd was created to be the developer of the new city. Its shareholders are Petronas, Khazanah Nasional Berhad (the government investment arm) and the Kumpulan Wang Amanah Negara. Putrajaya Holdings is building the new city in partnership with five of the nation's leading developers, Hong Leong Properties, Malaysian Plantations, Malaysian Resources Corporation Berhad, Peremba and SP Setia Berhad. Kuala Lumpur City Centre Berhad (KLCC Bhd.) is the project manager and was included in the development team because of their success in managing the construction of the Petronas Twin Towers project.

Design work started in 1993 and the first visions of the new city emerged in 1994. A group of five of Malaysia's leading architects produced schemes for what this new city might look like. Of these visions one particular concept emerged which was to define the future of the project – a Malaysianized garden city concept. Garden cities have a rather long intellectual history stemming from Ebenezer Howard's work at the end of the nineteenth century. Singapore also uses the term to describe itself and because of this it is curious that the Malaysians would adopt it as the defining concept for their new capital city, given the intense competition between these two countries.

Nevertheless, the garden city concept defined the development of the project. The winning concept established a city on a lake and utilized a series of formal beaux-arts inspired axes along which a sequence of nodes would be located. Each node would create the basis for identifiable precincts. The most important precinct, to the north of the site and sitting on top of a hill, would be the Government Precinct. Here the Prime Minister's Office and other important government departments were to be located. From here the rest of the city would unfold, responding to a series of the axes and a newly formed water body.

The concept's theme was reflected in its approach to landscape with buildings situated in lush vegetation. The concept incorporated a series of open spaces, including a wetland environment created by the construction of a dam on Sungai Chuau and Sungai Bisa, two small rivers. This vision guided the production of the first master plan, which was released in 1995. In the same year the project was named in memory of Malaysia's first Prime Minister, Tunku Abdul Rahman Putra Al-Haj (Jaya translates from the Malay for city).

The 1995 plan divided the Core Area of Putrajaya into five precincts, which persisted in the construction of the project – the Government Precinct, the Mixed Development Precinct, the Civic and Cultural Precinct, the Commercial Precinct and the Sports and Recreation Precinct. Also evident was the idea of a 4-kilometer long boulevard, which acts to create a sense of unity to the project by connecting across all of the precincts. It is the spine along which everything else hinges. Although the first master plan encapsulated the vision of a garden city, it failed to adequately deal with issues of infrastructure and the extreme topography of the site and so some time after its release another master planning effort was necessary to rectify critical shortcomings. The nature of the site was extremely hilly and it became

10.7 View across Putrajaya Lake (copyright Anand Krishnan 2002).

apparent that a new city could only be built with further study (Jebasingam Issace John 2000).

This new effort accepted the foundation of the 1995 master plan and worked toward developing a better relationship between the plan as it existed and the site. The choice of Perang Besar meant that inevitably any development would have to entail a considerable amount of cut and fill. The aim of the second planning effort was, therefore, to reduce the amount of earthworks needed to execute the vision and as a result of this to make the transportation infrastructure more efficient (Jebasingam Issace John 2000). Site clearance and preparation started in 1996.

The final version of the master plan maintains the idea of the five core precincts. The Government Precinct is located at the northern end of the core. The federal government ministries, departments and agencies are accommodated here. The Prime Minister's Office sits at a prime position in the Government Precinct looking down over the Dataran Putra (People's Square) to the Putra Boulevard, which extends from this point down through the Core precincts, forming the major axis in the development. From this spine the other precincts are orientated. The Mixed Development Precinct has commercial and government buildings, parks and open spaces, and residential areas. At the center of the core lies the Civic and Cultural Precinct, housing Putrajaya's museums, art galleries, theaters, archives and amphitheater. The Commercial Precinct forms the southern gateway into Putrajaya Island, at the other end of Putra Boulevard. It will become the commercial core of the new city. On the opposite shore of the lake, terminating the Putra Boulevard, the Sports and Recreation Precinct will be the center for recreational pursuits.

10.8 Residential complex in Putrajaya (copyright Anand Krishnan 2002).

Surrounding the core, separated by water and green space are a group of residential precincts. Sitting on the edge of the lake is the Grand Mosque of Putrajaya, which orients itself to the Kiblat axis extending toward Mecca. The imposing structure of the Prime Minister's residence also sits on the lake, commanding a prime position in the plan. Integral to the idea of a garden city is the creation of an extensive wetland system in the upper reaches of Sungai Chuau and Sungai Bisa, to the very north of the project. The total area of the wetlands is approximately 120 hectares. The aim of this system is to filter water before it arrives in Putrajaya Lake. Over twenty species of wetland plants are incorporated into the wetland systems.

By car from Kuala Lumpur one arrives into the oval loop road that forms the circulation for the Government Precinct. Despite passing through gates and entering a landscaped drive, one is actually quite surprised to arrive at the back entrance of the Prime Minister's Office. One has to move around the Prime Minister's Office to see the city unfolding on the lower elevations. While one is stunned and impressed at the grandeur of the scene below, most of the buildings in the Government Precinct, however, appear to be rather dull office buildings of little merit. The exception is the Prime Minister's Office, which is simply palatial. It is six stories tall and sits, looking down on the Dataran Putra. It is a large rectangular building, clad in brown stone and at its top sits an enormous onion shaped Islamic dome. From this vantage point one is able to view the Putra Boulevard under construction. Moving down and in front of the Prime Minister's Office one arrives at the ceremonial Dataran Putra, a large circular *square*, which has several levels paved in patterns inspired from Islamic geometry. Here formal ceremonies and military parades will be held. An enormous mosque dominates Dataran

10.9 The Perdana Putra Building is the palatial office of the Prime Minister of Malaysia, a green domed six-story granite edifice the size of several city blocks looming over manicured hills with green glass windows and surrounded by artificial mangrove lakes filled with bulrushes (copyright Anand Krishnan 2002).

10.10 The pink-domed Masjid Putra is a major focal point within Putrajaya, located at the termination of the Persiaran Perdana axis. The mosque consists of three main functional areas – the prayer hall, the "Sahn" or courtyard, learning facilities and function rooms. An impressive minaret built in five tiers, stands 116 m tall – the tallest minaret in the region. The mosque can accommodate 15,000 worshippers at any one time (copyright Anand Krishnan 2002).

Putra and makes it clear that Malaysia's identity is closely tied to the Islamic beliefs of its Malay citizenry.

The residential districts around the core are also under construction. They appear to be very well laid out versions of contemporary Malaysian residential subdivisions that one might expect in the more affluent of Kuala Lumpur's suburbs. Architecturally such housing incorporates a strange mixture of domestic vocabularies that would not be out of place in some new communities in the United States. The housing types vary and include detached bungalows, townhouses and high-rise residential buildings. This housing is earmarked for the government workers, though the plan

10.11 The Prime Minister's residence on the other side of the Putra Lake, derisively called "mahligai," or palace, by its critics (copyright Anand Krishnan 2002).

allows for a percentage of private sales as well (Jebasingam Issace John 2000).

Designing the capital city

Putrajaya follows in a tradition of designed administrative centers in the twentieth century. Most readers will be aware of cities such as Brasilia and Chandigargh. Putrajaya, however, in plan and articulation shares a closer association with Walter Burley Griffin's plan for Canberra. Not only do both capitals surround artificial lakes, the plan of Putrajaya would not look out of place in John Reps' critical compilation *Canberra 1912: Plans and Planners of the Australian Capital Competition*. In this book, Reps presents the top five entries in the 1912 competition for the Australian capital and explains the context from which they were derived (see Reps 1997). Each of the entries can be seen as attempts to define the "ideal" capital city for that time and in looking through them one is struck by how little capital city making has progressed in almost a century.

In examining Putrajaya, the language of the plan seems to be derived from the same vocabulary as some of the 1912 plans. One can clearly see elements of such famous garden cities as Letchworth and Hampstead Garden Suburb embedded in the planning of Putrajaya's streets. In addition, the formal and civic gestures of the plan appear inspired by City Beautiful renderings, recalling Daniel Burnham's famous 1909 design for the center of Chicago or the Senate Park Commission's plan for Central Washington D.C. of 1902. In comparing Putrajaya to the Canberra competition plans, it employs some of the same language as Eliel Saarinen's second placed scheme, with its combination of fluid curves and formal axes. In addition, Putrajaya's hierarchy of civic monuments resembles that of Griffin's plan with its emphasis on Canberra's Government Precinct.

It is interesting to compare the sketches and artists' renditions of the Canberra schemes to Putrajaya. John Reps reproduces several images from the 1912 competition in his book. One in particular stands out. In a site selection report of 1908, Charles Coulter depicted a vision, which captures the civic expression of what a capital city should be. In his watercolor rendering of a "Federal capital at Lake George" he depicted a "vision of monumental buildings topped by domes and towers clustered around the lakeshore or set on imposing hillside sites" (Reps 1997: 52). This vision is remarkable in that it was never fully realized in Canberra but in many respects is being completed in Putrajaya. Palatial structures sit on the crests of hills, their importance magnified by domes. Placement of these buildings is carefully orchestrated to create picturesque views across the water. Structures come down and meet the edge of the lake, constructing a civic edge to the

water. This is countered by softer edges from which views are taken of these important elements. The whole plan is an orchestration of civic power and national pride. Although the language of the architecture may vary, the massing and form of the buildings in Coulter's image are remarkably the same as that found in Putrajaya. This does not suggest that the designers of Putrajaya even knew of Coulter's drawings, although one would assume they had studied Canberra.

What it shows is that there is a kind of recipe deemed appropriate for government cities and that this recipe has not changed very much over the course of one hundred years. It also shows that such a recipe is valid despite the influence of globalization. Indeed such a recipe, with its ambition for local expression through constructed urban situations, may be more important because of the diminution of place under the rubric of

10.12 Charles Coulter "An Ideal City, Lake George, NSW." Accession No. R134. By permission of the National Library of Australia.

10.13 View toward Putrajaya Hospital showing the construction of the city in progress (copyright Anand Krishnan 2002).

globalization. This recipe provides a very particular set of elements, which are carefully combined to produce the appropriate level of civic grandeur. Such a recipe, although apparently universal, is used to create an expression of national achievement and identity. In this way Putrajaya, Canberra and even Washington D.C. share the fact that their creation was used by their nations to make a statement of national maturity. Their creation not only announces to the world a coming of age; it also expresses the nature and quality of a nation's sense of itself.

The plans of government cities also announce what a nation believes to be important. In this regard the plan for Putrajaya is significantly different from both Washington and Canberra. In Washington the Mall is the civic space of the city. The organization of this space expresses and represents the democratic system of American government. The long axis of the Mall focuses on the Capitol Building, which holds the House and Senate Office buildings, the Library of Congress and the Supreme Court. It is a symbol of the American people and their government; the meeting place of the nation's legislature. The short axis, important in the plan but subordinate in emphasis, focuses on the White House, the office of the President. In the American tradition of democracy it must be understood that the President is viewed as an ordinary citizen, who for a short period of time is asked to serve the people. Although the presidency is a powerful office, it is not seen in the same way as a king or ruler. The American President is an individual of and for the people of the United States. In its own way Canberra expresses and represents the democratic system of Australian government. The focus of the Canberra plan is the House of Parliament, where the two houses of government, the Senate and the House of Representatives, reside. This not only represents the core of the Australian Federal City; it represents the idea that it is the combined structure of an elected government that is the caretaker of the country.

In Putrajaya the focus for the plan is quite different. Despite being the Federal Administrative

10.14 Street scene within Putrajaya (copyright Anand Krishnan 2002).

Center, Putrajaya does not house Malaysia's Parliament House, as it is still situated near the Lake Gardens in Kuala Lumpur, where the House of Representatives and the Senate have been located since 1963. In its place is a precinct that accommodates the most important offices of the ruling Umno party. The most important building in Putrajaya is the Prime Minister's Office, which commands the highest elevation in Putrajaya and an imposing location in relation to the Putra Axis. The location of the Prime Minister's Office, although not directly on axis with the Boulevard, designates it as the most important building in Putrajaya and by extension the most important office in the land.

The dominance of the Prime Minister's Office in Putrajaya is an expression of the esteem to which Dr. Mahathir is held in Malaysia. He became Prime Minister on July 16, 1981 and is Malaysia's longest-serving Prime Minister as well as being one of the world's longest serving leaders. The seventy-six year old is credited with propelling Malaysia along its development miracle. But while this extraordinary man and the office that he holds are important to Malaysia it is surprising that the Parliament House, symbol of Malaysian democracy did not figure at all in the concept or making of Putrajaya. The idea that the Parliament House may move to Putrajaya has been discussed in the Malaysian Parliament. However "such a possibility depended on Putrajaya's future expansion . . . but it would require thorough study though" (Yatim 2000). Since Putrajaya aims to be a symbol of Malaysian city making this is somewhat surprising. As an expression of Malaysian nationhood and identity the omission of the Parliament House from the planning of Putrajaya can be read as a dimin-

10.15 Street scene in Kuala Lumpur. The comparison between the order of Putrajaya and disorder of Kuala Lumpur is part of the Malaysian government's attempts to present a cultivated image to the global economy.

ishing of parliament's presence at the expense of an exultation of Dr. Mahathir's twenty-year reign. This represents a marked difference to the expressions of both the Washington and Canberra plans.

The intelligent garden city

Putrajaya is similar to Canberra in its relationship to landscape. Neither city will ever develop the kind of mass of built form that one associates with cities such as New York, Chicago or Boston. Instead the city is a kind of engraving across the earth where roads become lines or traces through the landscape. These generate the inscription of the city within a cultivated landscape. The buildings themselves sit in a carefully articulated open space such that they have little to do with each other. The city is best appreciated from distant views or from elevated positions where one is able to see it as a whole. Only then will one appreciate the relationship of the individual pieces to the larger idea. Except for moments within the project, such as within Dataran Putra for example, one will not get this sense of the project as it utilizes a very low density of building and so the possibility of any urban experience is reduced. Rather, the experience is similar to being in a very large suburban office park.

This feeling is reinforced by the singularity of the programs within the various precincts and the articulation of buildings to each other. Having too much space in cities is just as bad as too little. Too much open space reduces the urban definition of a place, leads to buildings being situated at distance to each other and denies the possibility of an active street life. These kinds of places inevitably reinforce the primacy of the motor vehicle. In Putrajaya this leads to a lack of intensity that might support life in the project. The result is that as one moves through the space of the city there are few people to be seen, all of them being cloistered away in their office buildings. Canberra too struggles with this inevitability.

In addition to the low density urban development with the project, defined open space accounts for approximately 40 percent of the plan in Putrajaya. This allows for a series of interconnected public parks that are linked throughout the city. This web of green will allow for movement through the city on foot or bike and will separate the various precincts. While this is laudable, what is lacking is a tension between density of building and open space, which would heighten the power and presence of this green network.

10.16 The Prime Minister's Office, Putrajaya (copyright Anand Krishnan 2002).

10.17 View of the Putrajaya construction site (copyright Anand Krishnan 2002).

Despite the ambitions for an intelligent garden city, Putrajaya is not an environment that will hail a reconsideration of an urban ecology in the twenty-first century. Since Putrajaya is a project that claims to be an intelligent garden city one should expect to see a heightened level of articulation of issues relating to urban sustainability. An intelligent garden city might claim a territory as a precedent for green urban development or it might have become a model for innovative urban design that leads the world in urban ecological technology. Given that this is the most important project with the MSC, itself a twenty-first century project, one would expect that issues of urban sustainability and ecological technology would drive the formation of the project. Indeed, Cyberjaya does a better job at addressing these kinds of issues. Examples of large-scale attempts at urban sustainable development are still relatively rare, although there are some precedents. One example is the work currently underway in Vancouver with the South East False Creek development, which aims at developing a new way to conceive, design and maintain urban projects with higher ecological and sustainability standards. Putrajaya does include elements of wetland and certainly presents this aspect of the scheme in ecological terms but what is missing is a larger application of ecological perspective that would embrace the entire project.

While the amount of open space in Putrajaya may arguably contribute to the maintenance of healthy soils and habitats for plants and animals, the constructed environment of Putrajaya should also have contributed to our search for sustainability through using less energy and water, by reducing waste and pollution and by minimizing air emissions. This applies equally to the design of the buildings and infrastructure as it does the "remade" landscape of the lake and open spaces. Putrajaya's environmental investment is certainly the wetland, but to claim that this is environmental-ism is not sustainable. It would be different if the wetlands were purifying water for a polluted river system or natural habitat. However, the purification of water for a constructed decorative dam diminishes the environmental claim.

The intelligent garden city is only intelligent in terms of the provision of information infrastructure. This occurs in terms of the intelligent connectedness of each of the buildings through state of the art technology and also in the urban development process itself, which included the development of an integrated city planning and management system. This system is built on an enterprise-wide platform, which provides access control, database connectivity, communications and document management. This allows for electronic submission of development applications. The preparation of the master plan and urban design guidelines assists in the processing of development applications by automatically checking compliances of development applications to land use, height restrictions, density, coverage, plot-ratio, set-back guidelines, and assists in the processing of building plans, for example (Putrajaya Authority 2001). Certainly this system allows for faster and more cost effective development and management practices but it does not lead to a new way to conceive of urban development in ecological terms. While Putrajaya seems well positioned in these technological "intelligent" terms, it lacks a stronger conviction about its role in terms of intelligent approaches to urban development and sustainability.

Unlike projects such as Lujiazui, whose motivation is overtly commercial, Putrajaya's motivation is based on representing the civic and cultural ambitions of Malaysia. Given the issues we face with the environment, Malaysia could have staked a leading position in the global sphere by a commitment to the idea of urban ecology. Unfortunately, this was an opportunity missed.

Global capitals

Putrajaya provides Malaysia with two very important qualities. In the nation's search for Malaysianness, Putrajaya provides a physical manifestation of what this possibility might be. This is important in the global economy. Putrajaya gives Malaysia a built image of itself which can be marketed in the global economy to signify that it too is a global player and confident enough as a nation to express itself. In addition, Putrajaya provided Malaysia with an opportunity to reflect upon itself, to identify its core values, and to understand its origins and its potential in the future.

Putrajaya provides a different perspective for the consideration of global urban projects. More than any other it is making a conscious struggle with the tension between engagement and resistance to the forces of globalization. It provides an example of a nation aiming for difference with the very real understanding that in a world converging on sameness, difference will be a highly valuable commodity in the future global economy.

10.18 View within the government precinct of Putrajaya looking toward the Prime Minister's Office (copyright Anand Krishnan 2002).

11.1 View of Lujiazui from Puxi. The presentation of Shanghai's emergence into the global economy.

11 The Idea of the City – Critical Pasts and Futures

Make no little plans, they have no magic to stir men's blood. Make big plans, aim high in hope and work, remembering that a noble, logical diagram once recorded will never die.

Daniel Burnham

Implications for thinking about urbanism (or, what does this mean?)

In *The Overexposed City*, Paul Virilio describes his work as an exploration of "new ways of analyzing a city whose structure can no longer be seen in the materials and locations that realize it." For Virilio the passage of time as a way of understanding the city has shifted from mechanical means (train, car, etc.) to electronic ones, leading to fundamental changes in the way that the city is understood. In an age of increased informationalization he writes:

[that] the way one gains access to the city is no longer through a gate, an arch of triumph, but rather through an electronic audiencing system whose users are not so much inhabitants or privileged residents as they are interlocutors in permanent transit. From this moment on, breaks in continuity occur less within the boundary of a physical urban space or its cadastral register than within a span of time, a span that advanced technology and industrial redeployment have incessantly restructured through a series of interruptions and through successive or simultaneous transformations which have managed to organize the urban milieu to the point of bringing about a decline, an irreversible deterioration of urban sites ... The representation of the contemporary city is thus no longer determined by a ceremonial opening of gates, by a ritual of processions and parades, nor by a succession of streets and avenues. From now on, urban architecture must deal with the advent of a "technological space-time."

(Virilio 1986: 544)

Virilio suggests that the physical city is in decline and its relevance highly questionable. For him time has usurped physical space in the contemporary global city as the primary way we think about, access and understand the city. What Virilio's position fails to acknowledge, and others who would dismiss the material city, is that ultimately technological space-time must be grounded in some way in material presence. For the space of flows to function it requires physical nodes of some kind. While it may be true that the advent of technological space-time demands a rethinking of relationships in the material world, the fact of its presence is undeniable. Whether or not one buys into Virilio's position, it is clear that we need to rethink what a city is and what the good city should be. The global urban projects examined in this book are important visions of what the twenty-first century city might be – for better or for worse. They represent some of the largest designed, and therefore consciously constructed, urban projects built in the last several

11.2 View of Jin Mao Tower, Lujiazui.

decades. As such they provide us with mechanisms for this re-evaluation of the materiality of city space in a global age.

Urbanism and its absence

The global urban projects described in this book are similar in terms of their political and economic ambitions. In many respects they aim at the same ends. They set out to capture competitive position as pieces of global infrastructure and they aim to project an image that can be marketed in the global sphere. They are however different in the way those ambitions are articulated in physical terms. Most critically they share a similarity with regards to their urbanity. Some see them as expressions of a new kind of global urbanism (see Clark 1996). As we have seen there appears to be a dominant global agenda to each of them that overrides the possibility that these projects might become eventually integrated into the messiness of the "real" city. One can certainly trace urbanistic origins and each of the urban projects can be characterized into various ideas of the city – modernist urbanism, rational urbanism, empirical urbanism, etc. However, to varying degrees the overriding contribution of the global urban projects to the history of urbanism and to the field of urban design is that they share a common characteristic, which can be described as the conscious pursuit of an "absent" urbanism.

Absent urbanism is the deliberate construction of city form through the articulation of buildings, roadways, streets, parks, and sidewalks without any attempt to foster a social sphere. This avoidance guarantees that the global agenda will not be undermined. Cities by their nature are unpredictable and difficult to control. With global urban projects the presentation of a very particular image is critical to their real and perceived success and in order to control the presentation of this image the messiness of the urban situation

needs to be eliminated. In the making of these global urban projects the provision of a certain kind of commercial space, of a certain kind of commercial image and a certain kind of commercial return override considerations of the establishment and fostering of communities, neighborhoods, communicative action or social interactions. The ambition of the global urban project demands an order that means that these other accommodations become too risky. The global urban project raises the issue of the compatibility between the global agenda and this understanding of urbanity.

This deliberate avoidance recognizes that urbanity is not a predictable thing and at times it can even be ugly. Neighborhoods can be either good or bad depending on who you are for example. Cities and urban culture can be inclusive or exclusive. They can be open or prejudiced. This is one aspect of cities that has always been present. In his conclusion to *Cities and Civilization*, Peter Hall writes that the greatest cities have never been "earthly utopias," but rather;

> . . . places of stress and conflict and sometimes actual misery . . . places where the adrenalin pumps through the bodies of the people and through the streets on which they walk; messy places, sordid places sometimes, but places nevertheless superbly worth living in . . .
>
> (Hall 1998: 989)

The agendas that lie behind the creation of the global urban project are more than indifferent to this issue. There is a deliberate avoidance of the messiness of urbanity, which suggests that in the minds of those that create these projects the idea of urbanity and the idea of the global urban project are mutually exclusive and to include the messiness of life would weaken a project's potential as a piece of global infrastructure and diminish the power of the global image. In these projects we find the deliberate pursuit of a sanitized urban condition. This is a troubling conclusion for urban design in a global sphere.

Each of the global urban projects examined can be positioned within a certain lineage – modernist, rational or empirical. The articulation of some global urban projects goes beyond the abstraction of modernist urbanism to a new level of absent urbanism. Examples of this kind of project are Tokyo Rainbow Town, Minato Mirai 21 and Lujiazui. In the case of Lujiazui, it is one of the most successful of the global urban projects in terms of facilitating an image that can be marketed in the global market place. The project provides an interesting example of how urbanity can be corrupted. If one examines the design competition schemes from Richard Rogers, Massimiliano Fuksas, Toyo Ito and Dominique Perrault it is clear that they all present specific ideas of the city. Each scheme deals with how communal space might support and encourage a particular type of urban culture. Above all else this is the foundation for each project. Streets, squares, open spaces and parks are articulated as containers for this cultural ambition and form the basis of each proposals structure. The built elements become a backdrop to the structure of public space. The scale of the competition provided a tremendous opportunity for designers to manufacture propositions to support urban culture through the arrangement of their designs. Although each scheme presented a different vision for the idea of the city they shared a common acceptance that such an idea should be at the basis of their project.

The winning scheme takes a different and inverse position vis-à-vis the other entries. This scheme lacks an idea about urban culture and lacks the public structure evident in the other schemes. In a complete reversal of urban intention, the scheme agglomerates objects in a weak arrangement and sits them in space such that they do not relate to each other in any way. The scheme accepts the complete lack of any idea of the city as the basis for Lujiazui. Urban design is here reduced to the arrangement of high-rise office buildings. In this sense Lujiazui is an anti-urban project and the most dangerous if it spawns imitation, which given its success in political and financial terms would suggest that indeed this would be the case.

Lujiazui presents a vision of the global project as a vacuous social space. Ironically, the winning scheme for Lujiazui "adopts" some of the elements of the other competition schemes but does so in a way that lacks a fundamental understanding of what those elements are and what their purpose was in the original schemes. One example of this was the adoption of the idea of a central park space, which can be found in several of the competition entries. The built result in Lujiazui, however, is the resemblance of a social container in the form of the central park. However this is simply an ornamental space lacking in the ability to nurture social interaction. One only has to consider the uses that surround it to understand that the park is surrounded by high-rise office projects and will never be anything more. This is exacerbated by the fact that multi-lane roadways ring the park. At best the park offers a view from the office towers.

One might justify the absence of urbanism in Lujiazui by saying that the entire project exists not for itself, in the sense of making a place, but rather exists solely to manufacture an image that can be broadcast into the global market place. If this is indeed true we are witness to a corruption of urban design's agency to make cities. We have arrived at a troubling conclusion in that the most successful global project lacks any idea of the city. What value then do we assign to the idea of the city? Lujiazui represents a modern crisis in

11.3 View of central atrium space inside Jin Mao Tower, Lujiazui. Increasingly one's experience of the city is internal.

urbanism, the ultimate aspiration of globalization and a project whose functionality, as a piece of Shanghai's global infrastructure is without dispute, yet one that lacks any possibility to articulate or support an urbanity appropriate to Shanghai. If Lujiazui is a model for how China and the rest of the world should proceed then there is little hope for architecture and urban design, whose roles would simply be the arrangement of buildings and infrastructure. Urbanism, as a critical activity, finds no role here.

Projects such as Muang Thong Thani, Zhongguancun, Saigon South and the New Singapore Downtown display an obvious modernist parentage. This means that they propose an arrangement of buildings and infrastructure such that open space becomes residual and figural to varying degrees. These projects struggle with the same issues that modernism faced some thirty years ago. The abstraction of space in the modernist project to the purely functional denies the possibility that urbanity can find a host. These projects however are clearly critical in the sense that they respond to their host urban environments and propose another, different kind of urban environment. In most cases this can be described as a critique of the existing city as not being capable of supporting a "new" modern lifestyle. They are "progressist" (in Choay's terminology) in that they propose that society must change, become more efficient and technologically advanced, and the city being a part of that system must likewise change. These projects make clear that a new urban form is required to facilitate an efficient and technologically enabled society. However in their articulation the role of urban culture struggles to find place.

Putrajaya is an empirical project in that it relies on a particular aesthetic preference based within certain nostalgic references and employs picturesque devices of contextualism, allusionism and ornamentalism (see Stern 1977). The design of Putrajaya can be seen to be contextual in that individual buildings are part of the larger whole. Indeed as we have already seen the project is designed to be read and understood as a whole, separate and superior to the rest of Kuala Lumpur's urban fabric. It is allusionary in that it expresses a certain act of cultural and historical response in a particular scenography, which remakes semantic connections to the great capitals of the past. There is, in addition, a significant aspect of ornamentalism to both the architecture of the buildings and the articulation of the landscape. This can be seen in the design of the Prime Minister's Office and also in the design of Dataran Putra, which is paved in patterns inspired from Islamic geometry. This aims at eliciting a sense of grandeur by harking to a mythic nostalgia and by elevating specific cultural signifiers relevant to Malays and Malay history and symbolism. In this way the project establishes a connection to strong cultural and societal emotions, in order to reinforce its claim of representing Malaysia's capital. What the picturesque alone is not able to achieve is the generation of an urbanity in broadly defined terms. The dominance of the administrative and political agenda in the project denies a richer engagement with the possibility of urban culture. The core of the project is so singularly ceremonial that life is excluded and occurs instead on the outside of the project. This singular dominance flattens the urban vitality of the project such that it unfortunately should be equated with a government business park.

If the global urban projects presented here are important moments in the development of contemporary urbanism, how should we evaluate them in light of the declining relevance of the physical city and the dominance of absent urbanism? The answer, perhaps, is to re-evaluate the foundational concepts of urbanism to remind us of the basis for the field. This requires a reminder of the history of the origins and history of urbanism as a critical activity. If nothing else, the global urban projects examined in this book certainly raise this as a fundamental and necessary operation today – what is needed is a recalibration.

Recalibrating urbanism in light of its critical past

Urbanism is primarily concerned with how the physical form of cities can be arranged to produce certain kinds of social and cultural conditions. Necessarily the "idea of the city" relates to ways of thinking about what cities should be in light of new forces influencing the urban situation. While we might assume that this has always been the case François Choay reminds us that the terms *urbanización*, *urbanisme*, *town planning*, and *Städtebau*, which are used today to mean everything encompassing city planning and design, are constructs that date to the late nineteenth century (Choay 1969). The development of these "ideas of the city" responds to the emergence of a new series of forces influencing the form of the city under the influence of industrialization and developed through the twentieth century in response to internationalization.

The construction of terms such as *urbanización*, *urbanisme*, *town planning*, and *Städtebau*, marks a fundamental change in the relationship between Western society and the organization of cities. These terms emerge as a result of forces that challenged the way people thought about cities where for the first time cities were seen as parts of an economic network of production and consumption. Choay's argument is that until the Industrial Revolution the city was part of a semiotic system where the urban system was one of

11.4 View from the 88-story high observation deck of Jin Mao Tower. The new city unfolds.

communication and information. Both the inhabitants and the planners understood the relationships between elements within the city in the context of a set of rules and codes. By understanding these rules and codes, the city itself had meaning. Accordingly the citizen, in the process of living in the city, was integrated into the structure of society at any given time and any urban plan or project implicitly corresponded to that structure which it both instituted and controlled.

In medieval Europe this structure was related to the Church, the feudal system and corporate artisanship. In the Baroque period the urban order no longer had this inclusive significance. However the grand radial boulevards of Baroque planning were still designed with reference to the established power and the relationship between the urban system and other concurrent systems was still implicitly accepted by both inhabitants and planners. The greatest issue we have today is that in the global world the city is no longer part of this urban semiotic system and with this its relevance and meaning have dissipated. Our issue then is the very relevancy of the city and the emergence of urban design as a defined field of activity in the United States in the 1950s can be seen as a search for and the proposition for meaning in the city.

Choay goes on to describe how the social and cultural upheaval of the Industrial Revolution fundamentally altered how cities were thought about and designed. In these terms there is an obvious correspondence to the situation in the Asia Pacific Rim a century later, where technology and a new global order have likewise instigated social and cultural upheavals in cities. These later day upheavals have indeed also affected the way in which we think about and design in cities. Under the influence of industrialization, economics and capital determined the spatial organization of

cities and an individual's position in the structure of society became more complicated and confused. This process of alienation continued through the twentieth century and the emergence of globalization only exacerbated this alienation through the continued and accelerated abstraction of meaning in urban form. This is responsible for a plethora of criticism from all disciplines regarding the decline of cities and the concurrent demise of urbanity.

In response to the upheavals induced by industrialization there developed a growing sense that the city was out of control. Reminiscent of later-day critics such as James Kunstler and Andres Duany, Victor Considérant wrote in 1858 that "[b]ig cities . . . were formless masses, jumbles of houses . . . architectural chaos." In a similar way we have seen numerous attempts by Pacific Rim planners to address their corresponding urban chaos. In the nineteenth century these feelings of disenfranchisement produced what Choay describes as "critical planning," which arose from a group of urbanists critical of the current condition of the city. This produced a series of important texts and treatises, which were often precursors to various planning propositions – Haussmann's *Mémoires*, Stübben's *Der Städtebau* (1900), and Cerdá's *Teoria General de Urbanización* (1867) are examples. Given that there is no shortage of criticism about cities today it is interesting that despite the efforts of the Congress of New Urbanism (see www.cnu.org) there has not developed other new forms of "critical" planning in the United States. The Pacific Rim global urban projects can be seen, at some levels, to be critical planning in practice. However, the kind of treatise that existed in the nineteenth century is certainly absent.

The rise of what Choay defines as "urbanism" is precisely the questioning of what this social order should be and ultimately leads to the a-priori construction of a new and different one. This speculation was engaged in by a group of social and political reformers who aspired to nothing short of a complete restructuring of society, of which the city was one part. It was generated from the founders of socialism, with thinkers such as Robert Owen, Charles Fourier, Étienne Cabet, Karl Marx and Friedrich Engels. Robert Owen's visions of his "Owenite" villages of 1817 or Fourier's "Phalanstères" (1847) are examples of social propositions finding physical form as urban utopias. This was further elaborated by figures such as Arturo Soria with his "la ciudad lineal," (the linear city) in 1882, Tony Garnier with his "cité industrielle," (the industrial city) designed between 1899 and 1901 and Camillo Sitte with his book *The City Designed According to Artistic Principles*. Sitte analyzed classical, medieval and baroque spatial organization extracting and re-proposing common aspects. For Sitte the "modern disease of isolated construction," denied the possibility of urban space having a "community" role to play. In the organization of the built fabric the principles of irregularity, imagination and asymmetry were to be followed. The straight line, regularity and symmetry were condemned. One can see aspects of Sitte-esque ideas of the city reappearing in such later propositions as Gordon Cullen's *Townscape*.

The development of urbanism, understood here to be the critical appreciation of the current condition and the concurrent proposition for a new and different order (this includes social and cultural orders, unlike Sitte whose concerns were purely physical) can be first seen in Ebenezer Howard's "garden city" (1898). The wide acceptance of Howard's idea may in part be attributed to the fact that the garden city presents a rather ambiguous plan and instead relies on a series of principles, which are open to a variety of interpretations. Often these principles are applied wrongly. Howard intended the garden city to be a refuge from the alienating character of the city and critically also from the inadequacies of country life, in many respects derived from Soria. This new entity was to combine the social advantages of the city with the health advantages of the country. The connection between Howard's garden city idea and the development of the suburb fails to acknowledge that Howard was fundamentally concerned with a new idea of urbanity, not an idea for low density living.

In the twentieth century urbanism spawned a series of critical ideas of the city. In the Salon d'Atomne of 1922 in Paris, Le Corbusier exhibited his "ville contemporaine," a model city with a center composed of twenty 60-story skyscrapers. Around these were five- and six-story apartments and around that sports grounds, a park and industry. The contemporary city was to accommodate 3 million inhabitants. The plan was based on four principles: the solving of the problem of congestion at the center, an increase in population density, the expansion of the means of transport and an increase in parkland. Le Corbusier's ambition was to define an appropriate idea of the city, for him:

> Present day cities will not be able to meet the demands of modern life, if they are not adapted to new conditions ... In order to transform the cities, we must track down the fundamental principles of modern town planning.
>
> (Le Corbusier, *Urbanisme* 1966)

On the foundation of CIAM (Congrès Internationaux d'Architecture Moderne) in 1928, the Declaration of La Sarraz defined "town planning" as the organization of the functional conditions of collective life and not on aesthetic considerations. Significantly, this idea was about organizing social functions by means of land organization, the regulation of traffic and legislation. CIAM IV (1933) is generally considered the beginning of "modern" town planning, as it was here that the city was first split into four – dwellings, work, recreation and transportation – in order to facilitate a new kind of social order. The social components of modernism gave way to the aesthetic however. Hitchcock and Johnson's "International style," the vehicle that launched modernism in America, was preoccupied with the aesthetic at the expense of the social.

This preoccupation manifests itself in later work into the simple consideration of buildings and infrastructure and is certainly evident in some of the modernist global urban projects described previously. While this may have been a misreading of Le Corbusier's intention, open space in many modernist legacies was of little or no concern. Open space became, simply, the space between building objects and architects lost their ability to think about, deal with and design these in-between spaces. Whether this is due to a fundamental misunderstanding or a regrettable inevitability, the fact is that the in-between spaces in the city are precisely those spaces where urbanity was most likely to be manifest and its neglect led to somewhat obvious consequences. The legacy today can be clearly seen in many of the "modernist" projects examined in the previous chapters where large parts of the city fail to provide a framework that might support an urban culture.

In the late 1950s and early 1960s, just as CIAM urbanism was waning, a new consciousness about the idea of the city emerged. This new consciousness was in response to the abstraction of meaning in the city, attributable perhaps to the emergence of globalization. This emergence raised issues of place and the need for the reinforcement of cultural specificities in architectural and urban terms. These issues also manifest a return to the importance of history, as a way to reinforce meaning in the built form of the city. This new consciousness spawned the urban design programs at the Universities of Pennsylva-

nia and Harvard, soon to be followed by the Universities of Washington and Columbia. The origins of urban design were reactionary in the sense that they grew from a growing concern for the relevancy of the city in times of radical change. This also led to a diffraction of design thinking in terms of the city. The singularity of CIAM modernism gave way to an array of other critical explorations.

These critical reactions to CIAM urbanism can be characterized in two trajectories. On the one hand there developed a neo-empirical response to the "modern" city with the work of Gordon Cullen, Kevin Lynch, Robert Venturi, Denis Scott Brown, and later Colin Rowe and Fred Koetter. This trajectory presented a return to figural space that could be visually appealing and therefore, humanizing. Colin Rowe's perspective outlines the main agenda of the neo-empiricists in the "re-cycling" of meaning through the "remembrance" of history. Reacting against the singularity of the impoverished modern city, Rowe calls for a return to the messiness of vital urban situations, layered with multiple meanings. In many respects his call could be applied against the absence of urbanity in the global urban projects.

He writes that the design of cities should embody a:

> Remembrance of former function and value; shifting context; an attitude which encourages the composite; an exploitation and re-cycling of meaning; desuetude of function with corresponding agglomeration of reference; memory; anticipation; the connectedness of memory and wit; the integrity of wit; and since it is a proposition evidently addressed to people, it is in terms such as these, in terms of pleasures remembered and desired, of a dialectic between past and future, of an impacting of iconographic content, of a temporal as well as a spatial

11.5 View from the 88-story high observation deck of Jin Mao Tower down toward Century Boulevard, Lujiazui. The pedestrian public realm has been consumed by the global city.

collision, that resuming an earlier argument, one might proceed to specify an ideal city of the mind.

> (Rowe and Koetter 1978: 138)

In parallel to this trajectory arose a series of theorists who developed neo-rational ideas of the city. This can be seen in the work of people such as Robert and Leon Krier, Maurice Culot and Aldo Rossi. Rossi articulates his ideas on the city in *The*

Architecture of the City, which was published in Italian in 1966 and in English in 1982. Rossi's motivation was to view architecture from within the discipline, to deal with the facts of the city as a field of research leading to a recalibration of design agency. For Rossi architecture is about the articulation of ideas and the role of the architect is to bring those ideas into built form. In the introduction to the English edition, Peter Eisenman notes that Rossi proposes a two-fold "idea of the city" as ultimate data – an archeological artifact – and of the city as autonomous structure, which not only characterizes the city as an object, but more importantly, and perhaps inadvertently, redefines its subject – the architect. As opposed to the humanist architect of the sixteenth century and the functionalist architect of the twentieth century, Rossi's architect would seem to be an unheroic, autonomous researcher. Rossi's position is valuable because it suggests that cities are not simply the results of some unco-ordinated chaos and rather that they are the product of intellectual creation.

Contemporary urbanism

These two broad classifications define contemporary ideas of the city. In the American context the rise of New Urbanism is one manifestation of a contemporary neo-empirical idea of the city. New Urbanism is above all else driven by a concern for a particular aesthetic and set of social characteristics, invoking a mythic nostalgia for the New England townscape. This proposition, promoted through the Congress on New Urbanism, has reshaped the role of urban design in the American context, where the small, the local, and the immediate have become the realm of most urban design practice today. Keeping urban order in line with the myth of the small town has become a major preoccupation of "community" advocates in the United States. While these concerns have certain legitimacy New Urbanism cannot address all of the functional requirements of modern urban situations.

The neo-rational position has also been theoretically developed in the work and writings of people such as Rem Koolhaas. Koolhaas' work can be described as being preoccupied with how ideas produce results in the construction of architecture (in the sense of an intellectual construct) and how this results in the construction of the city. Koolhaas intellectualizes the phenomenon of the contemporary in order to develop constructs, which can be applied in operational means to the making of urban projects and continue the rational project of the city.

Such theoretical positions establish the basis for how one imagines urbanism, how one thinks a city should or should not be. For the New Urbanists this idea has a particular aesthetic and formal preference. For Koolhaas the idea does not follow any particular formal preference but operates within a range of acceptable possibilities. Both positions, however, clearly relate to particular possibilities for urbanism in a global context. New Urbanism can be seen as a complete reaction against the abstraction of the global order. Koolhaasian thinking is likewise a reaction, but one that seeks its *modus operandi* within the logic of the global. In this sense Koolhaas is more interesting for he raises the possibility of new urbanisms within the global sphere, rather than the reinvention of old urbanisms that deny the power of the global.

Koolhaas' position is a criticism of contemporary urban planning and urban design for its attachment to the idea of the "good" city as the historical European city. This attachment creates a fundamental lack of ability to understand contemporary challenges, and for a lack of ideas on how to deal with contemporary processes of urbanization. If this remains unresolved, the result will be the development of a city without history and without identity – to a generic city. This generic city (he refers to Singapore) represents sameness, repetition and a fundamental lack of design. The problem, however, is that this position has not found a way to relate an appreciation of the importance of coalitions of societal actors and forces to the description of a new urban form and in the end does not have a vision that helps us resolve the paradox between historicism and modernization.

Neither position is particularly applicable to the global urban projects discussed here. In the case of the New Urbanism the proliferation of particular urban outcomes fails to prove useful to the political and the economic agendas of cities in the Asia Pacific Rim. These cities, at this time in their development, require an engagement with the monumental that seems at odds with the community agenda of the neo-traditionalist designers who generally eschew such monumental and grand statements in favor of a "homely" vision. By the same token it seems doubtful that Koolhaas' position would necessarily generate any more useful outcomes. Koolhaas certainly deals far better with the issue of the monumental in his work but despite this the indifference toward a definite description of urbanity may lead to an abstraction of space similar to other modernist propositions.

In broad terms then this is the intellectual context around which urbanism is construed today. It is within these debates about the appropriateness of various ideas of the city that the operations of planning and urban design exist. The idea of urbanism as a critical capacity related to the production of city space is open to myriad possibilities.

Thinking the critical future of urbanism

Most discussions on the global economy focus on the hyper-mobility of capital, the possibility of instantaneous transmission of information and money around the globe, the centrality of information outputs to our economic systems and empha-size the neutralization of geography and of places. What is ignored, however, is that even the most advanced information industries need a material infrastructure of buildings and work processes, and considerable agglomeration, in order to operate in global markets. This requires conscious effort to arrange this material infrastructure and reinforces that indeed there is a role for urban design in this making.

The question at the heart of contemporary urban design practice is its relevancy in light of these global urban projects. There are several issues that need to be addressed. The first is that the making of the urban projects reinforces the centrality of design as an operative practice. These projects are not organic in the sense of evolving through a long period of time and being the result of a series of disparate actions. Rather they are created quickly and directly from a defined physical imagining, in other words they have a designed directedness. Second, these projects reinforce the importance of place in cities at a time when many global theorists suggest its diminution. Certainly there continues to be semantic issues in relation to the meaning and relevancy of place, but the importance of place in the global sphere is beyond repute. The reinforcement of the centrality of design and the importance of place combine to suggest myriad opportunities for urban design in the making of urban projects. Needless to say it remains to be seen if these opportunities will be fully taken up by the design professions.

It is evident from the global urban projects that despite the emergence of opportunities there has been a reduction in the autonomy of the design disciplines and a concurrent negation of design's ability to control outcomes. It appears that those that define the ultimate political agenda for the project have absorbed decision making and design's ability to influence that agenda has receded. Design has become an operation in

11.6 View from the 88-story high observation deck of Jin Mao Tower. One tower per block – this kind of urban situation is rapidly altering the landscape of cities in the Asia Pacific Rim, ultimately requiring a fundamental change in the way urban design approaches the city.

bringing form to agendas largely outside of its purview. In the global urban projects one can see various examples of this. Projects such as Saigon South, Muang Thong Thani and Putrajaya, however, do attempt to articulate another layer of meaning above the primary motivation of the project. In these projects one is able to find evidence of attempts to articulate a conscious idea, one that informs the physicality of the project and presents a vision for how a city should look, feel and function. Such projects show glimmers of an emerging urbanity – of an idea of the city – and in so doing suggest that there continues to be a role for design in the making of cities.

How one might define that role is certainly open to speculation. Fundamentally urbanism involves the articulation of a possible future, one based on the promise that this future will in some and varied ways be better than the present. This invariably involves moral and ideological judgments. Indeed the origins of urbanism, as we have seen, were based on such imperatives. Ideological positions are by their nature personal, based within a collection of social and cultural suppositions. It is therefore difficult to determine a set of beliefs that everyone will agree with. However, given the relevancy of our time and the conditions under which urban design operates globally today there should be a general set of principles around which urban design can cluster.

Given the transient nature of many belief systems today urban design must be a reflexive activity, constantly engaged in referencing the present and its origins. As a defined field of activity it locates itself between architecture and planning and indeed in the Sert trajectory of the discipline aims to rescue urbanism from the reductive analytical operations of planning. In many respects the issues faced by urban design in 1960 are ostensibly the same as today. In the beginning urban design reacted to the homogen-

ization and displacement wrought by both urban renewal and a move toward universalism in design. Today it must engage with and react to forces, which lead simultaneously toward a complicated hybrid urbanization, which includes homogenization and heterogenization. The field of urban design currently struggles with its capacity in this engagement. In the North American sphere of thinking urban design seems paralyzingly perplexed as to what issues it should be taking on. The field is dominated by discussions that either relate to the intellectual disinvestment of downtowns or the production of better forms of suburbia.

The tremendous growth in the world's population (most of which will be in cities) combined with an increasing awareness of the limited capacity of the environment, require a radical rethinking of urban design's engagement. Urban design should be nothing less than a search for new forms of settlement appropriate to the conditions of today. This will inevitably require the abandonment of accepted "conventions" of urban form, patterns and morphologies and a recalibration of definitions of the city to bring them in line with the currency of our time.

Urban design must reinforce its capacity for speculative visioning as a means to explore possibilities that may drive a new way of thinking about cities. Such speculation must open up a multitude of architectural possibilities to escape the current singular positions of modernism versus historicism, or urban versus suburban. This escape will nevertheless be grounded in a set of principles, which will guide the development of future urban projects. The basis for which should be the nurturing of life in the city. Meaning in urban situations is manifest through the social city. Urban design's role should be the articulation of meaning through the provision of a physical structure, which supports this social activity.

It is becoming increasingly evident that our continuing existence on this planet will heavily depend on our ability to manage resources. The intelligent use of resources toward an urban sustainability must be embraced by urban design. This will not merely involve the management of waste from urban projects but should fundamentally influence their creation, the way they are designed, the standards of construction and operation, the types of programs and their arrangement and the way in which the project situates itself into the existing context. This will involve the imagining and testing of new urban propositions.

Urban design should aim at the cultivation of urbanity. This means that it must construct the form, extent and nature of places for collective assembly. The city dweller reaps the benefits of living in the city through the occasion of chance encounters and the various occupations and distractions, which form part of the everyday urban experience (Lefebvre 1991: 121). The drama of life is extended in urban areas, simply because there are lots of people to interact with. There are definite benefits to density in urban situations for the creation of urban culture within a city through creating possibilities for communicative action (remembering Arendt).

A belief in the potential of urban design as an activity engaged in the making of cities is one that acknowledges that cities are the product of intellectual creation. We no longer inhabit holes in the ground that we simply arrive upon by accident or temporarily locate ourselves based on the dictates of game or water. Rather we inhabit environments made through intellectual and physical endeavors. Cities are made through thoughts and labor and being so, are in themselves the largest works of art known to humanity. As works of art they should be available for appreciation and possess an aesthetic validity, one that is certainly not restricting and encompassing but open and differentiated. Cities should be invested with desire, with emotion, with justice and with passion. For urban designers there should be no greater achievement than the accommodation of principles of living, of sustainability, and of community with beauty. This is the challenge to further global urban projects.

In an environment where capital is not place bound and is free to roam the globe in search of better investment opportunities, cities will have to attract private investment in order to stay competitive. While this necessarily raises the fact that in doing so some people benefit while others lose, for cities not to play this game creates the possibility that that city would be worse off than if it did. In addition to being competitive globally, cities must also be compassionate and aware of this plus and minus reality. To do this they will have to create environments where people will want to be. Urban design then, will have an essential role to play in creating environments of quality not only for the rich but for the poor as well. Above all else this is what will determine if cities will be competitive. The global urban project marks the realization that the city has a critical role to play in the competitive global economy. Increasingly city governments are realizing that the global urban project is a piece of infrastructure, a portal to the global flows of information, people and capital. For many nations in the Pacific Rim, lacking competitive infrastructure, the global project is seen as the most important development project. What has been missing from many of these projects, however, is a recognition that they simultaneously provide an opportunity for cities to create a constructed vision of an ideal self. In these projects lies the possibility to define specific ideas of the city, developed from a critical urbanism, one that is responsive to place, climate, culture and history, leading to the production of an emerging urbanity.

Bibliography

Abbas, Ackbar (1994) "Building on disappearance: Hong Kong, architecture and city," *Public Culture* 14: 441–59.

Abu-Lughod and Janet Lippman (1995) "Comparing Chicago, New York, and Los Angeles: testing some world city hypotheses," in Paul L. Knox and Peter J. Taylor (eds) *World Cities in a World System*, Cambridge and New York: Cambridge University Press, 171–91.

Agnew, J. (1984) "Devaluing place: people prosperity versus place prosperity and regional planning," *Environment and Planning D: Society and Space* 1: 35–45.

Albrow, Martin, *et al.* (1997) "The impact of globalization on sociological concepts, community, culture and milieu," in John Eade (ed.) *Living the Global City*, New York and London: Routledge, 20–36.

Amer, R. and Thayer, C. (1999) *Vietnamese Foreign Policy in Transition*, New York: St. Martin's Press.

Amin, A. (ed.) (1994) *Post-Fordism: A Reader*, Oxford: Blackwell.

Amin, A. (1997) "Placing globalization," *Theory, Culture and Society* 14: 123–37.

Amin, A. and Thrift, N. (1992) "Neo-Marshallian nodes in global networks," *International Journal of Urban and Regional Research*, Dec, 16(4): 571.

Anderson, Benedict (1983) *Imagined Communities: Reflections on the Growth and Spread of Nationalism*, New York and London: Verso. Reprinted 1991.

Appadurai, A. (1996) "Disjuncture and difference in the global economy," *Public Culture* 2(2): 1–24.

Architecture Australia (1992) *International City: MTT*, February: 32–5.

Architecture and Urbanism (1994) *Bernard Tschumi 1983–1993*, March: Special Issue.

Arefi, M. (1999) "Non-place and placelessness as narratives of loss: rethinking the notion of place," *Journal of Urban Design* 4(2): 179–94.

Arendt, H. (1958) *The Human Condition*, Chicago: University of Chicago Press.

Aronowitz, Stanley (1988) *Science as Power: Discourse and Ideology in Modern Society*, Minneapolis, MN: University of Minnesota Press.

Arrighi, Giovanni (1997) "Globalization and the rise of East Asia: lessons from the past, prospects for the future," paper prepared for the Seminar, "Latin America: globalization and integration," organized by the Instituto Brasileiro de Estudos Contemporaneos, Belo Horizonte, Brazil 25–6.

Ashihara, Yoshinobu (1989) *The Hidden Order: Tokyo through the Twentieth Century*, Tokyo: Kodansha International (in Japanese).

Asia Development Bank (2000) "Vietnam agricultural sector program interim report," by ANZDEC Limited with IFPRI and Lincoln International for ADB TA 3223-VIE, Hanoi.

Asia Development Bank (2001) www.adb.org/Documents/News/1999/pi1999089.asp

Asia Times Online (2000) "Environmental crisis overtakes Vietnam's economic zones," February 24, http://atimes.com/se-asia/

Asia Times Online (2001a) "Vietnam report," July 25, http://atimes.com/se-asia/

Asia Times (2001b) "HCMC Council," July 27, http://atimes.com/se-asia/

Askew, M. and Logan, W. (eds) (1994) *Cultural Identity and Urban Change in Southeast Asia: Interpretative Essays*, Geelong: Deakin University Press.

Bangkok Post (1994) "Year-end economic review," December 30, 63.

Bangkok Post (1996) "Chula study quote threats to economy," November 3, 2.

Bangkok Post (2000) "Impact centre lifts Bangkok land's image – regional exhibition hub," *Ultimate Goal*, Feb 22.

Beck, Ulrich (2000) "What is globalization," in D. Held and A. McGrew (eds) *The Global Transformations Reader*, Cambridge: Polity Press, 99–104.

Bello, W. (1997) "The end of the Asian miracle," http://www.stern.nyu.edu/~nroubini/asia/miracle.pdf

Bello, W., Cunningham, S. and Poh, L.K. (1998) *A Siamese Tragedy: Development and Disintegration in Modern Thailand*, London and New York: ZED Books.

Beng, C.H. (1993) "Responding to global challenges: the changing international economy," in G. Rodan (ed.) *Singapore Changes Guard: Social, Political and Economic Direction in the 1990s*, New York: Longman Cheshire, 101–15.

Berry, J. and McGreal, S. (eds) (1999) *Cities in the Pacific Rim: Planning Systems and Property Markets*, London: E & FN Spon.

Bestor, Theodore (1989) *Neighborhood Tokyo*, Tokyo: Kodansha International.

Bird, Jon (1993) "Dystopia on the Thames," in Jon Bird, *et al.* (eds) *Mapping the Futures: Local Cultures, Global Change*, London and New York: Routledge, 120–35.

Blanc, Cristina Szanton (1997) "The thoroughly modern 'Asian': capital, culture and nation in Thailand and the Philippines," in Aihwa Ong and Donald Nonini (eds) *Ungrounded Empires*, New York: Routledge, 261–86.

Borja, Jordi and Castells, M. (1997) *Local and Global: The Management of Cities in the Information Age*, London: Earthscan Publications: United Nations Center for Human Settlements (Habitat).

Breen, A. and Rigby, D. (1996) *The New Waterfront: A Worldwide Urban Success Story*, New York: McGraw Hill.

Broeze, Frank (ed.) (1989) *Brides of the Sea: Port Cities of Asia from the 16th to 20th Centuries*, Honolulu, HI: University of Hawaii.

Brotchie, J. et al. (eds) (1995) Cities in Competition: Productive and Sustainable Cities for the 21st Century, Melbourne: Longman Press,

Budd, L. and Whimster, S. (1992) (eds) Global Finance and Urban Living: A study of Metropolitan Change, London and New York: Routledge.

Campbell, D. et al. (eds) (1997) Regionalization and Labour Market Interdependence in East and Southeast Asia, Basingstoke: St. Martin's Press, New York: Macmillan.

Cannon, T. and Zhang, L.-Y. (1996) "Inter-region tension and China's reforms," in I. Cook, M. Doel and R. Li (eds) Fragmented Asia, Aldershot: Avebury: 75–101.

Castells, M. (1983) The City and the Grassroots, Berkeley: University of California Press.

Castells, M. (1989) The Informational City: Information Technology, Economic Restructuring and the Urban Regional Process, New York: Basil Blackwell.

Castells, M. (1997) The Power of Identity, Oxford: Blackwell Publishers.

Central Trading Development Group (CT&D) (2001) http://www.saigon.south.com/ss/docs/cdthome.htm

Chalermpow, Koanantakool (1993) Urban Life and Urban People in Transition, Bangkok: Thailand Development Research Institute.

Chan, Kam-wing and Xu Xueqiang (1985) "Urban population growth and urbanization in China since 1949: reconstructing a baseline," The China Quarterly 104: 583–613.

Chan Kam-wing (1996) "Post-Mao China: a two-class urban society in the making," International Journal of Urban and Regional Research 20(1): 134–50.

Chang, S.D. and Kwok, R.Y. (1990) "The urbanization of rural China," in R.Y. Kwok, W. Parish and A.G.O. Yeh (eds) Chinese Urban Reform – What Model Now? New York: M.E. Sharpe, 140–57.

Charms, E. (1999) "The new bubble burst in Thailand," IFU, National School of the Highways Departments, CNRS.

Chase Dunn, Christopher (1984) "Urbanization in the world system: new directions for research," in Michael Peter Smith (ed.) Cities in Transformation, Beverly Hills and London: Sage, 111–20.

Chen, P. (1973) "Social stratification in Singapore," Working paper No. 12, Department of Sociology, National University of Singapore.

Chin, C.B.N. and Mittelman, J.H. (1997) "Conceptualizing resistance to globalization," New Political Economy 2(1): 25–37.

China State Council (1984) Regulations on City Planning, Beijing: State Council (in Chinese).

Chiu, W.K., Ho, K.C. and Lui, Tai-lok (1997) City-States in the Global Economy: Industrial Restructuring in Hong Kong and Singapore, Boulder, CO: Westview Press.

Chiu-Sheng Lin, "Changing theoretical perspectives on urbanization in Asian developing countries," Third World Planning Review 16(1): 1–23.

Choay, F. (1969) The Modern City: Planning in the 19th Century, New York: George Braziller.

Choe, S.C. (1996) "The evolving urban system in North-East Asia," in F.C. Lo and Y.M. Yeung (eds) Emerging World Cities in Pacific Asia, Tokyo: United Nations University Press.

Choo, Chun-Wei (1997) "IT2000: Singapore's vision of an intelligent island," in P. Droege (ed.) Intelligent Environments, Amsterdam: Elsevier.

Chua, B. (1996) "Singapore: management of a city-state in Southeast Asia," in J. Ruland (ed.) The Dynamics of Metropolitan Management in Southeast Asia, Singapore: Institute of Southeast Asian Studies: 207–24.

CIA Factbook Online (2001) http://www.odci.gov/cia/publications/factbook/geos/hk.html, accessed February.

Clammer, J. Contemporary Urban Japan: a Sociology of Consumption, Oxford, UK and Malden, MA: Blackwell Publishers.

Clark, D. (1996) Urban World/Global City, London: Routledge.

Cohen, M. (ed.) (1996) "Preparing for the urban future," Woodrow Wilson Center, Washington, DC, distributed by the Johns Hopkins University Press.

Collins, G. and Flores, C. (1968) (eds) "Arturo Soria y la Ciudad Lineal, Madrid," Revista de Occidente.

Colquohoun, A. (1981) Essays in Architectural Criticism, Cambridge, MA: MIT Press.

Communist Party of Vietnam, Central Committee (2000) "Socioeconomic development strategy 2001–2010," (draft).

Cook, I., Doel, M. and Li, R. (eds) (1996) Fragmented Asia, Aldershot: Avebury.

Cooke, Philip (1986) "Modernity, postmodernity and the city," Theory, Culture and Society 5: 475–92.

Cooke, Philip (1988) "The postmodern condition and the city," Comparative Urban and Community Research 1: 62–80.

Cooper, J. (1996) "Muang Thong Thani Thailand," in Content, Form and Technique 2: 68–77.

Corbridge, S. and Thrift, N. (1994) Money, Power and Place, Oxford: Blackwell.

Cox, H. (1968) "The restoration of a sense of place: a theological reflection on the visual environment," Ekistics 25(151): 422–4.

Cox, Kevin (1997) Spaces of Globalization, New York: Guilford Press.

Cuff, D. (2000) The Provisional City: Los Angeles Stories of Architecture and Urbanism, Cambridge, MA and London: MIT Press.

Cyberjaya (2001) Cyberjaya promotional web page. http://www.cyberjaya-msc.com/project/1_project01.html, accessed July 8.

Daniels, P. (1993) "Service industries in the world economy," IBG Studies in Geography, Oxford: Blackwell.

Daniels, P. (1995) "Office development and information technology: sustaining the competitiveness of the City of London?" in J. Brotchie, M. Batty, E. Blakely, P. Hall and P. Newton (eds) Cities in Competition: Productive and Sustainable Cities for the 21st Century, Melbourne: Longman, 226–48.

Dau, Nguyen Dinh (1998) From Saigon to Ho Chi Minh City – 300 Year History, Vietnam: Land Service Science and Technics Publishing House.

Davis, D. et al. (eds) (1995) Urban Spaces in Contemporary China: the Potential for Autonomy and Community in Post-Mao China, Cambridge, England: Woodrow Wilson Center Press and New York: Cambridge University Press.

Davis, Mike (1990) City of Quartz, London: Verso.

Davis, Mike (1992) "Burning all illusions in LA," in Don Hazen (ed.) Inside the L.A. Riots, New York: Institute for Alternative Journalism, 97–100.

Dear, Michael (1986) "Postmodernism and planning," Society and Space 4: 367–84.

Dear, Michael (1991) "The premature demise of postmodern urbanism," Cultural Anthropology 6(4): 538–52.

Deutsche, Rosalyn (1991) "Boy's Town," Society and Space 9: 5–30.

Deyo, F. (1991) "Singapore developmental paternalism," in

S. Goldstein (ed.) *Mini-dragons: Fragile Economic Miracles in the Pacific*, Boulder, CO: Westview Press, 64–103.

Dicken, P. (1987) "A tale of two NICs: Hong Kong and Singapore at the crossroads," *Geoforum* 18: 151–64.

Dicken, P. (1994) "Global-local tensions: firms and states in the global space-economy," *Economic Geography* 70(2): 101–28.

Dicken, P. (1998) *Global Shift: Transforming the World Economy*, London: Paul Chapman.

Dirlik, A. (ed.) (1993) *What is the Rim? Critical Perspectives on the Pacific Region Idea*, Boulder, CO: Westview Press.

Dirlik, A. (1994) *After the Revolution: Waking to Global Capitalism*, Hanover: Wesleyan University Press.

Dirlik, A (1999) "Globalism and the politics of place," in K. Olds *et al.* (eds) *Globalization and the Asia-Pacific*, London: Routledge: 39–56.

Dobbs-Higginson, M.S. (1994) *Asia Pacific: Its Role in the New World Disorder*, Melbourne: Mandarin.

Dogan, Mattei and Kasarda, John D. (eds) (1988) *The Metropolis Era. Vol. 1: A World of Giant Cities; Vol. 2: Mega Cities*, Newbury Park CA: Sage Publications (includes Shanghai, New York City, Los Angeles, Tokyo, Mexico City, São Paulo).

Douglass, M. (1993) "The new Tokyo story: restructuring space and the struggle for place in a world city," in R.C. Hill and Fujita Kuniko (eds) *Japanese Cities in the World Economy*, Philadelphia, PA: Temple University Press, 83–119.

Douglass, M. (1995) "Global interdependence and urbanization: planning for the Bangkok mega-urban region," in T. McGee and I.M. Robinson (eds) *The Mega-Urban Regions of Southeast Asia*, Vancouver: UBC Press: 45–79.

Douglass, M. (1998) "East Asian urbanization: patterns, problems, prospects," Stanford Asia/Pacific Research Center Monograph, July.

Douglass, M. and Zoghlin, M. (1994) "Sustaining cities at the grassroots: livelihood, environment, and social networks in Suan Phlu, Bangkok," in *Third World Planning Review* 16(2): 171–200.

Dowall, D. (1992) "A second look at the Bangkok land and housing market," *Urban Studies* 29(1): 25–38.

Droege, P. (ed.) (1997) *Intelligent Environments*, Amsterdam: Elsevier.

Duffy, Francis (1997) *The New Office*, London: Conran Octopus.

Duffy, H. (1995). *Competitive Cities: Succeeding in the Global Economy*, London: Spon.

Dutt, A. (ed.) (1994) *Asian City: Processes of Deveiopment, Characteristics and Planning*, Amsterdam, Netherlands: Kluwer Academic Publishers.

Eade, John (ed.) (1997) *Living the Global City: Globalization as a Local Process*, London and New York: Routledge.

The Economist, January 8, 2000, "Goodnight, Vietnam."

Economist Intelligence Unit (2000) *Vietnam Country Report July 2000*, London: Economist Intelligence Unit.

Economist Intelligence Unit (2001) *Vietnam Country Report July 2001*, London: Economist Intelligence Unit.

Editing Committee (1989) *The History of Yokohama*, Yokohama: Public Information Center, Citizen Bureau, City of Yokohama (in Japanese).

Editorial Board of Shenzhen Special Economic Zone Yearbook (1992) *Shenzhen Statistical Yearbook 1991*, Shenzen: Shenzhen Special Economic Zone.

Ekins, Paul (1992) *A New World Order: Grassroots Movements for Global Change*, London: Routledge.

Entrikin, J.N. (1991) *The Betweenness of Place: Towards a Geography of Modernity*, Baltimore, MD: Johns Hopkins University Press.

Enright, M., Scott, E. and Dodwell, D. (eds) (1997) *The Hong Kong Advantage*, Oxford, New York: Oxford University Press.

Fainstein, Susan S. and Fainstein, Norman I. (1989) "Technology, the new international division of labor, and location: continuities and disjunctures," in R.A. Beauregard (ed.) *Economic Restructuring and Political Response*, Beverly Hills: Sage 17–39.

Fainstein, S., Gordon, I. and Harloe, M. (1992) *Divided Cities: New York and London in the Contemporary World*, Cambridge: Blackwell Publishers.

Fan, C. (1992) "Foreign trade and regional development in China," *Geographical Analysis* 24(3): 240–56.

Far Eastern Economic Review (1996) "Impossible mission," November 28, 18.

Far Eastern Economic Review (1998) "Off the market," June 25, 65.

Featherstone, M. (ed.) (1990) *Global Culture: Nationalism, Globalization and Modernity*, London: Sage.

Featherstone, M. (1993) "Global and local cultures," in J. Bird, B. Curtis, T. Putnam, G. Robertson and T. Tickner (eds) *Mapping Futures: Local Cultures, Global Change*, London and New York: Routledge, 169–87.

Forbes, D. (1996) *Asian Metropolis: Urbanization and the South-East Asian City*, Melbourne, New York: Oxford University Press.

Forbes, D. (1999) "Globalization, postcolonialism and new representations of the Pacific Asian metropolis," in K. Olds *et al.* (eds) *Globalization and the Asia-Pacific*, London: Routledge: 238–54.

Forbes, D. and Thrift, N. (1986) *The Price of War – Urbanization in Vietnam – 1954–1985*, London: Allen and Unwin.

Forbes, D. and Thrift, N. (1987) "International impacts on the urbanization process in the Asian region: a review," in Fuchs R. *et al.* (eds) *Urbanization and Urban Policy in Pacific Asia*, Boulder, CO: Westview Press: 67–87.

Forbes, D. and Thrift, N. (1997) "Regional integration, internationalization and the new geographies of the Pacific Rim," in R. Watters and T. McGee (eds) *Asia Pacific: New Geographies of the Pacific Rim*, London: C. Hurst: 115–35.

Foreign Affairs and International Cooperation Office of Shanghai Pudong New Area Administration, Promotional Material 2001.

Foster, H., Chuenyan Lai, D. and Naisheng Zhou (1998) *The Dragon's Head: Shanghai, China's Emerging Megacity*, Victoria, British Columbia: Western Geographical Press.

Francey, Daniel (2001) Series of interviews with Mr. Daniel Francey, Manager of International Marketing, Phu My Hung Corporation, Saigon South, Vietnam, May, June, September.

Friedmann, John (1986) "The world city hypothesis," *Development and Change* 17(1): 69–84.

Friedmann, John (1995) "Where we stand: a decade of world city research," in Paul L. Knox and Peter J. Taylor (eds) *World Cities in a World-System*, Cambridge: Cambridge University Press: 21–47.

Friedmann, J. and Wolff, G. (1982) "World city formation," *International Journal Of Urban And Regional Research* 6: 306–44.

Fu-chen Lo and Marcotullio, P. (1998) "Globalization and urban transformation in the Asia-Pacific region," UNU/IAS Working Paper No. 40, UNESCO.

Fu-chen Lo and Yue-man Yeung (eds) (1996) *Emerging World Cities in Pacific Asia*, Tokyo, New York, Paris: The Chinese University of Hong Kong and the United Nations University Press.

Fu-chen Lo and Yue-man Yeung (1998) "Urbanization and globalization," UNU/IAS Working Paper No. 39, UNESCO.

Fu-chen Lo and Yue-Man Yeung (eds) (1998) "Globalization and the world of large cities," New York: United Nations University Press.

Fuchs, R. (ed.) (1994) *Mega-city Growth and the Future*, Tokyo and New York: United Nations University Press.

Fuchs, R., Jones, G. and Pernia, E. (eds) (1987) *Urbanization and Urban Policy in Pacific Asia*, Boulder, CO: Westview Press.

Fujita, K. and Hill, Richard C. (1993) "Toyota city: industrial organization and the Local State in Japan," in Richard C. Hill and Kuniko Fujita (eds) *Japanese Cities in the World Economy*, Philadelphia, PA: Temple University Press, 175–202.

Giddens, Anthony (1991) *Modernity and Self-Identity: Self and Society in the Late Modern Age*, Stanford: Stanford University Press.

Gilbert, Alan (ed.) (1996) *The Mega-city in Latin America*, Tokyo: United Nations University Press.

Ginsburg, N., Koppel, B. and McGee, T. (eds) (1991) *The Extended Metropolis: Settlement Transition in Asia*, Honolulu, HI: University of Hawaii Press.

Goh, C.T. (1997) "Singapore and the East Asia miracle," in *Speeches: A Bimonthly Selection of Ministerial Speeches*, Singapore: Ministry of Information and the Arts.

Goh, K. and Chan, B. (1997) "Key social and economic trends, 1990–1995," www.Singstat.Gov.Sg/Ssn/2q97/Featl.Pdf, accessed 20 September 1999.

Golany, G., Hanaki, K. and Koide, O. (eds) (1998) *Japanese Urban Environment*, New York: Pergamon Press.

Gray, John (2000) *False Dawn: The Delusions of Global Capitalism*, New York: The New Press.

Guldin, G. (1992) *Urbanizing China*, Greenwood Press.

Hall, P. (1966) *The World Cities*, London: Weidenfeld and Nicolson.

Hall, P. (1987) "The geography of the post-industrial economy," in John F. Brotchie, Peter Hall and Peter W. Newton (eds) *The Spatial Impact of Technological Change*, New York: Croom Helm: 3–17.

Hall, P. (1990) "The disappearing city?" IURD Working Paper 506, Berkeley: Institute of Urban and Regional Development, University of California, March 1990.

Hall, P. (1995) *Cities of Tomorrow: An Intellectual History of Urban Planning and Design in the Twentieth Century*, Oxford (UK) and Cambridge, MA: Blackwell.

Hall, P. (1998) *Cities in Civilization: Culture, Innovation and Urban Order*, London: Weidenfeld and Nicolson.

Hall, P. and Newton, P.W. (eds) *The Spatial Impact of Technological Change*, New York: Croom Helm.

Hall, Peter and Pfeiffer, Ulrich (2000) *Urban Future 21. A Global Agenda for 21st-Century Cities*, London: E & FN Spon.

Hamnett, C. (1994) "Social polarisation in global cities: theory and evidence," *Urban Studies* 31: 401–24.

Hanru, H. and Obrist, U. (eds) (1997) *Cities on the Move*, Ostfildern-Ruit: Hatje, New York: Distributed Art Publishers.

Harasim, L. (ed.) (1993) *Global Networks: Computers and International Communication*, Cambridge, MA: MIT Press.

Harvey, D. (1973) *Social Justice and the City*, Baltimore, MD: Johns Hopkins University Press.

Harvey, D. (1978) "The urban process under capitalism," *International Journal of Urban and Regional Research* 2(1): 101–32.

Harvey, D. (1985a) *Consciousness and the Urban Experience*, Oxford: Blackwell.

Harvey, D. (1985b) *The Urbanization of Capital*, Oxford: Blackwell.

Harvey, D. (1988) "Urban places in the 'global village': reflections on the urban condition in late twentieth century capitalism," in L. Mazza (ed.) *World Cities and the Future of the Metropoles*, Electra, XVII Trienale: 21–32.

Harvey, D. (1989) *The Condition of Postmodernity*, Oxford: Blackwell.

Harvey, D. (1992) "Postmodern morality plays," *Antipode* 25(4): 300–26.

Harvey, D. (1993) "From space to place and back again: reflections on the condition of postmodernity," in Jon Bird *et al.* (eds) *Mapping the Futures*, New York and London: Routledge, 3–29.

Harvey, D. (1995) "Nature, politics and possibilities: a debate and discussion with David Harvey and Donna Haraway," *Environment and Planning D: Society and Space* 13: 507–27.

Harvey, D. (1996a) "On architects, bees and possible urban worlds," in C. Davidson (ed.) *Anywise*, New York: Anyone Corporation, 216–27.

Harvey, D. (1996b) *Justice, Nature and the Geography of Difference*, Oxford: Blackwell.

Haseyama, T., Hirata, A. and Yanagihara, T. (1983) *Two Decades of Asian Development and Outlook for the 1980's*, Tokyo: Institute of Developing Economies.

Hatch, W. and Yamamura, K. (1996) *Asia in Japan's Embrace*, Cambridge: Cambridge University Press.

Hefner, R. (ed.) (1998) *Market Cultures: Society and Values in New Asian Capitalisms*, Boulder, CO: Westview Press.

Held, D. and McGrew, A. (eds) (2000) *The Global Transformations Reader*, Cambridge: Polity Press.

Hidenobu, Jinnai (1995) *Tokyo: Spatial Anthropology*, Berkeley: University of California Press.

Hill, Richard C. and Kuniko, Fujita (1993a) "Global interdependence and urban restructuring in Japan," in Richard C. Hill and Fujita Kuniko (eds) *Japanese Cities in the World Economy*, Philadelphia, PA: Temple University Press, 280–98.

Hill, Richard C. and Kuniko, Fujita (eds) (1993b) *Japanese Cities in the World Economy*, Philadelphia, PA: Temple University Press.

Hill, Richard C. and Kuniko, Fujita (1995) "Osaka's Tokyo problem," *International Journal of Urban and Regional Research* 19(2): 181–93.

Hirst, Paul and Thompson, Grahame (1996) *Globalization in Question: The International Economy and the Possibilities of Governance*, Cambridge: Polity Press.

Ho Chi Minh City Department of Planning and Investment, 2001 http://www.hcminvest.gov.vn

Ho, K.C. (1998) "From port city to city state: forces shaping Singapore's built environment," in W. Kim, M. Douglass, S.-C. Choe and K.C. Ho (eds) *Culture and the City in East Asia*, Oxford: Clarendon Press: 212–33.

Holston, J. (1989) *The Modernist City: An Anthropological Critique of Brasilia*, Chicago: The University of Chicago Press.

Hong Ni Tiep (1980) "The architecture of Hanoi today and tomorrow," *Arckitektur CCCP* 7–8.

Hong Phuc Thang (1989) "On the problems of tradition and modernity in the planning and construction of Hanoi," *Hanoian Journal* 4.

Hoogvelt, Ankie (1999) *Globalization and the Postcolonial World: The New Political Economy of Development*, Baltimore, MD: Johns Hopkins University Press.

Hoogvelt, Ankie (2000) "Globalization and the postcolonial world," in D. Held and A. McGrew (eds) (2000) *The Global Transformations Reader*, Cambridge: Polity Press, 355–60.

Hook, B. (ed.) (1998a) *Shanghai and the Yangtze Delta: A City Reborn*, Hong Kong and New York: Oxford University Press.

Hook, B. (ed.) (1998b) *Beijing and Tianjin: Towards a Millennial Megalopolis*, Oxford, New York and Hong Kong: Oxford University Press.

Hugill, Peter J. (1995) *World Trade Since 1431. Geography, Technology, and Capitalism*, Baltimore, MD: Johns Hopkins University Press.

Hugill, Peter J. (1999) *Global Communications Since 1844: Geopolitics and Technology*, Baltimore, MD: Johns Hopkins University Press.

Hutton, T. (1997) "Service industries, economic restructuring and the spatial reconfigurations of Asian Pacific city-regions," in Asian Urban Research Network, Center for Human Settlements, University of British Columbia, Vancouver.

IFC (2000) *China's Emerging Private Enterprises*, Washington, DC.

International Monetary Fund (1997) "Globalisation: opportunities and challenges," *World Economic Outlook*, May.

ISIS (2001) The Institute of Strategic and International Studies (ISIS), Malaysia http://www.isis.org.my/isis/mbc/2020.htm, accessed July 6, 2001.

Ito, S. (2000) *Grand Design of Tokyo*, Tokyo: Keio University Press (in Japanese).

Jacobs, A. and Appleyard, D. (1982) "Toward an urban design manifesto," Working Paper, Institute of Urban and Regional Development, University of California, Berkeley, 384.

Jameson, Frederic (1983) "Postmodernism and consumer society," in Hal Foster (ed.) *The Anti-Aesthetic*, Port Townsend, WA: Bay Press, 111–25.

Jameson, Frederic (1984) "Postmodernism, or the cultural logic of late capitalism," *New Left Review* 146: 53–92.

Jameson, Frederic (1989). "Marxism and postmodernism," *New Left Review* 176 (July/August): 31–46.

Jameson, Frederic (1991) *Postmodernism, or, The Cultural Logic of Late Capitalism*, Durham, NC: Duke University Press.

Jao, Y.C. and Leung, C.K. (eds) (1986) *China's Special Economic Zones: Policies, Problems and Prospects*, Hong Kong: Oxford University Press.

Jebasingam Issace, John (2000) Interview with John Jebasingam Issace, Director, City Planning Department, Perbadanan Putrajaya, at Putrajaya, Malaysia, July 7.

Jiming, H. (1994) "Metropolis and communications," in Zheng Shiling (ed.) *The Renew and Redevelopment of Shanghai*, Shanghai: Tongji University Press, 73–90.

Jun, J. and Wright, D. (eds) (1996) *Globalization and Decentralization*, Washington, DC: Georgetown University Press.

Kahn, J. (2001) "U.S. accuses the Japanese of inflexibility on trade talks," October 31, Business Section, New York Times Online, http://www.nytimes.com/2001/10/31/business/world-business/31TRAD.html?todaysheadlines

Kaiyo Sangyo Kenkyu-kai Corporation (1987) *The Tokyo Bay 21st Century: Attractive Waterfront Planning*, Tokyo: Kajima Print Inc. (in Japanese).

Kaltenbruner, R. (1999) "East of planning: urbanistic strategies today," *Daidalos*, 72: 9–17.

Kanagawa Economy Laboratory Incorporated Foundation (ed.) (1979) *Yokohama and Port: Thinking About its History and Future*, Yokohama: Kanagawa Economy Laboratory (in Japanese).

Kansai Institute of Economic and Political Studies (1999) *Studies on Globalization Risk*, Osaka: Kansai University (in Japanese).

Kaothien, U. and Webster, D. (1998) "Globalization and urbanization: the case of Thailand," Input Paper: *World Development Report 2000*, World Bank.

Karan, P. and Stapleton, K. (eds) (1997) *The Japanese City*, Lexington, KY: The University of Kentucky Press.

Kern, Stephen (1983) *The Culture of Time and Space*, Cambridge, MA: Harvard University Press.

Khan, Zafar Shah (1991) "Patterns of direct foreign investment in China," World Bank Discussion Papers, Washington, DC: The World Bank.

Kim, W., Douglass, M., Choe, S.-C. and Ho, K.C. (eds) (1998) *Culture and the City in East Asia*, Oxford: Clarendon Press.

King, Anthony (1990) *Global Cities: Post-Imperialism and the Internationalization of London*. London and New York: Routledge.

King, Anthony (1996) *Re-Presenting the City: Ethnicity, Capital and Culture in the 21st Century*, New York: New York University Press.

Kira, M. and Tereda, M. (eds) (2000) *Japan, Towards Totalscape: Contemporary Japanese Architecture, Urban Planning and Landscape*, Rotterdam: NAI Publishers.

Kirkby, R.J.R. (1985) *Urbanization in China: Towns and Country in a Developing Economy 1949–2000 AD*, London: Croom Helm.

Knox, Paul (1995) "World cities and the organization of global space," in R.J. Johnston, Peter J. Taylor and Michael J. Watts (eds) *Geographies of Global Change*, Oxford: Blackwell, 232–47.

Knox, P.L. and Taylor, P.J. (eds) (1995) *World Cities in a World System*, Cambridge: Cambridge University Press.

Kokko, Ari (1998) "Vietnam – ready for *doi moi*?" *SSE/EFI Working Paper Series in Economics and Finance*, No. 286, December, Stockholm School of Economics.

Königs, U. (1999) "Scapes as a future model of the city," *Daidolos* 72: 18–27.

Koolhaas, R. (1998) *SMLXL*, New York: Monacelli Press.

Koolhaas, R. (2001) *Mutations*, Bordeaux: Actar Press Center d'Architecture.

Kotler, P. and Kartajaya, H. (2000) *Repositioning Asia: from Bubble Economy to Sustainable Economy*, Singapore: John Wiley (Asia).

Kueh, Y.Y. (1992) "Foreign investment and economic change in China," *The China Quarterly* 138: 637–90.

Kwan, C.H. (1994) *Economic Interdependence in the Asia-Pacific Region*, London: Routledge.

Kwok, R.Y. (1988) "Metropolitan development in China: a struggle between contradictions," *Habitat International* 12(4): 195–207.

Lampugnani, V. (ed.) (1993) *Hong Kong Architecture*, Munich, New York: Prestel-Verlage Press.

Larrain, J. (1994) *Ideology and Cultural Identity*, Cambridge: Polity Press.

Lash, S. and Friedmann, J. (eds) (1991) *Modernity and Identity*, Oxford: Blackwell.

Lau Siu-kai (1982) *Society and Politics in Hong Kong*, Hong Kong: The Chinese University Press.

Lau Siu-kai (1988) *The Ethos of the Hong Kong Chinese*, Hong Kong: The Chinese University Press.

Le Corbusier (1966) *Urbanisme*, nouvelle édition, preface de Jean Casson, Paris: Vincent, Freal et Cie.

Lefebvre, H. (1991) *The Production of Space*, Oxford and Cambridge, MA: Blackwell Press.

Levine, J. (2001) *Design and Vietnam*, http://www.architecture-asia.com/VIETNAM/Design&Vietnam1.htm, accessed March 2001.

Levitas, R. (1993) "The future of thinking about the future," in J. Bird, B. Curtis, T. Putnam, G. Robertson and T. Tickner (eds) *Mapping Futures: Local Cultures, Global Change*, London and New York: Routledge, 257–66.

Li, L.H., Tse, Raymond Y.C. and Ganesan, Sivaguru (1999) "Shanghai," in J. Berry and S. McGreal (eds) *Cities in the Pacific Rim: Planning Systems and Property Markets*, London: E & FN Spon, 45–66.

Lin, G.C.S. (1994) "Changing theoretical perspectives on urbanization in Asian developing countries," *Third World Planning Review* 16(1): 1–24.

Liss-Katz, S. (1998) "Fort Bonifacio global city," *City Space and Globalization*, Ann Arbor, MI: University of Michigan, 63–9.

Lo, C.P. (1987) "Socialist ideology and urban strategies in China," *Urban Geography* 8(5): 440–58.

Lo, F.C. and Yeung, Y.M. (eds) (1996) *Emerging World Cities in Pacific Asia*, Tokyo: United Nations University Press.

Logan, John R. and Molotch, Harvey L. (1987) *Urban Fortunes*, Berkeley: University of California Press.

Logan, W. (1995) "Heritage planning in post *doi moi* Vietnam," *Journal of the American Planning Association*, Summer.

Low, Murray (1997) "Representation unbound: globalization and democracy," in Kevin Cox (ed.) *Spaces of Globalization*, New York: Guilford Press, 240–80.

Lyotard, Jean-François. (1984) *The Postmodern Condition*, Minneapolis, MN: University of Minnesota Press.

McGee, T. and Robinson, I. (eds) (1995) *The Mega-Urban Regions of Southeast Asia*, Vancouver: University of British Columbia Press.

Machimura, Takashi (1992) "The urban restructuring process in Tokyo in the 1980s: transforming Tokyo into a world city," *International Journal of Urban and Regional Research* 16(1): 114–28.

Machimura, Takashi (1998) "Symbolic use of globalization in urban politics in Tokyo," *International Journal of Urban and Regional Research* 22(2): 183–94.

Mackerras, C. (1998) "History and culture," in B. Hook (ed.) *Beijing and Tianjin: Towards a Millennial Megalopolis*, Oxford, New York and Hong Kong: Oxford University Press, 1–30.

Mackie, J. (1998) "Business success among Southeast Asian Chinese," in Robert R. Hefner (ed.) *Market Cultures: Society and Values in New Asian Capitalisms*, Boulder, CO: Westview Press, 41–77.

Macleod, S. and McGee, T. (1996) "The Singapore–Johore–Riau growth triangle: and emerging extended metropolitan region," in F.C. Lo and Y.M. Yeung (eds) *Emerging World Cities in Pacific Asia*, Tokyo: United Nations University Press: 417–64.

McNulty, Sheila (2001) "Losing his grip," *Financial Times*, 27 February http://news.ft.com/ft/gx.cgi/ftc?pagename=View&c=Article&cid=FT33AUP0QJC&live=true, accessed February 2001.

Mahathir, M. (1991) "Vision 2020 – the way forward," text of the working paper presented by MBC Chairman and Prime Minister of Malaysia, Honourable Dato' Seri Dr. Mahathir Mohammad, at the 1st Plenary Meeting in Kuala Lumpur on February 28, http://www.jaring.my/isis/mbc/2020.htm

Mahathir, M. (1998) *Excerpts from the Speeches of Mahathir Mohamad on the Multimedia Super Corridor*, Kuala Lumpur: Pelanduk Publications.

Maki, Fumihiko (1997) "The city and inner space," *Japan Echo* 6(1): Spring.

Malone, P. (ed.) (1996) *City, Capital, Water*, London: Routledge.

MAMPU (1994) "Malaysian incorporated policy report," Prime Minister's Department, Kuala Lumpur.

Marcuse, Peter (1989). "'Dual city': a muddy metaphor for a quartered city," *International Journal of Urban and Regional Research* 13(4): 697–708.

Marcuse, Peter (1993) "What's new about divided cities," *International Journal of Urban and Regional Research* 17(3): 355–65.

Marcuse, Peter (1997a) "Walls of fear and walls of support," in Nan, Ellin (ed.) *Architecture of Fear*, New York: Princeton University Press, 101–14.

Marcuse, Peter (1997b) "Glossy globalization," in Peter, Droege (ed.) *Intelligent Environments*, Amsterdam: Elsevier Science Publishers.

Marcuse, Peter (1997c) "The enclave, the citadel, and the ghetto: what has changed in the post-Fordist U.S. city," *Urban Affairs Review* 33(2): 228–64.

Marcuse, Peter with Kempen, Ronald van (1997) "A new spatial order in cities?" *American Behavioral Scientist special issue, The New Spatial Order of Cities* 41(3): 285–99.

Marcuse, Peter and Kempen, Ronald van (eds) (1999) *Globalizing Cities: Is There a New Spatial Order?* Oxford: Blackwell.

Marshall, R. (1999) "Kuala Lumpur: competition and the quest for world city status," *Built Environment* 24(4).

Marshall, R. (2001) *Waterfronts in Post Industrial Cities*, London: Spon Press.

Martin, H.-P. and Schumann, H. (1997) *The Global Trap: Globalization and the Assault on Democracy and Prosperity*, London: Zed Books.

Meier, R. (1980) *Urban Futures Observed, in the Asian Third World*, Amsterdam: Elsevier Science.

Meier, R. (1982) "Shanghai: an introduction to its future," Institute of Urban and Regional Development, *UC Berkeley Working Paper No. 395*, November.

MIT Consulting Team, EC/BMA Project Team, BMA Department of City Planning (1996) *The Bangkok Plan: A Vision for the Bangkok Metropolitan Administration Area 1995–2005*, Discussion Draft.

Mittelman, J. (ed.) (1996) *Globalization: Critical Reflections*, Boulder, CO and London: Lynne Rienner Publishers.

Mittelman, J. (2000) *The Globalization Syndrome: Transformation and Resistance*, Princeton, NJ: Princeton University Press.

Montgomery, J. (1998) "Making a city: urbanity, vitality and urban design," *Journal of Urban Design* 3(1).

Moss, M. (1987) "Telecommunications and international financial centers," in John F. Brotchie, Peter Hall and Peter W. Newton (eds) *The Spatial Impact of Technological Change*, New York: Croom Helm: 75–88.

Nakamura, H. (1993) "Urban growth in prewar Japan," in Richard C. Hill and Kuniko Fujita (eds) *Japanese Cities in the World Economy*, Philadelphia, PA: Temple University Press, 26–52.

Nation Section (1999): *Business*, Jan 30, http://www.nation multimedia.com/page.arcview.php3?clid=6&id=1719&date=1999 -01-30&usrsess=1

Nien Newspaper (1998) "Ho Chi Minh City – changing the main development direction towards the south", 16 January.

Nikken Sekkei (1997) "Tu Liem planning and design report," unpublished.

Nonini, Donald (1997) "Shifting identities, positioned imaginaries: transnational traversals and reversals by Malaysian Chinese," in Aihwa Ong and Donald Nonini (eds) *Ungrounded Empires*, New York: Routledge, 203–27.

Nonini, Donald and Ong, Aihwa (1997) "Chinese transnationalism as an alternative modernity," in Aihwa Ong and Donald Nonini (eds) *Ungrounded Empires*, New York: Routledge, 3–38.

Ohno, H. (ed.) (1992) "Hong Kong: alternative metropolis," *Space Design*, March 19, 330.

Olds, K. (1995) "Globalization and the production of new urban spaces: Pacific Rim megaprojects in the late 20th century," *Environment and Planning* 27(11): 1713–43.

Olds, K. (2001) *Globalization and Urban Change: Capital, Culture, and Pacic Rim Mega-Projects, Oxford Geographical and Environmental Studies*, Oxford and New York: Oxford University Press.

Olds, K. *et al.* (eds) (1999) *Globalization and the Asia-Pacific: Contested Territories*, London: Routledge.

Paisley, E. (1996) "Asia's property perils," *Institutional Investor*, January.

People's Daily Newspaper (2000) "Pudong lures over $27.7 billion foreign capital," Tuesday April 18, http://english. peopledaily.com.cn

Perry, M. (1998) "The Singapore growth triangle in the global and local economy," in V.R. Savage, L. Kong and W. Neville (eds) *The Naga Awakens: Growth and Change in Southeast Asia*, Singapore: Times Academic Press: 87–112.

Perry, M., Kong, L. and Yeoh, B. (1997) *Singapore: A Developmental City State*, New York: John Wiley and Sons.

Porter, M. (1990) *The Competitive Advantage of Nations*, London: Macmillan.

Porter, M. *et al.* (2000) *The Global Competitiveness Report 2000*, Geneva: World Economic Forum.

Pudong New Area Administration (2001) http://pudong. shanghaichina.org/ accessed June 2001.

Putrajaya Authority (2001) *Putrajaya Authority Integrated City Planning and Management System, Malaysia*, http://www. novasprint.com/ref_putrajaya.htm, accessed December 2001.

Quah, S., Kong, C.S. and Chung, K.Y. (eds) (1991) *Social Class In Singapore*, Singapore: Times Academic Press Centre For Advanced Studies.

Rakatansky, M. (1993) *Massimo Cacciari: Architecture and Nihilism*, New Haven, CT: Yale University Press.

Reid, A. (1993) *Southeast Asia in the Age of Commerce, Vol. 2: Expansion and Crisis*, New Haven, CT: Yale University Press.

Reischauer, E. and Jansen, M. (1995) *The Japanese Today: Continuity and Change*, Cambridge, MA and London: The Belknap Press of Harvard University Press.

Relph, E. (1976) *Place and Placenessness*, London: Pion Press.

Reps, J. (1997) *Canberra 1912: Plans and Planners of the Australian Capital Competition*, Melbourne: Melbourne University Press.

Reza, A., Parsa, G. and Kawaguchi, Y. (1999) "Tokyo," in J. Berry and S. McGreal (eds) *Cities in the Pacific Rim: Planning Systems and Property Markets*, London: E & FN Spon: 107–27.

Rimmer, P. (1993a) "Transport and communications in the Pacific economic zone during the early 21st century," in Y.M. Yeung (ed.) *Pacific Asia in the 21st Century: Geographical and Developmental Perspectives*, Hong Kong: Chinese University Press: 195–232.

Rimmer, P. (1993b) "Reshaping Western Pacific Rim cities: exporting Japanese planning ideas," in Richard C. Hill and Kuniko Fujita (eds) *Japanese Cities in the World Economy*, Philadelphia, PA: Temple University Press, 257–79.

Rimmer, P. (ed.) (1997) *Pacific Rim Development: Integration and Globalization in the Asia-Pacific Economy*, Sydney: Allen and Unwin.

Rimmington, D. (1998) "History and culture," in B. Hook (ed.) *Shanghai and the Yangtze Delta: A City Reborn*, Oxford, New York: Oxford University Press, 1–29.

Rohwer, J. (1995) *Asia Rising*, London: Nicholas Brealey Publishing.

Roost, Frank (1998) "Recreating the city as entertainment center: the media industry's role in transforming Potsdamer Platz and Times Square," *Journal of Urban Technology* 5(2): 1–21.

Rose, Gillian (1993) "Some notes towards thinking about the spaces of the future," in Jon Bird *et al.* (eds) *Mapping the Futures: Local Cultures, Global Change*, London and New York: Routledge, 70–83.

Rowe, P. (1997) *Civic Realism*, Cambridge, MA: MIT Press.

Rowe, W.T. (1989) *Hankow: Conflict and Community in a Chinese City, 1796–1895*, Stanford, CT: Stanford University Press.

Ruano, M. (1999) "Strangers in Paradise," in *Instant China – Notes on an Urban Transformation*, 2G International Architecture Review no.10, Editorial Gustavo Gili, SA.

Robbins, B. (ed.) (1993) *The Phantom Public Sphere*, Minneapolis, MN: The University of Minnesota Press.

Robbins, E. (1998) "Thinking the city multiple," in *The Harvard Architectural Review 10, Civitas/What is city?*, Princeton Architectural Press, 36–45.

Robinson, R. and Goodman, D. (eds) (1996) *The New Rich in Asia*, London and New York: Routledge.

Rowe, C. and Koetter, F. (1978) *Collage City*, Cambridge, MA: MIT Press.

Rozman, G. (1990) "East Asian urbanization in the nineteenth century: comparisons with Europe," in Ad van der Worde, Akira Hayami and Jan de Vries (eds) *Urbanization in History*, London: Oxford University Press, 61–73.

Ruland, J. (ed.) (1996) *The Dynamics of Metropolitan Management in Southeast Asia*, Singapore: Institute of Southeast Asian Studies.

SaigonTourist, *Saigon – Ho Chi Minh*, Tourism Information Technology Center, CD-ROM.

Saito, T. (1990) *The Future of Yokohama New City*, Tokyo: Bunshindo Inc., second edition (in Japanese).

Sassen, Saskia (1988) *The Mobility of Labor and Capital*, Cambridge: Cambridge University Press.

Sassen, Saskia (1989) "New trends in the sociospatial organization of the New York city economy," in Robert A.

Beauregard (ed.) *Economic Restructuring and Political Response*, Newbury Park, CA: Sage.

Sassen, Saskia (1991) *The Global City: New York, London, Tokyo*, Princeton, NJ: Princeton University Press.

Sassen, Saskia (1993) "Miami: a new global city?" *Contemporary Sociology* 22(4): 471–80.

Sassen, Saskia (1994) *Cities in a World Economy*, Thousand Oaks, CA: Pine Forge Press (Sage Publications).

Sassen, Saskia (1995) "Urban impacts of economic globalism," in J. Brotchie, M. Batty, E. Blakely *et al.* (eds) *Cities in Competition: Productive and Sustainable Cities for the 2lst Century*, Melbourne: Longman Australia, 36–57.

Sassen, Saskia (1996) *Losing Control: Sovereignty in an Age of Globalization*, New York: Columbia University Press.

Sassen, Saskia (1998a) *Globalization and its Discontents*, New York: The New Press.

Sassen, Saskia (1998b) "Swirling that old wine around in the wrong bottle: a comment on white," *Urban Affairs Review* 33(4): 478–81.

Sassen, Saskia (1998c) "Hong Kong: strategic site/new frontier," in C. Davidson (ed.) *Anyhow*, Cambridge: MIT Press, 130–7.

Sassen-Koob, Saskia (1984) "The new labor demand in global cities," in Michael Peter Smith (ed.) *Cities in Transformation*, Beverly Hills, CA: Sage, 139–71.

Savage, L. (1998) "Shifting gears: union organizing in the low wage service sector," in L. Herod (ed.) *Organizing the Landscape*, Minneapolis, MN: University of Minnesota Press.

Savitch, H.V. (1988) *Post-Industrial Cities: Politics and Planning in New York, Paris, and London*, Princeton, NJ: Princeton University Press.

Scott, Alan (ed.) (1997) *The Limits of Globalization: Cases and Arguments*, London: Routledge.

Scott, Allen J. (1997) "The cultural economy of cities," *International Journal of Urban and Regional Research* 21(2): 323–39.

Seguchi, T. and Malone, P. (1996) "Tokyo: waterfront development and social needs," in P. Malone (ed.) *City Capital and Water*, London: Routledge, 164–94.

Seidensticker, E. (1990) *Tokyo Rising: The City Since the Great Earthquake*, Cambridge, MA: Harvard University Press.

Seidensticker, E. (1991) *Low City, High City: Tokyo from Edo to the Earthquake*, Cambridge, MA: Harvard University Press.

Serageldin, Ismail (1997) "A decent life," *Harvard Design Magazine* Winter/Spring.

Sert, J.L. (1942) *Can Our Cities Survive?*, Cambridge, MA: Harvard University Press.

Setchell, A.C. (1994) "Recent housing activity in Bangkok: has the boom benefited the poor?" 36th Annual Meeting of the Association of Collegiate Schools of Planning, Phoenix, Arizona, November 3–6.

Shanghai Lujiazui Ltd. (2001a) *The Planning and Architecture of Shanghai Lujiazui Central Area, the Volume of International Consultation, The Construction Industry*, Beijing: Press of China.

Shanghai Lujiazui Ltd. (2001b) *The Planning and Architecture of Shanghai Lujiazui Central Area, the Volume of Architectural Documentation, The Construction Industry*, Beijing: Press of China.

Shanghai Lujiazui Ltd. (2001c) *The Planning and Architecture of Shanghai Lujiazui Central Area, the Volume of Planning Revision, The Construction Industry*, Beijing: Press of China.

Shanghai Lujiazui Ltd. (2001d) *The Planning and Architecture of Shanghai Lujiazui Central Area, the Volume of Traffic and Transportation Planning, The Construction Industry*, Beijing: Press of China.

Shanghai Municipal Government (1997) *Atlas of Shanghai*, Shanghai: Shanghai Scientific and Technical Publishers.

Shapiro, Michael (1992) *Reading the Postmodern Polity*, Minneapolis, MN: University of Minnesota Press.

Shatkin, Gavin (1998). "Fourth world cities in the global economy: the case of Phnom Penh, Cambodia," *International Journal of Urban and Regional Research* 22(3): 378–93.

Shaw, Gareth and Williams, Allan M. (1993) *Critical Issues in Tourism: A Geographical Perspective*, London: Blackwell.

Shiling, Z. (1999) *Shanghai, An Everchanging Metropolis*, Shanghai: Tongji University.

Shiling, Z. and Jiaming, C. (1994) "Planning and administration of Shanghai as an international metropolis," in Zheng Shiling (ed.) *The Renewal and Redevelopment of Shanghai*, Shanghai: Tongji University Press, 43–72.

Shiozaki, Y. and Malone, P. (1996) "Tokyo, Osaka and Kobe: island city paradise?" in P. Malone (ed.) *City, Capital, Water*, London: Routledge, 134–63.

Short, J.R. and Kim, Y.-H. (1999) *Globalization and the City*, Harlow: Longman.

Siksna, A. (1998) "City center blocks and their evolution," *Journal of Urban Design* 3(3): October.

Simmonds, Roger and Hack, Gary (2000) *Global City Regions: Their Emerging Forms*, London: Carfax (Bangkok, Ankara, Boston, Madrid, South African Diego, Santiago, São Paulo, Seattle, Taipei, Tokyo, Midlands).

Singapore Government Department of Statistics (1996a) *Yearbook of Statistics, 1995*, Singapore: Department of Statistics, Ministry of Trade and Industry.

Singapore Government Department of Statistics (1996b) *General Household Survey 1995: Socio-demographic and Economic Characteristics*, Release No. 1. Singapore: Department of Statistics.

Singapore Government Department of Statistics (1997) *Yearbook of Statistics, 1996*, Singapore: Department of Statistics, Ministry of Trade and Industry.

Singapore Government Department of Statistics (2001) www.singstat.gov.sg/OFFICIALGUIDE/guide.html

Sit, V. (1981) *Urban Hong Kong*, Hong Kong: Summerson Eastern Publications.

Sit, V. (1995) *Beijing: The Nature and Planning of a Chinese Capital City*, New York: John Wiley & Sons.

Skinner, G.W. (1977) *The City in Late Imperial China*, Stanford, CA: Stanford University Press.

Smith, Anthony (1995) *Nations and Nationalism in a Global Era*, Cambridge, UK: Polity Press.

Smith, D. and Borocz, J. (eds) (1995) *A New World Order: Global Transformation in the Late Twentieth Century*, Westport, CT: Praeger.

Smith, Michael P. (1980) *The City and Social Theory*, Oxford: Blackwell.

Smith, Michael P. (ed.) (1984) *Cities in Transformation*, Beverly Hills, CA and London: Sage.

Smith, Michael P. (1988) *City, State, and Market*, Oxford: Blackwell.

Smith, Michael P. (1989) "Urbanism: medium or outcome of human agency?" *Urban Affairs Quarterly* (March): 353–8.

Smith, Michael P. (1997) "The global city – whose social construct is it anyway?" *Urban Affairs Review* 33.

Social Watch (2001) *Country Report 2001: Vietnam: Achievements and Challenges* http://unpan1un.org/intradoc/groups/public/documents/apcity/unpan002366.pdf

Soja, Edward J. (1986) "Taking Los Angeles apart: some fragments of a critical human geography," *Society and Space* 4: 259.

Soja, Edward J. (1989) *Postmodern Geographies: The Reassertion of Space in Critical Social Theory*, New York: Verso Press.

Soja, Edward J. (1996) *Thirdspace: Journeys to Los Angeles and Other Real-and-Imagined Places*, Cambridge, MA: Blackwell.

Soja, Edward J. (2000) *Postmetropolis: Critical Studies of Cities and Regions*, Oxford: Blackwell.

Starr, Amory (2000) *Naming the Enemy: Anti-Corporate Social Movements Confront Globalization*, London: Zed Books.

STB (State Statistical Bureau) (1990) *The Forty Years of Urban Development*, Beijing: China Statistical Information and Consultancy Service Center.

STB (1991) *China Statistical Yearbook (1991)*, Beijing: State Statistical Bureau.

Stelux (1997) "Announcement of results for year ended 31st March 1997."

Stern, R. (1977) "At the edge of modernism: some methods paradigms and principles for modern architecture at the edge of the modern movement," *Architectural Design* 47(4).

Stiglitz, Joseph (2000) *What's Wrong with the International Monetary Fund*, http://www.thenewrepublic.com/041700/stiglitz041700.html

Storey, R. (1995) *Ho Chi Minh City (Saigon)*, Victoria, Australia and Berkeley, CA: Lonely Planet Publications.

Storper, Michael (1997) "Territories, flows, and hierarchies in the global economy," in K. Cox (ed.) *Spaces of Globalization*, New York: Guilford, 19–44.

Straits Times Interactive (1997) PM Goh's vision of a new era for Singapore. http://llweb3.asial.com.sg/archive/st/4/pages/q06071.html, accessed 9 May.

Strand, D. (1990) "A perspective on popular movements in Beijing 1919–1989," Duke University, NC: Asian Pacific Studies Institute.

Stubbs, J. and Clarke, G. (eds) (1995) "Megacity management in the Asian Pacific region: policy issues and innovative approaches," Proceedings of the Regional Seminar on Megacities Management in Asia and the Pacific, Asian Development Bank and United Nations/World Bank Urban Management Programme for Asia and the Pacific, Manila, Philippines, 24–30 October, Asian Development Bank Manila, Philippines.

Sudjik, D. (1992) *100 Mile City*, London: André Deutsch.

Sudjik, D. (1993) "Bangkok's instant city," *Blueprint*, London: July–Aug., n.99, 17–19.

Sung, Yung-Wing *et al.* (1995) *The Fifth Dragon: The Emergence of the Pearl River Delta*, Singapore, Reading, MA: Addison Wesley Press.

Tafuri, M. (1986) *Modern Architecture*, New York: Electa/Rizzoli.

Tamney, J. (1991) *The Struggle Over Singapore's Soul: Western Modernisation and Asian Culture*, Berlin: Walter de Gruyter.

Tamura, A. (1989) *The City of Yokohama Story*, Tokyo: Jiji Tsushin-sha (in Japanese).

Tan, Sumiko (1999) *Home, Work, Play*, Singapore: Urban Redevelopment Authority.

Tarrow, Sidney (1998) *Power in Movement: Social Movements and Contentious Politics*, Cambridge: Cambridge University Press.

Taylor, B. (1989) "From export center to world city," *American Planning Association Journal* 55 (Summer): 309–22.

Taylor, N. (1998) "The elements of townscape and the art of urban design," *Journal of Urban Design* 4(2).

Theobald, W.F. (ed.) (1995) *Global Tourism: The Next Decade*, Oxford: Butterworth Heinemann.

Thrift, N. (1996) *Spatial Formations*, Thousand Oaks, CA and London, Sage Publications.

Thrift, N. (1998) *Cities and Global Economic Change*, London: Routledge.

Thrift, N. and Leyshon, A. (1997) *Money/Space*, London: Routledge.

Tokyo Metropolitan Government (1999a) *Planning Tokyo*, Tokyo: Tokyo Metropolitan Government.

Tokyo Metropolitan Government (1999b) *Vision 2000 Plan*, Tokyo: Tokyo Metropolitan Government.

Tokyo Metropolitan Government (2001) Description of Tokyo Plan 2000, http://www.toshikei.metro.tokyo.jp/plan/pl_index-e.html, accessed June 2001.

Town Planning Office (1988) *Town Planning in Hong Kong*, Hong Kong: Buildings and Lands Department.

Tran, E. (1997) *Doi moi* in Vietnam a small tiger's growth spurt comes to an end," http://www.columbia.edu/cu/cear/issues/fall97/graphics/regional/tran/tran.htm, accessed April 2000.

Tran Thi Que and Vo Tri Thanh (2001) Social Watch Organization, Uruguay, http://www.socwatch.org.uy/, accessed March 2001.

Tsinghua (2000) Unpublished design report from Zhongguancun Science and Technology Park design competition documents, in Chinese, translated by Ge Zhong of Tsinghua University.

United Nations (1993) The *East Asian Miracle: Economic Growth and Public Policy*, Oxford: Oxford University Press.

United Nations (1996a) *The World's Largest Cities*, New York: United Nations.

United Nations (1996b) *An Urbanizing World – Global Report on Human Settlements 1996*, New York: United Nations Center for Human Settlements, Oxford University Press.

United Nations (1998) *World Urbanization Prospects: The 1996 Revision*, New York: United Nations Department of Economic and Social Affairs, Population Division.

United Nations (2000) Population Information Network (POPIN) with support from the UN Population Fund (UNFPA) www.popin.org, accessed December 2000.

United Nations (2001) Economic and Social Commission for Asia and the Pacific, http://www.unescap.org/, accessed June 2001.

UNDP (1996) *Human Development Report*, Oxford and New York: Oxford University Press.

UNESCO (1995) *Our Creative Diversity: Report of the World Commission on Culture and Development*, Paris: United Nations.

Urban Redevelopment Authority of Singapore (1996) *New Downtown – Ideas for the City of Tomorrow*, Singapore: URA.

Urban Redevelopment Authority of Singapore (2001) *27 April 2001 URA releases the 1st quarter 2001 real estate information.*

Van Nghien (2000) Hoang, Chairman of Hanoi's People's Committee and Mayor of Hanoi, "Hanoi on the threshold of the 21st century, opportunities and challenges," http://www.unesco.org/cpp/uk/news/nghien.htm

Vernoorn, A. (1998) *Re Orient – Change in Asian Societies*, Melbourne: Oxford University Press.

Vietnam Government General Statistics Office (2000) "Vietnam living standards survey 1997–1998," Hanoi: Vietnam Government.

Vietnam Government Ministry of Planning and Investment (2000) "Law on foreign investment in Vietnam," Hanoi: Vietnam Government.

Vietnam Government Ministry of Planning and Investment (2001a) http://www.vnn.vn/investment/open_door/plan_invest.html

Vietnam Government (2001b) Ministry of Planning and Investment Vietnam Trade Network (VITRANET) http://www.vitranet.com.vn/fdi/default_e.htm, accessed June 2001.

Vietnam Panorama (2001) Vietnam Economic Performance in 2000, http://www.vietnampanorama.com/business/bizindex.html#Review, accessed January 2001.

Virilio, P. (1986) "The overexposed city," from "L'espace critique," ZONE 1–2, in K. Michael Hays (ed.) (1998) Architecture Theory Since 1968, Cambridge, MA: MIT Press.

Virilio, P. (1993) "Speed and vision: the incomparable eye," Daidalos 47, 96–105.

Virilio, P. (1997) "Speed and information: cyberspace alarm!" in P. Riemans (trans.) ctheory, 27 September.

Vogel, E. (1989) One Step Ahead in China, Cambridge, MA: Harvard University Press.

Vogel, E. (1991) The Four Little Dragons: The Spread of Industrialization in East Asia, Cambridge, MA: Harvard University Press.

Von Schaik, L. (1993) "Muang Thong Thani: Australians design an Asian city" in Architecture Australia, July/August, 28–35.

Wade, Robert (1996) "Globalization and its limits: reports on the death of the national economy are greatly exaggerated," in Suzanne Berger and Ronald Dore (eds) National Diversity and Global Capitalism, Ithaca, NY and London: Cornell University Press, 60–88.

Wallach, B. (1996) Losing Asia: Modernization and the Culture of Development, Baltimore, MD: Johns Hopkins University Press.

Ward, Peter (1995) "The successful management and administration of world cities: mission impossible?" in Paul L. Knox and Peter J. Taylor (eds) World Cities in a World System, New York: Cambridge University Press, 298–314.

Waters, M. (1995) Globalization, London: Routledge.

Watters, R. and McGee, T. (eds) (1997) Asia Pacific: New Geographies of the Pacific Rim, London: C. Hurst.

Watts, K. (1992) "National urban development policies and strategies," Third World Planning Review 14(2): 113–29.

Webster, D. (1995) "The urban environment in Southeast Asia: challenges and opportunities," in Southeast Asian Affairs, ISEAS.

Weiss, Linda (1997) "Globalization and the myth of the powerless state," New Left Review 225: 3–27.

White, James W. (1998a). "Old wine, cracked bottle?: Tokyo, Paris, and the global city hypothesis," Urban Affairs Review 33(4): 451–77.

White, James W. (1998b) "Half-empty bottle or no bottle at all? A rejoinder to Sassen and Smith," Urban Affairs Review 33(4): 489–91.

White, L. and Cheng, L. (1998) "Government and politics," in B. Hook (ed.) Shanghai and the Yangtze Delta: A City Reborn, Oxford, New York: Oxford University Press, 30–73.

Whyte, M.K. and Parish, W.L. (1984) Urban Life in China, New York: Praeger.

Williams, J. (1996) "Rapid economic development in Singapore and the future of the PAP," Journal of Contemporary Asia 26: 164–79.

Wonghanchao, W. (1996) Housing Industry in Bangkok – Thailand, College Station, Texas: Texas A&M University.

Woodside, A. (1976) Community and Revolution in Modern Vietnam, New York: Houghton Mifflin Press.

World Architecture (1997) "World architecture survey 1997," 62.

World Bank (1990) Financial Sector Policy in Thailand: A Macroeconomic Perspective, Washington, DC: World Bank.

World Bank (1991) World Development Report 1991: The Challenge of Development, New York: Oxford University Press.

World Bank (1993) The East Asian Miracle, Washington, DC: Oxford University Press.

World Bank (1995) Vietnam Environment Program and Policy Priorities for a Socialist Economy in Transition, Washington, DC: World Bank.

World Bank (1996) China 2020: Development Challenges in the New Century, Washington, DC.

World Bank (1997a) World Development Report 1997: The State in a Changing World, New York: Oxford University Press.

World Bank (1997b) China 2020: Sharing Rising Incomes, Washington, DC: World Bank.

World Bank (1999a) Global Economic Prospects and Developing Countries, Washington, DC.

World Bank (1999b) A Tale of Two Cities in Vietnam.

World Bank (2000a) World Development Report 2000: Attacking Poverty, New York: Oxford University Press.

World Bank (2000b) World Development Indicators 2000, Washington, DC: World Bank.

World Bank (2000c) World Development Report 1999–2000: Entering the 21st Century, Oxford, New York: Oxford University Press.

World Bank (2000d) Thailand Economic Monitor, World Bank Bangkok, December.

World Bank (2001) Sector Notes – Thailand, Washington, DC, http://wbln0018.worldbank.org/IFCExt/spiwebsite1.nsf/9456cd2430750aa9852568890061dfd0/c8f108565999988385256a2400527c39?OpenDocument

Wu Jianyong et al. (1997) Beijing Chengshi Shenghuo Shi (History of Urban Life in Beijing), Beijing: Kaiming Press (in Chinese).

Wu Wei (1994) "Pudong new area's present ecological environment and related matters", in Zheng Shiling (ed.) The Renew and Redevelopment of Shanghai, Shanghai: Tongji University Press, 170–85.

Xu, Xueqiang (1984a) "Characteristics of urbanization in China – changes and causes of urban population growth and distribution," Asian Geographer 3: 1529.

Xu, Xueqiang (1984b) "Trends and changes of the urban system in China," Third World Planning Review 6(1): 47–60.

Xu, Xueqiang and Li Si-ming (1990) "China's open door policy and urbanization in the Pearl River Delta," International Journal of Urban and Regional Studies 14(1): 49–69.

Yamada, H. (1989) Revaluation of Tokyo, Tokyo: PHP Research Laboratory (in Japanese).

Yamazawa, I., Hirata, A. and Yokota, K. (1991) "Evolving patterns of comparative advantage in the Pacific economies," in M. Ariff (ed.) The Pacific Economy: Growth and External Stability, Sydney: Allen and Unwin, 213–32.

Yang Kaizhong and Li Guoping et al. (2000) Chixu Shoudu: Beijing Xin Shiji Fazhan Zhanlue (The Sustainable Capital: The Development Strategy of Beijing in the New Century), Guanzhou: Guangdong Education Press (in Chinese).

Yatim, Datuk Dr Rais (2000) quoted from http://www.cari. com.my/News/Now/1275.htm

Yeh, Anthony Gar-on (1985) "Physical planning," in K.Y. Wong and D.K.Y. Chu (eds) *Modernization in China: The Case of the Shenzhen Special Economic Zone*, Hong Kong: Oxford University Press, 108–30.

Yeung, Y.M. (1987) "Cities that work: Hong Kong and Singapore," in R. Fuchs, G. Jones and E. Pernia (eds) *Urbanization and Urban Policies in Pacific Asia*, Boulder, CO: Westview Press.

Yeung, Y.M. (1990) *Changing Cities of Pacific Asia: A Scholarly Interpretation*, Hong Kong: Chinese University Press.

Yeung, Y.M. (1995) "Pacific Asia's world cities in the new global economy," *Urban Futures* 19: 81–7.

Yeung, Yue-man and Xu-wei Hu (eds) (1992) *China's Coastal Cities: Catalysts for Modernization*, Hawaii: University of Hawaii Press.

Yokohama Convention and Visitors Bureau (2001) General Information, http://www.city.yokohama.jp/me/ycvb/english/tourism/index.html

Yokohama Minato Mirai 21 Corporation (1984–2001) Minato Mirai 21 Information Brochure Vol. 1 though 63 (in Japanese).

Yokohama Minato Mirai 21 Corporation (1996) "Basic agreement on town development under Minato Mirai 21", *Minato Mirai 21*, Yokohama: Town Development Council.

Yokohama Minato Mirai 21 Corporation (2000) "Yokohama Minato Mirai 21 overview of planning and individual operations," Publicity Brochure, Yokohama: MM21 Corporation.

Yokohama Minato Mirai 21 Corporation (2001) http://web.infoweb.ne.jp/mm21/ accessed January 2001.

Yokohama Minato Mirai 21 Corporation (2001) "Minato Mirai 21 Information Brochure," Vol. 63, March (in Japanese).

Yokohama City Government (2001) http://www.city.yokohama.jp/

Yuan, L. and Choo, M. (1995) "Singapore as a global city: strategies and key issues," *Urban Futures* 19: 90–6.

Yue-Man Yeung (1994) *Urban Research in Asia: Problems, Priorities, and Prospects*, Hong Kong Institute of Asia-Pacific Studies, 25 pp.

Yusuf S., and Wu, W. (1997) *The Dynamics of Urban Growth in Three Chinese Cities*, Washington, DC: World Bank Publication.

Yusuf, S. Wu, W. and Evenett, S. (eds) (2000) *Local Dynamics in an Era of Globalization: 21st Century Catalysts for Development*, New York: Oxford University Press.

Zhang Hui Min (1999) "Presentation at waterfronts in post industrial cities at Harvard Design School," October 8, 1999.

Zhao Wan Liang (2000) Discussion between Zhao Wan Liang, Senior Urban Planner and Richard Marshall, at the Shanghai Urban Planning and Design Research Institute, Shanghai, 28 June, 2000.

Zhengyuan Fu (1993) *Autocratic Tradition and Chinese Politics*, Cambridge: Cambridge University Press.

Zhongguancun Administration Commission (2001) http://www.zgc.gov.cn, accessed May 2001.

Zukin, Sharon (1988) "The postmodern debate over urban form," *Theory, Culture and Society*, 431.

Zukin, Sharon (1991a) *Landscapes of Power: from Detroit to Disney World*, Berkeley: University of California Press.

Zukin, Sharon (1991b) "Postmodern urban landscapes: mapping culture and power," in S. Lash and J. Friedmann (eds) *Modernity and Identity*, Oxford: Blackwell.

Zukin, Sharon (1992) "The city as a landscape of power: London and New York as global financial capitals," in L. Budd and S. Whimster (eds) *Global Finance and Urban Living: A study of Metropolitan Change*, London and New York: Routledge, 195–223.

Zukin, Sharon (1995) *The Cultures of Cities*, Cambridge, MA: Blackwell.

Zukin, S., Baskerville, R., Greenberg, M., Guthreau, C. *et al.* (1998) "From Coney Island to Las Vegas in the urban imaginary: discursive practices of growth and decline," *Urban Affairs Review*, May 1998.

Index